HEYWOOD'S

DRAMATIC WORKS.

THE DRAMATIC WORKS OF THOMAS HEYWOOD NOW FIRST COLLECTED WITH ILLUSTRATIVE NOTES AND A MEMOIR OF THE AUTHOR IN SIX VOLUMES

Aut prodeffe folent aut delectare

VOLUME THE FOURTH

NEW YORK
RUSSELL & RUSSELL · INC

THE DRAMATIC WORKS OF THOMAS HEYWOOD

REISSUED, 1964, BY RUSSELL & RUSSELL, INC.

REPRINTED IN SIX VOLUMES FROM THE EDITION OF 1874

LIMITED TO 400 SETS

L. C. CATALOG CARD NO: 64—23468

PRINTED IN THE UNITED STATES OF AMERICA

THE

ENGLISH

TRAVELLER.

AS IT HATH BEENE

Publikely acted at the Cock-pit

in Drury-lane:

By Her Maiefties feruants.

Written by Thomas Heyvvood.

Aut prodeffe folent, aut delectare————

LONDON,
Printed by *Robert Raworth* : dwelling in Old Fifh-ftreet,
neere Saint *Mary Maudlins* Church. 1633.

Dramatis Perſonæ.

Geraldine. *Dalauill,* }	Two yong Gentlemen.
Olde Wincott	The husband.
His Wife	A yong Gentlewoman.
Prudentilla	Siſter to the wife.
Reignald	A paraſiticall ſeruing-man.
Robin	A countrey ſeruing-man.
Lionell	A riotous Citizen.
Blanda	A Whore.
Scapha	A Bawde.
Rioter	A Spend-thrift.
Two Gallants	His Companions.
Roger the Clowne	Seruant to Olde Wincott.
Two proſtitutes	Companions with Blanda.
Olde Lionell	A Merchant father to yong Lionell.
A Seruant	To Olde Lionell.
Olde Mr. Geraldine	Father to yong Geraldine.
An Vſurer *and his man.*	
A Gentleman	Companion with Dalauill.
Beſſe	Chambermaid to Miſtris Wincott.
A Tauerne Drawer	
Maſter Ricott	A Merchant.

The *Owner* of the houſe, ſuppoſed to be poſſeſt.

To the Right
WORSHIPFVLL
Sir HENRY APPLETON,
Knight Barronet, &c.

NOBLE SIR,

Or many reafons I am induced, to prefent this Poem, to your fauourable acceptance ; and not the leaft of them that alternate Loue, and thofe frequent curtefies which interchangably paft, betwixt your felfe and that good old Gentleman, mine vnkle (Mafter *Edmund Heywood*) whom you pleafed to grace by the Title of Father : I muft confeffe, I had altogether flept (my weaklines and bafhfullneffe difcouraging mee) had they not bin waken'd and animated, by that worthy Gentleman your friend, and my countreyman, Sir *William Eluiſh*, whom (who for his vnmerited loue many wayes extended towards me,) I much honour ; Neither Sir, neede you to thinke it any vnderualuing of your worth, to vndertake the patronage of a Poem in this nature, fince the like hath beene done by Roman *Lælius*, *Scipio*, *Mecænas*, and many other mighty Princes and Captaines, Nay, euen by *Auguſtus Cæfar* himfelfe, concerning whom *Ouid* is thus read, *De trifti* : *lib.* 2.

The Epiftle Dedicatorie.

Infpice ludorum fumptus Augufte tuorum
Empta tibi magno, talia multa leges
Hæc tu fpectafti, fpectandaque fæpe de defti
Maieftas adeo comis vbique tua est.

So highly were they refpected in the moft flourifhing eftate of the Roman Empire ; and if they haue
beene vilefied of late by any Separifticall humorift,
(as in the now queftioned *Hiftrio-maftix*) I hope by
the next Terme, (*Minerua afsiftente*) to giue fuch fatisfaction to the world, by vindicating many particulars
in that worke malicioufly exploded and condemned,
as that no Gentleman of qualitie and iudgement, but
fhall therein receiue a reafonable fatisfaction ; I am
loth by tedioufneffe to grow troublefome, therefore
conclude with a gratefull remembrance of my feruice
intermixt with Miriads of zealous wifhes for your
health of body, and peace of minde, with fuperabun-
dance of Earths bleffings, and Heauens graces, euer
remaining ;

Yours moft obferuant,

Thomas Heywood.

To the Reader.

F *Reader thou haſt of this Play beene an auditour? there is leſſe apology to be vſed by intreating thy patience. This* Tragi-Comedy *(being one referued amongſt two hundred and twenty, in which I haue had either an entire hand, or at the leaſt a maine finger, comming accidentally to the* Preſſe, *and I hauing Intelligence thereof, thought it not fit that it ſhould paſſe as* filius populi, *a Baſtard without a Father to acknowledge it : True it is, that my Playes are not expoſed vnto the world in Volumes, to beare the title of* Workes, *(as others) one reaſon is, That many of them by ſhifting and change of Companies, haue beene negligently lost, Others of them are ſtill retained in the hands of ſome Actors, who thinke it againſt their peculiar profit to haue them come in Print, and a third, That it neuer was any great ambition in me, to bee in this kind Volumniouſly read. All that I haue further to ſay at this time is onely this : Cenſure I intreat as fauourably, as it is expoſed to thy view freely, euer*

Studious of thy Pleaſure and Profit,

Thomas Heywood.

The Prologue.

 Strange *Play you are like to haue, for know,*
We vfe no Drum, nor Trumpet, nor Dumbe
*   fhow ;*
No Combate, Marriage, not fo much to day,
As Song, Dance, Mafque, to bumbafte out a
Play ;
Yet thefe all good, and ftill in frequent vfe
With our beft Poets ; *nor is this excufe*
Made by our Author, *as if want of skill*
Caus'd this defeCt ; it's rather his felfe will :
Will you the reafon know ?   There haue fo many
Beene in that kind, that Hee defires not any
At this time in His Sceane, no helpe, no ftraine,
Or flafh that's borrowed from an others braine ;
Nor fpeakes Hee this that Hee would haue you feare it,
He onely tries if once bare Lines will beare it ;
Yet may't afford, fo pleafe you filent fit,
Some Mirth, fome Matter, and perhaps fome Wit.

THE
ENGLISH
TRAVELLER.

Actus primus.   Scena prima,

Enter young Geraldine and master Dalauill.

Dal. H friend, that I to mine owne Notion
Had ioyned but your experience ; I
haue the Theoricke, But you the
Practicke.

Y. Ger. I perhaps, haue seene what you haue
onely read of.

Dal. There's your happinesse.
A Scholler in his study knowes the starres,
Their motion and their influence, which are fixt,
And which are wandering, can decipher Seas,
And giue each seuerall Land his proper bounds ;
But set him to the Compasse, hee's to seeke,
When a plaine Pilot can, direct his course
From hence vnto both th' Indies ; can bring backe
His ship and charge, with profits quintuple.

I haue read Ieruſalem, and ſtudied Rome,
Can tell in what degree each City ſtands,
Deſcribe the diſtance of this place from that,
All this the Scale in euery Map can teach,
Nay, for a neede could punctually recite
The Monuments in either ; but what I
Haue by relation only, knowledge by trauell
Which ſtill makes vp a compleat Gentleman,
Prooues eminent in you.
 Y. Ger. I muſt confeſſe,
I haue ſeene Ieruſalem and Rome, haue brought
Marke from th' one, from th' other Teſtimony,
Know Spaine, and France, and from their ayres haue
  fuckt
A breath of euery language : but no more
Of this diſcourſe ſince wee draw neere the place
Of them we goe to viſit.

Enter Clowne.

 Clo. Noble maſter Geraldine, worſhipfull maſter
Dalauill.
 Dal. I ſee thou ſtill remember'ſt vs.
 Clo. Remember you, I haue had ſo many memo-
randomes from the multiplicities of your bounties, that
not to remember you were to forget my ſelfe, you are
both moſt ingeniouſly and nobly welcome.
 Y. Ger. And why ingeniouſly and nobly ?
 Clo. Becauſe had I giuen your welcomes other
attributes then I haue done, the one being a Souldier,
and the other ſeeming a Scholler, I ſhould haue lied
in the firſt, and ſhewed my ſelfe a kind of blockhead
in the laſt.
 Y. Ger. I ſee your wit is nimble as your tongue,
But how doth all at home ?
 Clo. Small doings at home ſir, in regard that the
age of my Maſter correſponds not with the youth of
my Miſtris, and you know cold Ianuary and luſty May
ſeldome meet in coniunction.

Dal. I doe not thinke but this fellow in time may for his wit and vnderftanding make Almanackes ?

Clo. Not fo fir, you being more iudicious then I, ile giue you the preeminence in that, becaufe I fee by proofe you haue fuch iudgement in times and feafons.

Dal. And why in times and feafons ?

Clo. Becaufe you haue fo feafonably made choife, to come fo iuft at dinner time; you are welcome Gentlemen, ile goe tell my Mafter of your comming.

Exit Clowne.

Dal. A pleafant knaue.

Y. Ger. This fellow I perceiue
Is well acquainted with his Mafters mind,
Oh tis a good old man.

Dal. And fhee a Lady
For Beauty and for Vertue vnparraleld,
Nor can you name that thing to grace a woman
Shee has not in a full perfeçtion,
Though in their yeeres might feeme difparity
And therefore at the firft, a match vnfit ;
Imagine but his age and gouernement,
Withall, her modefty, and chafte refpeçt ;
Betwixt them, there's fo fweet a fimpathie,
As crownes a noble marriage.

Y. Ger. 'Tis acknowledged,
But to the worthy gentleman himfelfe,
I am fo bound in many courtefies,
That not the leaft, by all th' exprefsion
My Labour, or my Induftry can fhew,
I will know how to cancell.

Dal. Oh you are modeft.

Y. Ger. Hee ftudies to engroffe mee to himfelfe,
And is fo wedded to my company,
Hee makes mee ftranger to my Fathers houfe,
Although fo neere a neighbour.

Dal. This approues you,
To be moft nobly propertied, that from one
So exquifite in Iudgement, can Attraçt
So affeçtionate an eye.

Y. Ger.   Your Carracter,
I muſt beſtow on his vnmerrited loue,
As one that know I haue it, and yet ignorant
Which way I ſhould deſerue it : Heere both come.

Enter old Mr. Wincott, Wife, Prudentilla *the ſiſter, and
the* Clowne.

Winc.   Gentlemen, welcome, but what neede I vſe
A word ſo common, vnto ſuch to whom
My houſe was neuer priuate ; I expect
You ſhould not looke for ſuch a needles phraſe,
Eſpecially you Maſter Geraldine,
Your Father is my neighbour, and I know you,
Euen from the Cradle, then I loued your Infancy,
And ſince your riper growth better'd by trauell ;
My wife and you, in youth were play-fellowes,
And nor now be ſtrangers ; as I take it,
Not aboue two yeeres different in your Age.
    Wife.   So much hee hath out ſtript mee.
    Winc.   I would haue you
Thinke this your home, free as your Fathers houſe,
And to command it, as the Maſter on't ;
Call bouldly heere, and entertaine your friends,
As in your owne poſſeſsions, when I ſee't,
Ile ſay you loue me truely, not till then ;
Oh what a happineſſe your Father hath,
Farre aboue mee, one to inherit after him,
Where I (Heauen knowes) am childleſſe.
    Y. Ger.   That defect
Heauen hath ſupplied in this your vertuous Wife,
Both faire, and full of all accompliſhments,
My Father is a Widower, and heerein
Your happineſſe tranſcends him.
    Wife.   Oh Maſter Geraldine,
Flattery in Men's an adiunct of their ſex,
This Countrie breeds it, and for that, ſo farre
You needed not to haue trauell'd.
    Y. Ger.   Trueth's a word,

That fhould in euery language relifh well,
Nor haue I that exceeded.
   Wife. Sir, my Husband
Hath tooke much pleafure in your ftrange difcourfe
About Ierufalem and the Holy Land ;
How the new Citie differs from the old,
What ruines of the Temple yet remayne,
And whether Sion, and thofe hills about,
With thefe Adiacent Townes and Villages,
Keepe that proportioned diftance as wee read :
And then in Rome, of that great Piramis
Reared in the Front, on foure Lyons Mounted,
How many of thofe Idoll Temples ftand,
Firft dedicated to their Heathen gods,
Which ruined, which to better vfe repayred,
Of their Panthæon, and their Capitoll,
What Structures are demolifh't, what remaine.
   Winc. And what more pleafure to an old mans
      eare,
That neuer drew, faue his owne Countries aire,
Then heare fuch things related. I doe exceed him
In yeeres, I muft confeffe, Yet he much older
Then I in his experience.
   Prud. Mafter Geraldine,
May I bee bould to aske you but one queftion,
The which I'de be refolued in.
   Y. Ger. Any thing, that lies within my knowledge.
   Winc. Put him too't,
Doe Sifter, you fhall finde him (make no doubt)
Moft pregnant in his anfwere.
   Prud. In your trauells
Through France, through Sauoye, and through Italy,
Spaine, and the Empire, Greece and Paleftine,
Which breedes the choyceft beauties.
   Y. Ger. Introath Lady,
I neuer caft on any in thofe parts
A curious eye of cenfure, fince my Trauell
Was onely aymed at Language, and to know :

Thefe paft me but as common obiects did.
Seene, but not much regarded.
   Prud. Oh you ftriue
To expreffe a moft vnheard of modeftie,
And feldome found in any Traueller,
Efpecially of our Countrey, thereby feeking
To make your felfe peculiar.
   Y. Ger. I fhould be loath
Profeffe in outward fhew to be one Man.
And prooue my felfe another.
   Prud. One thing more,
Were you to marry, You that know thefe clymes,
Their ftates and their conditions, out of which
Of all thefe countries would you chufe your wife.
   Y. Ger. Ile anfwere you in briefe, (as I obferue)
Each feuerall clime for obiect, fare, or vfe,
Affords within it felfe, for all of thefe
What is moft pleafing to the man there borne ;
Spaine, that yeelds fcant of food, affords the Nation
A parfimonious ftomach, where our appetites
Are not content but with the large exceffe
Of a full table ; where the pleafing'ft fruits
Are found moft frequent, there they beft content ;
Where plenty flowes, it askes abundant Feafts ;
For fo hath prouident Nature dealt with all ;
So in the choyce of Women, the Greeke wan-
   tons
Compel'd beneath the Tnrkifh flauery,
Vaffaile themfelues to all men, and fuch beft
Pleafe the voluptious, that delight in change ;
The French is of one humor, Spaine another,
The hot Italian hee 's a ftraine from both,
All pleafed with their owne nations, euen the Moore.
Hee thinks the blackeft the moft beautifull ;
And Lady, fince you fo farre taxe my choyce,
Ile thus refolue you ; Being an Englifh man,
Mong'ft all thefe Nations I haue feene or tri'd,
To pleafe me beft, heere would I chufe my bride.

Pru. And happy were that Lady, in my thoughts,
Whom you would deine that grace too.
  Wife. How now Sifter,
This is a fafhion that's but late come vp,
For maids to court their husbands.
  Winc. I would wife
It were no worfe, vpon condition,
They had my helping hand and purfe to boote,
With both in ample meafure ; oh this Gentleman,
I loue, nay almoft doate on.
  Wife. Ya'ue my leaue,
To giue it full exprefsion.
  Winc. In thefe armes then,
Oh had my youth bin bleft with fuch a fonne,
To haue made my eftate to my name hereditary,
I fhould haue gone contented to my graue,
As to my bed ; to death, as to my fleepe ;
But Heauen hath will in all things, once more
    welcome,
And you fir, for your friends fake.
  Dal. Would I had in mee,
That which he hath, to haue clam'd it for mine owne,
How euer, I much thanke you.

Enter Clowne.

  Winc. Now fir, the newes with you.
  Clo. Dancing newes fir,
For the meat ftands piping hot vpon the dreffer,
The kitchin's in a heat, and the Cooke hath fo beftir'd
    himfelfe,
That hee's in a fweat. The Iacke plaies Muficke, and
    the Spits
Turne round too't.
  Winc. This fellowes my beft clocke,
Hee ftill ftrikes trew to dinner.
  Clo. And to fupper too fir, I know not how the day
goes with you, but my ftomacke hath ftrucke twelue,
I can affure you that.

Winc. You take vs vnprouided Gentlemen,
Yet fomething you fhall finde, and wee would rather
Giue you the entertaine of houfhold guefts,
Then complement of ftrangers, I pray enter.

Exeunt. Manet Clo.

Clo. Ile ftand too't, that in good hofpitality, there
can be nothing found that's ill, he that's a good
houfe-keeper, keepes a good table, a good table, is
neuer without good ftooles, good ftooles, feldome
without good guefts, good guefts, neuer without good
cheere, good cheere, cannot bee without good ftomackes, good ftomackes, without good digeftion, good
digeftion, keepes men in good health, and therefore
all good people, that beare good minds, as you loue
goodneffe, be fure to keepe good meat and drinke in
your houfes, and fo you fhall be called good men, and
nothing can come on't but good, I warrant you.

Exit.

Actus Primus.   Scena Secundus.

Enter two feruing-men Reignald *and* Robin.

Reig. Away you Corridon.

Rob. Shall I bee beate out of my Mafters houfe
thus ?

Reig. Thy Mafter, wee are Lords amongft our
felues,
And heere we Liue and Reigne, Two yeeres already
Are paft of our great Empire, and wee now
Write, Anno Tertio.

Rob. But the old man liues,
That fhortly will depofe you.

Reig. Ith' meane time,
I, as the mighty Lord and Senefhcall
Of this great houfe and caftle, banifh thee,

The very fmell ath' kitchin, bee it death,
To appeare before the dreffer.
    Rob. And why fo ?
    Reig. Becaufe thou ftink'ft of garlike, is that breath
Agreeing with our Pallace, where each Roome,
Smells with Muske, Ciuit, and rich Amber-greece,
Alloes, Cafsia, Aromaticke-gummes,
Perfumes, and Pouders, one whofe very garments
Scent of the fowlds and ftables, oh fie, fie,
What a bafe naftie rogue tis.
    Rob. Yet your fellow.
    Reig. Then let vs put a Cart-Horfe in rich
        trappings,
And bring him to the Tilt-yard.
    Rob. Prancke it, doe,
Wafte, Ryot, and Confume, Mifpend your Howres
In drunken Surfets, lofe your dayes in fleepe,
And burne the nights in Reuells, Drinke and Drab,
Keepe Chriftmaffe all yeere long, and blot leane
        Lent
Out of the Calender ; all that maffe of wealth
Got by my Mafters fweat and thrifty care,
Hauocke in prodigall vfes ; Make all flie,
Powr't downe your oylie throats, or fend it fmoaking
Out at the tops of chimnies : At his departure,
Was it the old mans charge to haue his windowes
Glifter all night with Starres ? his modeft Houfe
Turn'd to a common Stewes ? his Beds to pallats
Of Lufts and Proftitutions ? his Buttrey hatch
Now made more common then a Tauernes barre,
His Stooles that welcom'd none but ciuill guefts,
Now onely free for Pandars, Whores and Bawdes,
Strumpets, and fuch.
    Reig. I fuffer thee too long,
What is to me thy countrey ; or to thee
The pleafure of our Citie ? thou haft Cowes,
Cattell, and Beeues to feed, Oues and Boues,
Thefe that I keepe, and in this pafture graze.
Are dainty Damofellaes, bonny Girles ;

If thou be'ft borne to Hedge, Ditch, Thrafh and
      Plough
And I to Reuell, Banquet and Carrowfe ;
Thou Peffant, to the Spade and Pickaxe, I
The Battoone and Steeletto, thinke it onely
Thy ill, my good, our feuerall lots are caft,
And both muft be contented.
      Rob.   But when both our feruices are queftioned.
      Reig.   Looke thou to one,
My anfwere is prouided.

Enter *Y. Lionell.*

      Rob.   Farewell Musk-Cat.   *Exit.*
      Reig.   Adue good Cheefe and Oynons, ftuffe thy
      guts
With Specke and Barley-pudding for difgeftion,
Drinke Whig and fowre Milke, whileft I rince my
      Throat,
With Burdeaux and Canarie.
      Y. Lio.   What was hee ?
      Reig.   A Spie Sir,
One of their Hindes oth' countrey, that came prying
To fee what dainty fare our kitchin yeelds,
What Guefts we harbour, and what rule we keepe,
And threats to tell the old man when he comes ;
I thinke I fent him packing.
      Y. Lio.   It was well done.
      Reig.   A whorefon-Iack-an-apes, a bafe Baboone,
To infinuate in our fecrets.
      Y. Lio.   Let fuch keepe, the Countrey where their
charge is.
      Reig.   So I faid Sir.
      Y. Lio.   And vifit vs when we command them
      thence,
Not fearch into our counfels.
      Reig.   'Twere not fit.
      Y. Lio.   Who in my fathers abfence fhould com-
      mand,
Saue I his only fonne ?

Reig.   It is but iuftice.

Y. Lio.   For am not I now Lord?

Reig.   *Dominus fac totum.*

And am not I your Steward?

Y. Lio.   Well remembred,

This night I have a purpofe to bee Merry,

Iouiall and Frollicke, how doth our cafh hold out?

Reig.   The bag's ftill heauy.

Y. Lio.   Then my heart 's ftill light.

Reig.   I can affure you, yet tis pritty deepe,

Tho fcarce a mile to th' bottome.

Y. Lio.   Let mee haue

to Supper, Let mee fee, a Ducke——

Reig.   Sweet Rogue.

Y. Lio.   A Capon——

Reig.   Geld the Rafcall.

Y. Lio.   Then a Turkey——

Reig.   Now fpit him for an Infidell.

Y. Lio.   Greene Plouer, Snite,

Partridge, Larke, Cocke, and Pheffant.

Reig.   Nere a Widgin?

Y. Lio.   Yes, wait thy felfe at Table.

Reig.   Where I hope your felfe will not be abfent.

Y. Lio.   Nor my friends.

Reig.   Weele haue them then in plenty.

Y. Lio.   Cauiare, Sturgeon, Anchoues, pickle
        Oyfters : Yes.

And a Potato Pie; befides all thefe,

What thou think'ft rare and coftly.

Reig.   Sir, I know

What 's to be done; the ftocke that muft be fpent,

Is in my hands, and what I haue to doe,

I will doe fuddenly.

Y. Lie.   No Butchers meat,

Of that, beware in any cafe.

Reig.   I ftill remember,

Your father was no Grafier, if he were,

This were a way to eate vp all his Fields,

Hedges and all.

Y. Lio.   You will be gone fir.

Reig.   Yes, and you are ith' way going.   *Exit.*

Y. Lia.   To what may young men beft compare
    themfelues?

Better to what, then to a houfe new built?
The Fabricke ftrong, the Chambers well contriu'd,
Polifht within, without, well beautifi'd;
When all that gaze vpon the Edifice,
Doe not alone commend the workemans craft,
But either make it their faire prefident
By which to build another, or at leaft,
Wifh there to inhabite: Being fet to fale,
In comes a flothfull Tenant, with a Family
As lafie and debofht; Rough tempefts rife,
Vntile the roofe, which by their idleneffe,
Left vnrepaired, the ftormy fhowres beat in,
Rot the maine Poftes and Rafters, fpoile the Roomes,
Deface the Seelings, and in little fpace,
Bring it to utter Ruine, yet the fault,
Not in the Architector that firft reared it,
But him that fhould repaire it: So it fares
With vs yong men; Wee are thofe houfes made,
Our Parents raife thefe Structures, the foundation
Laid in our Infancy; and as wee grow
In yeeres, they ftriue to build vs by degrees,
Story on ftory higher; vp at height,
They cover vs with Councell, to defend vs
From ftormes without: they polifh vs within,
With Learnings, Knowledge, Arts and Difciplines;
All that is nought and vicious, they fweepe from vs,
Like Duft and Cobwebs, and our Roomes concealed,
Hang with the coftlieft hangings; Bout the Walls,
Emblems and beautious Symbols pictured round;
But when that lafie Tenant, Loue, fteps in,
And in his Traine, brings Sloth and Negligence,
Luft, Difobedience, and profufe Exceffe;
The Thrift with which our fathers tiled our Roofes,
Submits to euery ftorme and Winters blaft.

Enter *Blanda* a Whore, and *Scapha* a Bawde.

And yeelding place to euery riotous finne,
Giues way without, to ruine what's within :
Such is the ftate I ftand in.

   Blan. And how doth this Tire become me ?

   Sca. Rather aske, how your fweet carriage,
And Court behauiour, doth beft grace you, for Louers
   regard,
Not fo much the outward habit, as that which the
   garment couers.

   Y. Lio. Oh heer's that Haile, Shower, Tempeft,
   Storme, and Guft,
That fhatter'd hath this building ; Let in Luft,
Intemperance, appetite to Vice ; withall,
Neglect of euery Goodneffe ; Thus I fee,
How I am fincking in mine owne difeafe,
Yet can I not abide it.

   Bla. And how this Gowne ? I prethee view mee
   well,
And fpeake with thy beft Iudgement.

   Sca. What doe you talke of Gownes, and Orna-
   ments ;
That haue a Beautie, pretious in it felfe,
And becomes any thing.

   Y. Lio. Let me not liue, but fhe fpeaks nought but
   truth,
And ile for that reward her.

   Bla. All's one to mee, become they mee, or not,
Or bee I faire, or fowle, in others eyes,
So I appeare fo to my Lionell,
Hee is the glaffe, in whom I iudge my face,
By whom in order, I will dreffe thefe curles,
And place thefe Iewels, onely to pleafe him,
Why do'ft fmile.

   Sca. To heere a Woman, that thinks her felfe fo
wife, fpeake fo foolifhlie, that knowes well, and does
ill.

   Bla. Teach me wherein I erre.

Sca. Ile tell thee Daughter ; In that thou knoweſt
thy felfe to bee beloued of fo many, and fetleſt thy
affeċtion, only vpon one ; Doth the Mill grinde onely,
when the Wind fits in one corner ?   Or Shipps onely
Saile, when it's in this, or that quarter?   Is hee a
cunning Fencer, that lies but at one Guard?   Or he a
Skilfull Muſician, that plaies but on one String?   Is
there but one way to the Wood ?   And but one
Bucket that belongs to the Well ?   To affeċt one, and
defpife all other, becomes the precife Matron, not the
Proſtitute ; the loyall Wife, not the loofe Wanton :
Such haue I beene, as you are now, and fhould learne,
to Saile with all Windes, defend all Blowes, make
Muficke with all Strings, know all the wayes, to the
Wood, and like a good trauelling Hackney, learne to
drinke of all Waters.

Y. Lio.   May I mifcarry in my Blandaes loue ;
If I that old damnation, doe not fend
To Hell, before her time.

   Bla.   I would not haue you Mother, teach me
      ought,
That tends to injure him.

   Sca.   Well looke too 't when 'tis too late, and then
repent at leafure, as I haue done : Thou fee'ſt, heeres
nothing but Prodigallity and Pride, Wantoning, and
Waſting, Rioting, and Reuelling, Spoyling, and Spend-
ing, Gluttony, and Gormondiſing, all goes to Hauocke,
and can this hold out?   When he hath nothing left,
to helpe himfelfe, how can he Harbour thee ?   Looke
at length, to Drinke from a dry Bottle, and feed from
an emptie Knap-facke, looke too 't, 'twill come to
that.

   Y. Lio.   My parfemony fhall begin in thee,
And inſtantly, for from this houre, I vow,
That thou no more fhalt Drinke vpon my coſt,
Nor taſte the fmalleſt Fragment from my Board ;
Ile fee thee ſtarue ith' ſtreet firſt.

   Sca.   Liue to one man ? a ieaſt, thou may'ſt afwell,
tie thy felfe to one Gowne ; and what Foole, but will

change with the Fafhion, Yes, doe, Confine thy felfe
to one Garment, and vfe no Varietie, and fee how
foone it will Rot, and turne to Raggs.

Y. Lio. Thofe Raggs, be thy Reward ; Oh my
    fweet Blanda,
Onely for Thee, I wifh my Father dead,
And neere to Roufe vs from our Sweet delight ;
But for this Hag, this Beldam, fhee whofe backe,
Hath made her Items, in my Mercers Bookes,
Whofe rauenous Guts, I haue Stuft with Delicates,
Nay euen to Surfit ; and whofe frozen Blood,
I haue Warmed with Aquauitæ ; Be this day
My laft of Bounty, to a Wretch Ingrate,
But vnto Thee, a new Indenture Sealed,
Of an affection fixt, and Permanent,
Ile loue thee ftill, bee 't but to giue the lye,
To this old Cancker'd Worme.

Bla. Nay, be not angrie.

Y. Lio. With thee, my Soule fhall euer be at peace,
But with this loue feducer, ftill at Warre.

Enter Rioter *and two* Gallants.

Sca. Heere me but fpeake.

Y. Lio. Ope but thy lips againe, it makes a way,
To haue thy Tongue pluck'd out.

Rio. What all in Tempeft ?

Y. Lio. Yes, and the Storme, raifed by that
    Witches Spells,
Oh 'tis a Damn'd Inchantreffe.

Rio. What's the bufineffe ?

Bla. Onely fome few words, flipt her vnawares,
For my Sake, make her peace.

Rio. You charge me deepely,
Come Friend, will you be Moou'd at womens Words,
A man of your knowne iudgement ?

Y. Lio. Had you but heard,
The damn'd Erronious Doctrine that fhee taught,
You would haue iudg'd her to the Stake.

Bla. But Sweet heart,
Shee now Recants thofe Errours, once more Number
her
Amongft your Houfhold feruants.

Rio. Shall fhe beg, and be denyed ought from you?
Bla. Come this Kiffe, Shall end all former quarells.

Rio. 'Tis not pofsible,
Thofe Lippes fhould mooue in vaine, that two wayes
plead;
Both in their Speech, and Silence.

Y. Lio. You haue preuail'd,
But vpon this Condition, noway elfe,
Ile Senfure her, as fhee hath Sentenc'd thee;
But with fome fmall Inuerfion.

Rio. Speake, how's that?
Bla. Not too feuere, I prethee, fee poore wretch,
Shee at the barre, ftands quaking.

Y. Lio. Now, hold vp?
Rio. How man, how?
Y. Lio. Her hand, I meane; And now il'e fen-
tence thee,
According to thy Councell giuen to her:
Saile by one Winde; Thou fhalt, to one tune Sing,
Lie at one Guard, and Play but on one String,
Hencefoorth, I will Confine thee to one Garment,
And that fhall be a caft one, Like thy felfe
Iuft, paft all Wearing, as thou paft all Vfe,
And not to be renewed, til't be as Ragged,
As thou art Rotten.

Bla. Nay fweet.
Y. Lio. That for her Habbit.
Sca. A cold Sute, I haue on't.
Y. Lio. To preuent Surfit,
Thy Diet, fhall bee to one Difh confin'd,
And that too Rifled, with as vncleane hands,
As ere were laid on thee.

Sca. What hee fcants me in Victuals, would he
but alow mee in Drinke.

Y. Lio. That fhall be the refufe of the Flagons,
Iacks,
And Snuffes, fuch as the naftieft Breathes fhall leaue ;
Of Wine, and Strong-water, neuer hope,
Hencefoorth to Smell.

Sca. Oh me, I Faint already.

Y. Lio. If I fincke in my State, of all the reft,
Be thou excufed, what thou propofed to her,
Beldam, is now againft thy felfe decreed,
Drinke from drie fprings, from empty Knap-facks
feede.

Sca. No burnt Wine, nor Hot-waters.

She Swounds.

Y. Lio. Take her hence.

Bla. Indeede you are too cruell.

Y. Lio. Yes to her,
Onely of purpofe, to be kind to thee ;
Are any of my Guefts come ?

Rio. Feare not Sir,
You will haue a full Table.

Y. Lio. What, and Muficke ?

Rio. Beft Confort in the Citie, for fixe parts.

Y. Lio. Wee fhall haue Songs then ?

Rio. Bith' eare.   *Whifpers.*

Y. Lio. And Wenches ?

Rio. Yes bith' eye.

Bla. Ha, what was that you faid ?

Rio. We fhall haue fuch to beare you company,
As will no doubt content you.

Y. Lio. Euer then :
In Youth there is a Fate, that fwayes vs ftill,
To know what's Good, and yet purfue what's Ill.

Exeunt omnes.

Actus Secundus.   Scena Prima.

Enter old Mafter Wincott, *and his* Wife.

Winc. And what's this Dalauill ?

Wife. My apprehenfion,
Can giue him no more true exprefsion,
Then that he firft appeares, a Gentleman,
And well conditioned.

Winc. That for outward fhew;
But what in him haue you obferued elfe,
To make him better knowne?

Wife. I haue not Eyes,
To fearch into the inward Thoughts of Men,
Nor euer was I ftudied in that Art,
To iudge of Mens affection by the face;
But that which makes me beft opinion'd of him,
Is, That he's the Companion, and the Friend
Beloued of him, whom you fo much commend,
The Noble Mafter Geraldine.

Winc. Thou haft fpoke,
That which not onely crownes his true defert,
But now inftates him in my better thoughts,
Making his Worth, vnqueftioned.

Wife. Hee pretends
Loue to my fifter Pru. I haue obferu'd him,
Single her out, to priuate conference.

Winc. But I could rather, for her owne fake, wifh
Young Geraldine would fixe his thoughts that way,
And fhee towards him; In fuch Affinity,
Truft me, I would not vfe a fparing hand.

Wife. But Loue in thefe kindes, fhould not be
    compel'd,
Forc'd, nor Perfwaded; When it freely Springs,
And of it felfe, takes voluntary Roote,
It Growes, it Spreads, it Ripens, and brings foorth,
Such an Vfurious Crop of timely Fruit,
As crownes a plentious Autume.

Enter *Clowne.*

Winc. Such a Harueft,
I fhould not be th' vngladdeft man to fee,
Of all thy fifters friends: Now, whence come you?

Clo. Who, I Sir, From a Lodging of Lardgeffe, a

Houfe of Hofpitality, and a Pallace of Plenty; Where there's Feeding like Horfes, and Drinking like Fifhes; Where for Pints, w'are ferued in Pottles; and in ftead of Pottle-pots, in Pailes; in ftead of Siluer-tanckards, we drinke out of Water-tanckards; Clarret runs as freely, as the Cocks; and Canarie, like the Conduits of a Coronation day; Where there's nothing but Feeding and Frollicking; Caruing in Kifsing; Drinking, and Dauncing; Muficke and Madding; Fidling and Feafting.

Winc. And where, I pray thee, are all thefe Reuels kept?

Clo. They may be rather called Reakes then Reuells; As I came along by the doore, I was call'd vp amongft them; Hee-Gallants, and Shee-Gallants, I no fooner look'd out, but faw them out with their Kniues, Slafhing of Shoulders, Mangling of Legs, and Lanching of Loynes, till there was fcarce a whole Limbe left amongft them.

Winc. A fearefull Maffacre.

Clo. One was Hacking to cut off a Necke, this was Mangling a Breft, his Knife flip from the Shoulder, and onely cut of a Wing, one was picking the Braines out of a Head, another was Knuckle deepe in a Belly, one was Groping for a Liuer, another Searching for the Kidneyes; I faw one plucke the Sole from the Body (Goofe that fhe was to fuffer't) another prickt into the Breaft with his one Bill, Woodcocke to indure it.

Wife. How fell they out at firft?

Clo. I know not that, but it feemes, one had a Stomacke, and another had a Stomacke; But there was fuch biting and tearing with their teeths, that I am fure, I faw fome of their poore Carcafles pay for't.

Winc. Did they not fend for Surgeons?

Clo. Alas no, Surgeons helpe was too late; There was no ftitching vp of thofe Wounds, where Limbe was pluckt from Limbe; Nor any Salue for thofe Scarrs, which all the Plaifter of Paris cannot Cure.

Winc.   Where grew the quarrell firſt ?

Clo.   It ſeemes it was firſt Broacht in the Kitchin;
Certaine creatures being brought in thither, by ſome of
the Houſe ; The Cooke being a Colloricke fellow, did
ſo Towſe them and Toſſe them, ſo Plucke them and
Pull them, till hee left them as naked as my Naile,
Pinioned ſome of them like Fellons ; Cut the Spurres
from others of their Heeles ; Then downe went his
Spits, Some of them he ranne in at the Throat, and
out at the Back-ſide : About went his Baſting-Ladle,
where he did ſo beſawce them, that many a ſhrode
turne they had amongſt them.

Wife.   But in all this, How did the Women ſcape ?

Clo.   They fared beſt, and did the leaſt hurt that
I ſaw ; But for quietneſſe ſake, were forc'd to ſwallow
what is not yet digeſted, yet euery one had their ſhare,
and ſhee that had leaſt, I am ſure by this time, hath
her belly full.

Winc.   And where was all this hauocke kept ?

Clo.   Marry Sir, at your next neighbours, Young
Maſter Lionell, Where there is nothing but Drinking
out of Dry-Fats, and Healthing in Halfe-Tubs, his
Gueſts are fed by the Belly, and Beggers ſerued at his
Gate in Baskets ; Hee's the Adamant of this Age, the
Daffadill of theſe dayes, the Prince of Prodigallity, and
the very Cæſar of all young Citizens.

Winc.   Belike then, 'twas a Maſſacre of meat, not
as I apprehended ?

Clo.   Your grauity hath geſt aright; The chiefeſt
that fell in this Battell, were wild Fowle and tame
Fowle ; Pheſſants were wounded in ſtead of Alfareſſe,
and Capons for Captaines, Anchoues ſtood for An-
tiants, and Cauiare for Corporals, Diſhes were aſſaulted
in ſtead of Ditches, and Rabbets were cut to pieces
vpon the rebellings, ſome loſt their Legs, whil'ſt other
of their wings were forc'd to flie ; The Pioner vnder-
mind nothing but Pie-cruſt ; And——

Winc.   Enough, enough, your wit hath plai'd too
long vpon our patience ;

Wife, it grieues me much both for the yong and old
 man, the one,
Graces his head with care, endures the parching heat
 and biting cold,
The terrours of the Lands, and feares at Sea in trauell,
 onely to gaine
Some competent eftate to leaue his fonne ;
Whiles all that Merchandife, through Gulfes, Croffe-
 Tides,
Pirats and Stormes, he brings fo farre, Th' other
Heere Shipwrackes in the Harbour.
 Wife. Tis the care of Fathers ; and the weakeneffe
Incident to youth, that wants experience.

 Enter Y. Geraldine, Dallauill, Prudentilla, *laughing.*

 Clo. I was at the beginning of the Battell,
But heere comes fome, that it feemes
Were at the rifling of the dead Carcaffes ;
For by their mirth, they haue had part of the Spoile.
 Winc. You are pleafant, Gentlemen, what I en-
 treat,
Might be the Subieᴄt of your pleafant fport,
It promifeth fome pleafure ?
 Prud. If their recreation
Bee, as I make no queftion, on truth grounded,
'twill beget fudden laughter.
 Wife. What's the Proieᴄt ?
 Dal. Who fhall relate it.
 Winc. Mafter Geraldine, if there be any thing can
 pleafe my Eare,
With pleafant foundes, your Tongue muft be the In-
 ftrument,
On which the String muft ftrike.
 Dal. Bee't his then.
 Prud. Nay heare it, 'tis a good one.
 Wife. Wee intreat you, Poffeffe vs oth' Nouell.
 Winc. Speake, good Sir.
 Y. Ger. I fhall then, with a kind of Barbarifme,

Shaddow a Ieaſt, that askes a ſmoother Tongue,
For in my poore diſcourſe, I doe proteſt,
'twill but looſe his luſter.

Wife.   You are Modeſt.

Winc.   Howeuer, ſpeake, I pray; For my ſake
doo't ?

Clo.   This is like a haſtie Pudding, longer in eating,
then it was in making.

Y. Ger.   Then thus it was, this Gentleman and I,
Paſt but iuſt now, by your next Neighbours houſe,
Where as they ſay, dwels one Young Lionell.

Clo.   Where I was to night at Supper.

Winc.   An vnthrift Youth, his Father now at Sea.

Y. Ger.   Why that's the very Subiect, vpon which
It ſeemes, this Ieſt is grounded, there this Night,
Was a great feaſt.

Clo.   Why ſo I told you, Sir.

Winc.   Bee thou ſtill dumbe, 'tis hee that I would
heare.

Y. Ger.   In the height of their Carowſing, all their
braines,
Warm'd with the heat of Wine ; Diſcourſe was offer'd,
Of Ships, and Stormes at Sea ; when ſuddenly,
Out of his giddy wildneſſe, one conceiues
The Roome wherein they quafft, to be a Pinnace,
Moouing and Floating ; and the confuſed Noiſe,
To be the murmuring Windes, Guſts, Marriners ;
That their vnſtedfaſt Footing, did proceed
From rocking of the Veſſell : This conceiu'd,
Each one begins to apprehend the danger,
And to looke out for ſafety, flie ſaith one
Vp to the Maine-top, and diſcouer ; Hee
Climbes by the bed poſt, to the Teaſter, there
Reports a Turbulent Sea and Tempeſt towards ;
And wills them if they'le ſaue their Ship and liues,
To caſt their Lading ouer-board ; At this
All fall to Worke, and Hoyſte into the Street,
As to the Sea, What next come to their hand,
Stooles, Tables, Treſſels, Trenchers, Bed-ſteds, Cups,

Pots, Plate, and Glaffes ; Heere a fellow Whiftles,
They take him for the Boat-fwaine, one lyes ftrugling
Vpon the floore, as if he fwome for life,
A third, takes the Bafe-violl for the Cock-boate,
Sits in the belly on't, labours and Rowes ;
His Oare, the Sticke with which the Fidler plaid ;
A fourth, beftrides his Fellowes, thinking to fcape
As did Arion, on the Dolphins backe,
Still fumbling on a gitterne.

 Clo. Excellent Sport.

 Winc. But what was the conclufion ?

 Y. Ger. The rude multitude,
Watching without, and gaping for the fpoyle
Caft from the windowes, went bith' eares about it ;
The Conftable is called to Attone the broyle,
Which done, and hearing fuch a noife within,
Of eminent Ship-racke ; enters the houfe, and finds
  them
In this confufion, They Adore his ftaffe,
And thinke it Neptunes Trident, and that hee
Comes with his Tritons, (fo they cal'd his watch)
To calme the Tempeft, and appeafe the Waues ;
And at this point, wee left them.

 Clo. Come what will, ile fteale out of Doores,
And fee the end of it, that's certaine. *Exit.*

 Winc. Thanks Mafter Geraldine, for this difcourfe,
Introath it hath much pleafed mee, but the night
Begins to grow fafte on vs, for your parts,
You are all young, and you may fit vp late,
My eyes begin to fummon mee to fleepe,
And nothing's more offenfiue vnto Age,
Then to watch long and late.

 Y. Ger. Now good Reft with you.

 Dal. What faies faire Prudentilla ? Maids and
  Widdows,
And wee young Batchelors, fuch as indeed
Are forc'd to lie in Solitary beds,
And fleepe without difturbance, wee methinks,
Should defire later houres ; when Married Wiues,

That in their amorous armes, hug their delights ;
To often wakings fubiect ; their more haft,
May better bee excufed.

    Prud. How can you,
That are as you confeffe, a fingle man,
Enter fo farre into thefe Mifticall fecrets
Of Mariage, which as yet you neuer prooued.

    Dal. There's Lady, an inftinct innate in man,
Which prompts vs to the apprehenfions
Of th' vfes wee were borne to ; Such we are
Apteft to learne ; Ambitious moft to know,
Of which our chiefe is Marriage.

    Prud. What you Men
Moft meditate, wee Women feldome dreame of.

    Dal. When dreame Maids moft ?

    Prud. When thinke you ?

    Dal. When you lie vpon your Backs, come come,
      your Eare.   *Exit* Dal. *and* Prud.

    Y. Ger. Wee now are left alone.

    Wife. Why fay wee be who fhould be iealous
      of vs ?
This is not firft of many hundred Nights,
That wee two haue beene priuate, from the firft
Of our acquaintance, when our Tongues but clipt
Our Mothers-tongue, and could not fpeake it plaine,
Wee knew each other ; As in ftature, fo
Increaft our fweet Societie ; Since your trauell,
And my late Marriage, Through my Husbands loue,
Mid-night hath beene as Mid-day, and my Bed-
    chamber,
As free to you, as your owne Fathers houfe,
And you as welcome too't.

    Y. Ger. I muft confeffe,
It is in you, your Noble Courtefie,
In him, a more then common confidence,
And in this Age, can fcarce find prefident.

    Wife. Moft trew, it is withall an Argument,
That both our vertues are fo deepe impreft
In his good thoughts, hee knowes we cannot erre.

Y. Ger. A villaine were hee, to deceiue fuch truft,
Or (were there one) a much worfe Carracter.

Wife. And fhe no leffe, whom either Beauty, Youth,
Time, Place, or opportunity could tempt,
To iniure fuch a Husband.

Y. Ger. You deferue, euen for his fake, to be for
euer young;
And hee for yours, to haue his Youth renew'd;
So mutuall is your trew coniugall Loue;
Yet had the Fates fo pleaf'd

Wife. I know your meaning.
It was once voyc'd, that wee two fhould haue Matcht,
The World fo thought, and many Tongues fo fpake,
But Heauen hath now difpof'd vs otherwayes;
And being as it is, (a thing in me,
Which I proteft, was neuer wifht, nor fought)
Now done, I not repent it.

Y. Ger. In thofe times,
Of all the Treafures of my Hopes and Loue,
You were th' Exchequer, they were Stor'd in you;
And had not my vnfortunate Trauell croft them,
They had bin heere referued ftill.

Wife. Troath they had,
I fhould haue beene your trufty Treafurer.

Y. Ger. Howeuer let vs Loue ftill, I intreat :
That, Neighbour-hood and breeding will allow;
So much the Lawes Diuine and Humaine both,
Twixt Brother and a Sifter will approue;
Heauen then forbid, that they fhould limit vs
Wifh well to one another.

Wife. If they fhould not,
Wee might proclaime, they were not Charitable,
Which were a deadly fin but to conceiue.

Y. Ger. Will you refolue me one thing ?

Wife. As to one,
That in my Bofome hath a fecond place,
Next my deere Husband.

Y. Ger. That's the thing I craue,
And onely that, to haue a place next him.

Wife. Prefume on that already, but perhaps,
You meane to ftretch it further.

Y. Ger. Onely thus farre,
Your Husbands old, to whom my Soule doth wifh,
A Nefters age, So much he merits from me ;
Yet if (as proofe and Nature daily teach)
Men cannot alwayes liue, efpecially
Such as are old and Crazed ; Hee be cal'd hence,
Fairely, in full maturity of time,
And we two be referu'd to after life,
Will you conferre your Widow-hood on mee ?

Wife. You aske the thing, I was about to beg ;
Your tongue hath fpake mine owne thoughts.

Y. Ger. Vow to that.

Wife. As I hope Mercy.

Y. Ger. 'Tis enough, that word
Alone, inftates me happy ; Now fo pleafe you,
Wee will diuide, you to your priuate Chamber,
I to find out my friend.

Wife. Nay Mafter Geraldine,
One Ceremonie refts yet vnperform'd,
My Vow is paft, your oath muft next proceed,
And as you couet to be fure of me,
Of you I would be certaine.

Y. Ger. Make ye doubt ?

Wife. No doubt ; but Loue's ftill Iealous, and in
that
To be excufed ; You then fhall fweare by Heauen,
And as in all your future Acts, you hope
To thriue and profper ; As the Day may yeeld
Comfort, or the Night reft, as you would keepe
Entire, the Honour of your Fathers houfe,
And free your Name from Scandall and Reproach,
By all the Goodneffe that you hope to enioy,
Or ill to fhun——

Y. Ger. You charge me deeply Lady.

Wife. Till that day come, you fhall referue your
felfe

A fingle man ; Conuerfe nor company
With any Woman, Contract nor Combine,
With Maid, or Widow ; which expected houre,
As I doe wifh not hafte, fo when it happens,
It fhall not come vnwelcome ; You heare all,
Vow this.

Y. Ger.   By all that you haue faid, I fweare,
And by this Kiffe Confirme.

Wife.   Y'are now my Brother,
But then, my fecond Husband.   *Exeunt.*

Enter Y. Lionell, Rioter, Blanda, Scapha, *two* Gallants, *and two* Wenches, *as newly wak'd from fleepe.*

Y. Lio.   Wee had a ftormy night on't.

Bla.   The Wine ftill workes,
And with the little reft they haue tooke to night,
They are fcarce come to themfelues.

Y. Lio.   Now 'tis a Calme,
Thankes to thofe gentle Sea-gods, that haue brought vs
To this fafe Harbour ; Can you tell their names ?

Sca.   He with the Painted-ftaffe, I heard you call
Neptune.

Y. Lio.   The dreadfull god of Seas,
Vpon whofe backe neere ftucke March flees.

1. *Gall.*   One with the Bill, keepes Neptunes Porpofes,
So *Ouid* fayes in 's Metamorphofis.

2. *Gall.*   A third the learned Poets write on,
And as they fay, His name is Triton.

Y. Lio.   Thefe are the Marine gods, to whom my
father
In his long voyage prayes too ; Cannot they
That brought vs to our Hauen, bury him
In their Abiffe ?   For if he fafe ariue,
I with thefe Sailors, Syrens, and what not,
Am fure heere to be fhipwrackt.

1. *Wen.*   Stand vp ftiffe.

Rio.   But that the fhip fo totters : I fhall fall.

1. *Wen.*   If thou fall, Ile fall with thee.

Rio.   Now I fincke,
And as I diue and drowne, Thus by degrees,
Ile plucke thee to the bottome.   *They fall.*

Enter Reignald.

Y. Lio.   Amaine for England, See, fee,
The Spaniard now ftrikes Saile.
  Reig.   So muft you all.
  1. *Gall.*   Whence is your fhip, from the *Bermoothes* ?
  Reig.   Worfe, I thinke from Hell :
We are all Loft, Split, Shipwrackt, and vndone,
This place is a meere quick-fands.
  2. *Gall.*   So we feared.
  Reig.   Wher's my young Mafter ?
  Y. Sio.   Heere man, fpeake, the Newes ?
  Reig.   The Newes is, I, and you——
  Y. Lio.   What ?
  Reig.   Shee, and all thefe——
  Bla.   I ?
  Reig.   We and all ours, are in one turbulent Sea
Of Feare, Difpaire, Difafter and mifchance fwallowed :
Your father, Sir——
  Y. Lio.   Why, what of him ?
  Reig.   He is, Oh I want breath.
  Y. Lio.   Where ?
  Reig.   Landed, and at hand.
  Y. Lio.   Vpon what coaft ?   Who faw him ?
  Reig.   I, thefe eyes.
  Y. Lio.   Oh Heauen, what fhall I doe then ?
  Reig.   Aske ye me
What fhall become of you, that haue not yet
Had time of ftuddy to difpofe my felfe ;
I fay againe, I was vpon the Key,
I faw him land, and this way bend his courfe ;
What drunkard's this, that can out fleepe a ftorme
Which threatens all our ruines ?   Wake him.
  Bla.   Ho, Rioter, awake.
  Rio.   Yes, I am wake ;

How dry hath this Salt-water made me ; Boy,
Giue me th' other Glaffe.
    Y. Lio. Arife, I fay,
My Fathers come from Sea.
    Rio. If he be come, Bid him be gone againe.
    Reig. Can you trifle
At fuch a time, when your Inuentions, Braines,
Wits, Plots, Deuices, Stratagems, and all
Should be at one in action ? each of you
That loue your fafeties, lend your helping hands,
Women and all, to take this drunkard hence,
And to beftow him elfe where.
    Bla. Lift for Heauens fake.   *They carry him in.*
    Reig. But what am I the neerer, were all thefe
Conuey'd to fundry places and vnfeene ;
The ftaine of our diforders ftill remaine,
Of which, the houfe will witneffe, and the old man
Muft finde when he enters ; And for thefe

Enter againe.

I am here left to anfwere : What is he gone ?
    Y. Lio. But whither ? But into th' felfe fame houfe
That harbours him ; my Fathers, where we all
Attend from him furprifeall.
    Reig. I will make
That Prifon of your feares, your Sanctuaiy ,
Goe get you in together.
    Y. Lio. To this houfe ?
    Reig. Your Fathers, with your Sweet-heart, thefe
    and all ;
Nay, no more words but doo 't.
    Bla. That were to betray vs to his fury.
    Reig. I haue 't heere,
To Baile you hence at pleafure ; and in th' interim,
Ile make this fuppofed Goale, to you, as fafe
From the iniur'd old mans iuft incenfed fpleene,
As were you now together ith' Low-Countreyes,

Virginia, or ith' Indies.

   Bla. Prefent feare,
Bids vs to yeeld vnto the faint beliefe
Of the leaft hoped fafety.

   Reig. Will you in ?

   Omn. By thee we will be counfell'd.

   Reig. Shut them faft.

   Y. Lio. And thou and I to leaue them ?

   Reig. No fuch thing,
For you fhall beare your Sweet-heart company,
And helpe to cheere the reft.

   Y. Lio. And fo thou
Meaneft to efcape alone ?

   Reig. Rather without,
Ile ftand a Champion for you all within ;
Will you be fwai'd ? One thing in any cafe
I muft aduife ; The gates boulted and lockt,
See that 'mongft you no liuing voyce be heard ;
No not fo much as a Dog to howle,
Or Cat to mewe, all filence, that I charge ;
As if this were a meere forfaken houfe,
And none did there inhabite.

   Y. Lio. Nothing elfe ?

   Reig. And though the old man thunder at the
    gates
As if he meant to ruine what he had rear'd,
None on their liues to anfwere.

   Y. Lio. 'Tis my charge ;
Remaines there nothing elfe ?

   Reig. Onely the Key ;
For I muft play the goaler for your durance,
To bee the Mercurie in your releafe,

   Y. Lio. Me and my hope, I in this Key deliuer
To thy fafe truft.

   Reig. When you are faft you are fafe,
And with this turne 'tis done : What fooles are thefe,
To truft their ruin'd fortunes to his hands
That hath betrai'd his owne ; And make themfelues

Prifoner to one deferues to lie for all,
As being caufe of all ; And yet fomething prompts me,
Ile ftand it at all dangers ; And to recompence
The many wrongs vnto the yong man done :
Now, if I can doubly delude the old,
My braine, about it then ; All's hufht within,
The noife that fhall be, I muft make without ;
And he that part for gaine, and part for wit,
So farre hath trauell'd, ftriue to foole at home :
Which to effect, Art muft with Knauery ioyne,
And fmooth Diffembling meet with Impudence ;
Ile doe my beft, and howfoere it prooue,
My praife or fhame, 'tis but a feruants loue.

Enter old Lionell *like a ciuill Merchant, with Water-*
men, and two feruants with Burdens and Caskets.

 Old Lio. Difcharge thefe honeft Sailors that haue
  brought
Our Chefts a fhore, and pray them haue a care,
Thofe merchandife be fafe we left aboord :
As Heauen hath bleft vs with a fortunate Voyage,
In which we bring home riches with our healthes,
So let not vs prooue niggards in our ftore ;
See them paid well, and to their full content.
 1. *Ser.* I fhall Sir.
 Old Lio. Then returne : Thefe fpeciall things,
And of moft value, weele not truft aboord ;
Meethinkes they are not fafe till they fee home,
And there repofe, where we will reft our felues,
And bid farewell to Trauell ; for I vow,
After this houre no more to truft the Seas,
Nor throw mee to fuch danger.
 Reig. I could wifh
You had tooke your leaue oth' Land too.
 Old Lio. And now it much reioyceth me, to thinke
What a moft fudden welcome I fhall bring,
Both to my Friends and priuate Family.

Reig. Oh, but how much more welcome had he
beene,
That had brought certaine tidings of thy death.

Old Lio. But foft, what's this? my owne gates
fhut vpon me,
And barre their Mafter entrance? Whofe within
there?
How, no man fpeake, are all afleepe or dead,
That no foule ftirres to open?   *Knocks aloud.*

Reig. What madde man's that, who weary of his
life,
Dares once lay hand on thefe accurfed gates?

Old Lio. Whofe that? my feruant Reignald.

Reig. My old Mafter,
Moft glad I am to fee you; Are you well Sir?

Old Lio. Thou fee'ft I am.

Reig. But are you fure you are?
Feele you no change about you? Pray you ftand off.

Old Lio. What ftrange and vnexpected greetings
this,
That thus a man may knocke at his owne gates,
Beat with his hands and feet, and call thus loud,
And no man giue him entrance?

Reig. Said you Sir;
Did your hand touch that hammer?

Old Lio. Why, whofe elfe?

Reig. But are you fure you toucht it?

Old Lio. How elfe, I prethee, could I haue made
this noife?

Reig. You toucht it then?

Old Lio. I tell thee yet I did.

Reig. Oh for the love I beare you,
Oh me moft miferable, you, for your owne fake,
Of all aliue moft wretched; Did you touch it?

Old Lio. Why, fay I did?

Reig. You haue then a finne committed,
No facrifice can expiate to the Dead;
But yet I hope you did not.

Old Lio. 'Tis paft hope,

The deed is done, and I repent it not.

    Reig. You and all yours will doo't. In this one raſhnes,

You haue vndone vs all; Pray be not deſperate,

But firſt thanke Heauen that you haue eſcapt thus well ;

Come from the gate, yet further, further yet,

And tempt your fate no more ; Command your ſer-
uants

Giue off and come no neerer, they are ignorant,

And doe not know the danger, therefore pity

That they ſhould periſh in 't ; 'Tis full ſeuen moneths,

Since any of your houſe durſt once ſet foot

Ouer that threſhold.

    Old Lio. Preethee ſpeake the cauſe ?

    Reig. Firſt looke about, beware that no man heare,

Command theſe to remooue.

    Old Lio. Be gone. *Exit* Seruants. Now ſpeake.

    Reig. Oh Sir, This houſe is growne Prodigious,

Fatall, Difaſterous vnto you and yours.

    Old Lio. What Fatall? what Difaſterous ?

    Reig. Some Hoſt that hath beene owner of this houſe,

In it his Gueſt hath ſlaine ; And we ſuſpect

'Twas he of whom you bought it.

    Old Lio. How came this

Diſcouer'd to you firſt ?

    Reig. Ile tell you Sir,

But further from the gate : Your ſonne one night

Suppt late abroad, I within ; Oh that night,

I neuer ſhall forget ; Being ſafe got home,

I ſaw him in his chamber laid to reſt ;

And after went to mine, and being drowſie,

Forgot by chance, to put the Candle out ;

Being dead aſleepe ; Your ſonne affrighted, calls

So loud, that I ſoone waken'd ; Brought in light,

And found him almoſt drown'd in fearefull ſweat ;

Amaz'd to ſee't, I did demand the cauſe :

Who told me, that this murdered Ghoſt appeared,

His body gafht, and all ore-ftucke with wounds ;
And fpake to him as followes.

   Old Lio. Oh proceed,
'Tis that I long to heare.

   Reig. I am, quoth he,
A Tranf-marine by birth, who came well ftored
With Gold and Iewels, to this fatall houfe ;
Where feeking fafety, I encounter'd death :
The couetous Merchant, Land-lord of this rent,
To whom I gaue my life and wealth in charge ;
Freely to enjoy the one, rob'd me of both :
Heere was my body buried, here my Ghoft
Muft euer walke, till that haue Chriftian right ;
Till when, my habitation muft be here :
Then flie yong man, Remooue thy family,
And feeke fome fafer dwelling : For my death,
This manfion is accurft ; 'Tis my poffefsion,
Bought at the deere rate of my life and blood,
None enter here, that aymes at his owne good.
And with this charge he vanifht.

   Old Lio. Oh my feare,
Whither wilt thou tranfport me ?

   Reig. I intreat keepe further from the gate, and
    flie.

   Old Lio. Flie whither ? Why doeft not thou flie
too ?

   Reig. What need I feare, the Ghoft and I am
friends.

   Old Lio. But Reignald.

   Reig. Tufh, I nothing haue deferued,
Nor ought tranfgreft : I came not neere the gate.

   Old Lio. To whom was that thou fpakeft ?

   Reig. Was 't you Sir nam'd me ?
Now as I liue, I thought the dead man call'd,
To enquire for him that thunder'd at the gate
Which he fo dearely pai'd for : Are you madd,
To ftand a fore-feene danger ?

   Old Lio. What fhall I doe ?

   Reig. Couer your head and flie ; Left looking
    backe,

You fpie your owne confufion.

    Old Lio. Why doeft not thou flie too ?

    Reig. I tell you Sir,
The Ghoft and I am friends.

    Old Lio. Why didft thou quake then ?

    Reig. In feare left fome mifchance may fall on you,
That haue the dead offended ; For my part,
The Ghoft and I am friends : Why flie you not,
Since here you are not fafe ?

    Old Lio. Some bleft powers guard me.

    Reig. Nay Sir, ile not forfake you : I haue got the
    ftart ;
But ere the goale, 'twill aske both Braine and Art.

                                 Exeunt.

Aĕus Tertius. *Scena Prima.*

Enter old Mafter Geraldine, Y. Geraldine, *Mafter*
    Wincott, *and* Wife, Dalauill, Prudentilla.

    Winc. We are bound to you, kind Mafter Geral-
    dine,
For this great entertainement ; Troath your coft
Hath much exceeded common neighbour-hood :
You haue feafted vs like Princes.

    Old Ger. This, and more
Many degrees, can neuer counteruaile
The oft and frequent welcomes giuen my fonne :
You haue tooke him from me quite, and haue I thinke,
Adopted him into your family,
He ftaies with me fo feldome.

    Win. And in this,
By trufting him to me, of whom your felfe
May haue both vfe and pleafure, y'are as kind
As money'd men, that might make benefit
Of what they are poffeft, yet to their friends

In need, will lend it gratis.

 Wife. And like fuch,
As are indebted more then they can pay ;
Wee more and more confeſſe our ſelues engaged
To you, for your forbearance.

 Prud. Yet you ſee,
Like Debtors, ſuch as would not breake their day ;
The Treaſure late receiued, wee tender backe,
The which, the longer you can ſpare, you ſtill
The more ſhall binde vs to you.

 Old Ger. Moſt kind Ladies,
Worthy you are to borrow, that returne
The Principall, with ſuch large vſe of thanks.

 Dal. What ſtrange felicitie theſe Rich men take,
To talke of borrowing, lending, and of vſe ;
The vſurers language right.

 Winc. Y'aue Maſter Geraldine,
Faire walkes and gardens, I haue praiſed them,
Both to my Wife and Siſter.

 Old Ger. You would ſee them,
There's no pleaſure that the Houſe can yeeld,
That can be debar'd from you ; prethee Sonne,
Be thou the Vſher to thoſe Mounts and Profpects
May one day call thee Maſter.

 Y. Ger. Sir I ſhall ;
Pleaſe you to walke.

 Prud. What Maſter Dalauill,
Will you not beare vs company.

 Dal. 'Tis not fit
That wee ſhould leaue our Noble hoſt alone,
Be you my Friends charge, and this old man mine.

 Prud. Well, bee't then at your pleaſure. *Exeunt.*

   Manet Dalauill *and* Old Geraldine.

 Dal. You to your Profpects, but there's proiect
  heere
That's of another Nature ; Worthy Sir,
I cannot but approue your happineſſe,
To be the Father of ſo braue a Sonne,

So euery way accomplifh't and made vp,
In which my voice is leaft : For I alaffe,
Beare but a meane part in the common quier,
When with much lowder accents of his praife,
So all the world reports him.

   Old Ger. Thanke my Starres,
They haue lent me one, who as he alwayes was,
And is my prefent ioy ; If their afpect
Be no wayes to our goods Maleuolent,
May be my Future comfort.

   Dal, Yet muft I hold him happie aboue others,
As one that Solie to himfelfe inioyes
What many others aime at ; But in vaine.

   Old Ger. How meane you that ?

   Dal. So Beautifull a Miftreffe.

   Old Ger. A Miftreffe, faid you ?

   Dal. Yes Sir, or a Friend,
Whether you pleafe to ftile her.

   Old Ger. Miftrefle ? Friend ?
Pray be more open languag'd.

   Dal. And indeed,
Who can blame him to abfent himfelfe from home,
And make his Fathers houfe but as a grange,
For a Beautie fo Attractiue ? Or blame her,
Huging fo weake an old Man in her armes,
To make a new choice, of an equall youth,
Being in him fo Perfect ? yet introath,
I thinke they both are honeft.

   Old Ger. You haue Sir,
Poffeft me with fuch ftrange fancies.

   Dal. For my part,
How can I loue the perfon of your Sonne,
And not his reputation ? His repaire
So often to the Houfe, is voyct by all,
And frequent in the mouthes of the whole Countrey,
Some equally addicted, praife his happineffe ;
But others, more Cenforious and Auftere,
Blame and reprooue a courfe fo difolute ;
Each one in generall, pittie the good man,

As one vnfriendly dealt with, yet in my confcience,
I thinke them truely Honeft.

 Old Ger. 'Tis fufpitious.

 Dal. True Sir, at beft ; But what when fcandal-
ous tongues
Will make the worft ? and what good in it felfe,
Sullie and ftaine by fabulous mif-report ;
For let men liue as charie as they can,
Their liues are often queftioned ; Then no wonder,
If fuch as giue occafion of fufpition,
Be fubiect to this fcandall : What I fpeake,
Is as a Noble Friend vnto your Sonne ;
And therefore, as I glory in his Fame,
I fuffer in his wrong ; for as I liue,
I thinke, they both are honeft.

 Old Ger. Howfoeuer,
I wifh them fo.

 Dal. Some courfe might be deuif'd,
To ftop this clamor ere it grow too wrancke ;
Left that which yet but inconuenience feemes,
May turne to greater mifchiefe ; This I fpeake
In Zeale to both, in foueraine care of him
As of a Friend ; And tender of her Honour,
As one to whom I hope to be allyed,
By Marriage with her Sifter.

 Old Ger. I much thanke you,
For you haue cleerely giuen me light of that,
Till now I neuer dreamt on.

 Dal. 'Tis my Loue,
And therefore I intreat you, make not mee
To be the firft reporter.

 Old Ger. You haue done
The office of a Noble Gentleman,
And fhall not be fo iniur'd.

 Enter againe as from Walking Winc. Wife, Y. Ger.
      Prud.

 Winc. See Mafter Geraldine,
How bold wee are, efpecially thefe Ladies

Play little better then the theeues with you,
For they haue robb'd your Garden.

Wife. You might Sir,
Better haue term'd it faucenes, then theft ;
You fee we blufh not, what we tooke in priuate,
To weare in publicke view.

Prud. Befides, thefe cannot
Be mift out of fo many ; In full fields,
The gleanings are allow'd.

Old Ger. Thefe and the reft,
Are Ladies, at your feruice.

Winc. Now to horfe,
But one thing ere wee part, I muft intreat ;
In which my Wife will be ioynt futer with me,
My Sifter too.

Old Ger. In what, I pray.

Winc. That hee
Which brought vs hither, may but bring vs home ;
Your much refpected Sonne.

Old Ger. How men are borne,
To woe their owne difafters ?

Wife. But to fee vs
From whence he brought vs Sir, that's all.

Old Ger. This fecond motion makes it Palpable :
To note a Womans cunning ; Make her husband
Bawde to her owne laciuious appetite,
And to Solicite his owne fhame.

Prud. Nay Sir,
When all of vs ioyne in fo fmall a fuit,
It were fome iniurie to be deni'd.

Old Ger. And worke her Sifter too ; What will
    not woman
To accomplifh her owne ends : But this difeafe,
Ile feeke to Phificke ere it grow too farre :
I am moft forrie to be vrg'd fweet Friends,
In what at this time I can no wayes grant ;
Moft, that thefe Ladies fhould be ought deni'd,
To whom I owe all Seruice, but occafions
Of weighty and important confcequence,

Such as concerne the beft of my Eftate,
Call him afide ; excufe vs both this once,
Prefume this bufineffe is no fooner ouer,
But hee's at his owne freedome.

Winc.   'Twere no manners
In vs to vrge it further, wee will leaue you,
With promife Sir, that he fhall in my will,
Not be the laft remembred.

Old Ger.   Wee are bound to you ;
See them to Horfe, and inftantly returne,
Wee haue Imployments for you.

Y. Ger.   Sir I fhall.

Dal.   Remember your laft promife.

Old Ger.   Not to doo 't,
I fhould forget my felfe : If I finde him falfe
To fuch a friend, be fure he forfeits me ;
In which to be more punctually refolu'd,
I haue a proiect how to fift his foule,
How 'tis enclin'd ; whether to yonder place,

Enter Y. Geraldine.

The cleare bright Pallace, or blacke Dungeon : See,
They are onward on the way, and hee return'd.

Y. Ger.   I now attend your pleafure.

Old Ger.   You are growne perfect man, and now
      you float
Like to a well built Veffell ; 'Tweene two Currents,
Vertue and Vice ; Take this, you fteere to harbour
Take that, to eminent fhipwracke.

Y. Ger.   Pray your meaning.

Old Ger.   What fathers cares are, you fhall neuer
      know,
Till you your felfe haue children, Now my ftuddy,
Is how to make you fuch, that you in them
May haue a feeling of my loue to you.

Y. Ger.   Pray Sir expound your felfe ; for I proteft
Of all the Languages I yet haue learn'd,
This is to me moft forraine.

Old Ger.   Then I ſhall ;
I haue liued to ſee you in your prime of youth
And height of Fortune, ſo you will but take
Occaſion by the forehead ; to be briefe,
And cut off all ſuperfluous circumſtance,
All the ambition that I ayme at now,
Is but to ſee you married.
   Y. Ger.   Married Sir.
   Old Ger.   And to that purpoſe, I haue found out
    one,
Whoſe Youth and Beauty may not onely pleaſe
A curious eye ; But her immediate meanes,
Able to ſtrengthen a ſtate competent,
Or raiſe a ruined Fortune.
   Y. Ger.   Of all which,
I haue beleeue me, neither need nor vſe ;
My competence beſt pleaſing as it is ;
And this my ſingularity of life,
Moſt to my mind contenting.
   Od Ger.   I ſuſpect, but yet muſt proue him further ;
Say to my care I adde a Fathers charge,
And couple with my counſell my command ;
To that how can you anſwere ?
   Y. Ger.   That I hope :
My duty and obedience ſtill vnblam'd,
Did neuer merit ſuch auſterity ;
And from a father neuer yet diſpleas'd.
   Old Ger.   Nay, then to come more neere vnto the
    point ;
Either you muſt reſolue for preſent marriage,
Or forfeit all your intereſt in my loue.
   Y. Ger.   Vn-ſay that language, I intreat you Sir,
And doe not ſo oppreſſe me ; Or if needs
Your heauy impoſition ſtand in force,
Reſolue me by your counſell ; With more ſafety
May I infringe a ſacred vow to heauen,
Or to oppoſe me to your ſtrict command ?
Since one of theſe I muſt.
   Old Ger.   Now Dalauill,

I finde thy words too true.

 Y. Ger. For marrie, Sir, I neither may, nor can.

 Old Ger. Yet whore you may ;

And that's no breach of any vow to Heauen :

Pollute the Nuptiall bed with Michall finne ;

Afperfe the honour of a noble friend ;

Forfeit thy reputation, here below,

And th' intereft that thy Soule might claime aboue,

In yon bleft City : Thefe you may, and can,

With vntoucht confcience : Oh, that I fhould liue

To fee the hopes that I haue ftor'd fo long,

Thus in a moment ruin'd : And the ftaffe,

On which my old decrepite age fhould leane ;

Before my face thus broken : On which trufting,

I thus abortiuely, before my time,

Fall headlong to my Graue.   *Falls on the earth.*

 Y. Ger. It yet ftands ftrong ;

Both to fupport you vnto future life,

And fairer comfort.

 Old Ger. Neuer, neuer fonne :

For till thou canft acquit thy felfe of fcandall,

And me of my fufpition ; Heere, euen heere,

Where I haue meafur'd out my length of earth ;

I fhall expire my laft.

 Y. Ger. Both thefe I can :

Then rife Sir, I intreat you ; And that innocency,

Which poyfon'd by the breath of Calumnie,

Caft you thus low, fhall, thefe few ftaines wipt off,

With better thoughts erect you.

 Old Ger. Well, Say on.

 Y. Ger. There's but one fire from which this
  fmoake may grow :

Namely, the vnmatcht yoake of youth ; And

In which, If euer I occafion was,

Of the fmalleft breach ; the greateft implacable mifchiefe

Adultery can threaten, fall on me ;

Of you may I be difauow'd a fonne ;

And vnto Heauen a feruant : For that Lady,
As fhe is Beauties mirror, fo I hold her
For Chaftities examples : From her tongue,
Neuer came language, that ariued my eare,
That euen cenfurious *Cato*, liu'd he now,
Could mif-interpret ; Neuer from her lips,
Came vnchafte kiffe ; Or from her conftant eye,
Looke fauouring of the leaft immodefty :
Further——
   Old Ger. Enough ; One onely thing remaines,
Which on thy part perform'd, affures firme credit
To thefe thy proteftations.
   Y. Ger. Name it then.
   Old Ger. Take hence th' occafion of this common
    fame ;
Which hath already fpread it felfe fo farre,
To her difhonour and thy preiudice,
From this day forward, to forbeare the houfe :
This doe vpon my blefsing.
   Y. Ger. As I hope it,
I will not faile your charge.
   Old Ger. I am fatisfied.   *Exeunt.*

Enter at one doore an Vfurer *and his Man, at the other,*
  Old Lionell *with his feruant : In the midft* Reignald.

   Reig. To which hand fhall I turne me ; Here's my
    Mafter
Hath bin to enquire of him that fould the houfe,
Touching the murder ; Here's an Vfuring-Rafcall,
Of whom we haue borrowed money to fupply
Our prodigall expences ; Broke our day,
And owe him ftill the Principall and Vfe :
Were I to meet them fingle, I haue braine
To oppofe both, and to come off vnfcarr'd ;
But if they doe affault me, and at once,
Not *Hercules* himfelfe could ftand that odds :
Therefore I muft encounter them by turnes ;
And to my Mafter firft : Oh Sir, well met.
   Old Lio. What Reignald ; I but now met with the
    man,

Of whom I bought yon houfe.

    Reig.   What, did you Sir?
But did you fpeake of ought concerning that
Which I laft told you.

    Old Lio.   Yes, I told him all.

    Reig.   Then am I caft: But I pray tell me Sir,
Did he confeffe the murder?

    Old Lio.   No fuch thing;
Moft ftiffely he denies it.

    Reig.   Impudent wretch;
Then ferue him with awarrant, let the Officer
Bring him before a Iuftice, you fhall heare
What I can fay againft him; Sfoot deni't:
But I pray Sir excufe me, yonder's one
With whom I haue fome bufineffe; Stay you here,
And but determine what's beft courfe to take,
And note how I will follow't.

    Old Lio.   Be briefe then.

    Reig.   Now, If I can afwell put off my Vfe-man,
This day, I fhall be mafter of the field.

    Vfu.   That fhould be Lionells man.

    Man.   The fame, I know him.

    Vfu.   After fo many friuolous delaies,
There's now fome hope. He that was wont to fhun vs,
And to abfent himfelfe, accoafts vs freely;
And with a pleafant countenance: Well met Reignald,
What's this money ready?

    Reig.   Neuer could you
Haue come in better time.

    Vfu.   Where's your mafter,
Yong Lionell, it fomething troubles me,
That hee fhould breake his day.

    Reig.   A word in priuate.

    Vfu.   Tufh, Priuate me no priuates, in a word,
Speake, are my moneys ready?

    Reig.   Not fo loud.

    Vfu.   I will be louder yet; Giue me my moneys,
Come, tender me my moneys.

    Reig.   We know you haue a throat, wide as your
    confcience;

You need not vfe it now——Come, get you home.

Vfu. Home?

Reig. Yes, home I fay, returne by three a Clocke,
And I will fee all cancell'd.

Vfu. 'Tis now paft two, and I can ftay till three,
Ile make that now my bufineffe, otherwayes,
With thefe lowd clamors, I will haunt thee ftill;
Giue me my Vfe, giue me my Principall.

    Reig. This burre will ftill cleaue to me ; what, no
      meanes
To fhake him off; I neere was caught till now :
Come come, y'are troublefome.

Vfu. Preuent that trouble,
And without trifling, pay me downe my cafh ;
I will be fool'd no longer.

Reig. So fo fo.

Vfu. I haue beene ftill put off, from time to time,
And day to day ; thefe are but cheating tricks,
And this is the laft minute ile forbeare
Thee, or thy Mafter : Once againe, I fay,
Giue me my Vfe, giue me my Principall.

Reig. Pox a this vfe, that hath vndone fo many ;
And now will confound mee.

Old Lio. Haft thou heard this?

Ser. Yes Sir, and to my griefe.

Old Lio. Come hither Reignald.

Reig. Heere Sir ; Nay, now I am gone.

Old Lio. What vfe is this?
What Principall hee talkes of? in which language
Hee names my Sonne ; And thus vpbraideth thee,
What is't you owe this man?

Reig. A trifle Sir,
Pray ftop his mouth; And pay't him.

Old Lio. I pay, what?

Reig. If I fay pay't him ; Pay't him.

Old Lio. What's the Summe?

Reig. A toy, the maine about fiue hundred pounds ;
And the vfe fiftie.

Old Lio. Call you that a toy?

To what vfe was it borrowed? At my departure,
I left my Sonne fufficient in his charge,
With furplus, to defray a large expence,
Without this neede of borrowing.
 Reig. 'Tis confeft,
Yet ftop his clamorous mouth; And onely fay,
That you will pay't to morrow.
 Old Lio. I paffe my word.
 Reig. Sir, if I bid you doo't; Nay, no more
  words,
But fay you'le pay't to morrow.
 Old Lio. Ieaft indeed,
But tell me how thefe moneys were beftowed?
 Reig. Safe Sir, I warrant you.
 Old Lio. The Summe ftill fafe,
Why doe you not then tender it your felues?
 Reig. Your eare fir; This fumme ioyn'd to the reft,
Your Sonne hath purchaft Land and Houfes.
 Old Lio. Land, do'ft thou fay?
 Reig. A goodly Houfe, and Gardens.
 Old Lio. Now ioy on him,
That whil'ft his Father Merchandis'd abroad,
Had care to adde to his eftate at home:
But Reignald, wherefore Houfes?
 Reig. Now Lord Sir,
How dull you are; This houfe poffeft with fpirits,
And there no longer ftay; Would you haue had
Him, vs, and all your other family,
To liue, and lie ith' ftreets; It had not Sir,
Beene for your reputation.
 Old Lio. Blefsing on him,
That he is growne fo thriftie.
 Vfu. 'Tis ftrooke three,
My money's not yet tender'd.
 Reig. Pox vpon him,
See him difcharged, I pray Sir.
 Old Lio. Call vpon me
To morrow Friend, as early as thou wilt;
Ile fee thy debt defraid.

Vfu. It is enough, I haue a true mans word.

Exit. Vfurer and man.

Old Lio. Now tell me Reignald,
For thou haft made me proud of my Sonnes thrift;
Where, in what Countrey, doth this faire Houfe ftand.

Reig. Neuer in all my time, fo much to feeke;
I know not what to anfwere.

Old Lio. Wherefore ftuddieft thou?
Vfe men to purchafe Lands at a deere rate,
And know not where they lie?

Reig. 'Tis not for that;
I onely had forgot his name that fould them,
'Twas let me fee, fee.

Old Lio. Call thy felfe to minde.

Reig. Non-pluft or neuer now; Where art thou
braine?
O Sir, where was my memory; 'Tis this houfe
That next adioynes to yours.

Old Lio. My Neighbour Ricots.

Reig. The fame, the fame Sir; Wee had peni-
worths in't;
And I can tell you, haue beene offer'd well
Since, to forfake our bargaine.

Old Lio. As I liue,
I much commend your choice.

Reig. Nay, 'tis well feated,
Rough-caft without, but brauely lined within;
You haue met with few fuch bargaines.

Old Lio. Prethee knocke,
And call the Mafter, or the feruant on't;
To let me take free view on't.

Reig. Puzzle againe on Puzzle; One word Sir,
The Houfe is full of Women, no man knowes,
How on the inftant, they may be imploy'd;
The Roomes may lie vnhanfome; and Maids ftand
Much on their cleanlineffe and hufwiferie;
To take them vnprouided, were difgrace,
'Twere fit they had fome warning; Now, doe you

Fetch but a warrant, from the Iuftice Sir ;
You vnderftand mee.

   Old Lio.   Yes, I˙doe.

   Reig.   To attach
Him of fufpeċted murder, Ile fee't feru'd ;
Did he deny't ?   And in the intrim, I
Will giue them notice, you are now ariu'd,
And long to fee your purchafe.

   Old Lio.   Councell'd well ;
And meet fome halfe houre hence.

   Reig.   This plunge well paft,
All things fall euen, to Crowne my Braine at laft.

                           Exeunt.

         Enter Dalauill *and a* Gentleman.

   Gent.   Where fhall we dine to day ?

   Dal.   At th' Ordinarie.
I fee Sir, you are but a ftranger heere ;
This Barnet, is a place of great refort ;
And commonly vpon the Market dayes,
Heere all the Countrey Gentlemen Appoint,
A friendly meeting ; Some about affaires
Of Confequence and Profit ; Bargaine, Sale,
And to conferre with Chap-men, fome for pleafure,
To match their Horfes ; Wager in their Dogs,
Or trie their Hawkes ; Some to no other end,
But onely meet good Company, difcourfe,
Dine, drinke, and fpend their Money.

      Enter Old Geraldine *and* Yong Geraldine.

   Gent.   That's the Market, Wee haue to make this
      day.

   Dal.   'Tis a Commoditie, that will be easily vented :
What my worthy Friend,
You are happily encounter'd ; Oh, y'are growne
      ftrange,
To one that much refpeċts you ; Troath the Houfe

Hath all this time feem'd naked without you;
The good Old Man doth neuer fit to meat,
But next his giuing Thankes, hee fpeakes of you;
There's fcarce a bit, that he at Table taftes,
That can digeft without a Geraldine,
You are in his mouth fo frequent : Hee and Shee
Both wondering, what diftafte from one, or either,
So fuddenly, fhould alianate a Gueft,
To them, fo deerely welcome.
    Old Ger. Mafter Dalauill,
Thus much let me for him Apoligie;
Diuers defignes haue throng'd vpon vs late,
My weakenefle was not able to fupport
Without his helpe; He hath bin much abroad,
At London, or elfe where; Befides 'tis Terme;
And Lawyers muft be followed, feldome at home,
And fcarcely then at leafure.
    Dal. I am fatisfied,
And I would they were fo too, but I hope Sir,
In this reftraint, you haue not vs'd my name?
    Old Ger. Not, as I liue.
    Dal. Y'are Noble——Who had thought
To haue met with fuch good Company; Y'are it
    feeme
But new alighted; Father and Sonne, ere part,
I vow weele drinke a cup of Sacke together;
Phificians fay, It doth prepare the appetite
And ftomacke againft dinner.
    Old Ger. Wee old men,
Are apt to take thefe courtefies.
    Dal. What fay you Friend?
    Y. Ger. Ile but enquire for one, at the next
    Inne,
And inftantly returne.
    Dal. 'Tis enough.   *Exit.*

    Enter Beffe *meeting* Y. Geraldine.

    Y. Ger. Beffe : How do'ft thou Girle?

Beff. Faith we may doe how we lift for you, you
  are growne fo
Great a ftranger : We are more beholding
To Mafter Dalauill, Hee's a conftant Gueft :
And howfoere to fome, that fhall bee namelefe,
His prefence may be gracefull ; Yet to others——
I could fay fomewhat.
    Y. Ger. Hee's a noble fellow,
And my choice friend.
    Beff. Come come, he is, what he is ; and that the
  end will prooue.
    Y. Ger. And how's all at home ?
Nay, weele not part without a glaffe of wine,
And meet fo feldome : Boy.

Enter Drawer.

Drawer. Anon, anon Sir.
    Y. Ger. A Pint of Clarret, quickly. *Exit* Drawer.
Nay, fit downe : The newes, the newes, I pray thee ;
I am fure, I haue beene much enquir'd of
Thy old Mafter, and thy young Miftris too.
    Beff. Euer your name is in my Mafters mouth, and
  fometimes too
In hers, when fhe hath nothing elfe to thinke of :
Well well, I could fay fomewhat.

Enter Drawer.

Drawer. Heere's your wine Sir.   *Exit.*
    Y. Ger. Fill Boy : Here Beffe, this glaffe to both
  their healths ;
Why do'ft weepe my wench ?
    Beff. Nay, nothing Sir.
    Y. Ger. Come, I muft know.
    Beff. Introath I loue you Sir,
And euer wifht you well ; You are a Gentleman,
Whom alwayes I refpected ; Know the paffages
And priuate whifperings, of the fecret loue

Betwixt you and my Miſtris; I dare ſweare,
On your part well intended : But——
   Y. Ger. But what ?
   Beſſ. You beare the name of Land-lord, but
    another
Inioyes the rent ; You doate vpon the ſhadow,
But another he beares away the ſubſtance.
   Y. Ger. Bee more plaine.
   Beſſ. You hope to inioy a vertuous widdow-hood ;
But Dalauill, whom you eſteeme your friend,
Hee keepes the wife in common.
   Y. Ger. Y'are too blame,
And Beſſe, you make me angry ; Hee's my friend,
And ſhe my ſecond ſelfe ; In all their meetings,
I neuer ſaw ſo much as caſt of eye
Once entertain'd betwixt them.
   Beſſ. That's their cunning.
   Y. Ger. For her ; I haue beene with her at all
    houres,
Both late and early ; In her bed-chamber,
And often ſingly vſher'd her abroad :
Now, would ſhe haue bin any mans aliue,
Shee had bin mine ; You wrong a worthy Friend,
And a chaſte Miſtris, y'are not a good Girle ;
Drinke that, ſpeake better of her, I could chide you,
But I'le forbeare ; What you haue raſhly ſpoke,
Shall euer heere be buried.
   Beſſ. I am ſorry my freeneſſe ſhould offend you,
But yet know, I am her Chamber-maid.
   Y. Ger. Play now the Market-maid,
And prethee bout thy buſineſſe.
   Beſſ. Well, I ſhall——that man ſhould be ſo fool'd.
                              Exit.

   Y. Ger. Shee a Proſtitute ?
Nay, and to him my troath plight, and my Friend ;
As poſsible it is, that Heauen and Earth
Should be in loue together, meet and kiſſe,
And ſo cut off all diſtance : What ſtrange frenſie
Came in this wenches braine, ſo to ſurmiſe ?

Were fhe fo bafe ? his noblenefſe is fuch,
He would not entertaine it for my fake :
Or he fo bent ? His hot and luſt burnt appetite
Would be foone quencht, at the meere contemplation
Of her moſt Pious and Religious life.
The Girle was much too blame ; Perhaps her Miſtris
Hath ſtirr'd her anger, by fome word or blow,
Which fhe would thus reuenge ; Not apprehending
At what a high price Honour's to be rated ;
Or elfe fome one that enuies her rare vertue,
Might hire her thus to brand it ; Or, who knowəs
But the yong wench may fixe a thought on me ;
And to diuert me from her Miſtris loue,
May raife this falfe afperfion ? howfoeuer,

> *Enter* Clo. *with a letter.*

My thoughts on thefe two columnes fixed are,
She's good as frefh, and purely chaſte as faire.

Clo. Oh Sir, you are the Needle, and if the whole
County of Middlefex had bin turn'd to a meere Bottle
of Hay, I had bin inioyn'd to haue found you out, or
neuer more return'd backe to my old Maſter : There's
a Letter Sir.

Y. Ger. I know the hand that fuperfcrib'd it well ;
Stay but till I perufe it, and from me
Thou fhalt returne an anfwere.

Clo. I fhall Sir : This is Market-day, and heere
acquaintance commonly meet ; and whom haue I
encounter'd ? my gofsip Pint-pot, and brim full ; nay,
I meane to drinke with you before I part, and how
doth all your worfhipfull kindred ? your fiſter Quart,
your pater-Pottle, (who was euer a Gentlemans fellow)
and your old grandfier Gallon ; they cannot chufe but
be all in health, fince fo many healthes haue beene
drunke out of them : I could wifh them all heere, and
in no worfe ſtate then I fee you are in at this prefent ;
howfoeuer gofsip, fince I haue met you hand to hand,
I'le make bould to drinke to you——Nay, either you
muſt pledge me, or get one to doo't for you ; Doe you
open your mouth towards me ? well, I know what you

would fay ; Heere Roger, to your Mafter and Miftris,
and all our good friends at home ; gramercy gofsip, if
I fhould not pledge thee, I were worthy to be turn'd
out to Graffe, and ftand no more at Liuery ; And now
in requitall of this courtefie I'le begin one health to
you and all your fociety in the Celler, to Peter Pipe,
Harry Hogfhead, Bartholomew Butt and little mafter
Randall Rundlet, to Timothy Tafter, and all your
other great and fmall friends.

   Y. Ger. Hee writes mee heere,
That at my difcontinuance hee's much grieu'd ;
Defiring me, as I haue euer tender'd
Or him or his, to giue him fatisfaction
Touching my difcontent ; and that in perfon,
By any priuate meeting.

   Clo. I Sir, 'tis very true ; The Letter fpeakes no
    more
Then he wifht me to tell you by word of mouth.

   Y. Ger. Thou art then of his councell ?

   Clo. His Priuy and pleafe you.

   Y. Ger. Though neere fo ftrict hath bin my
    fathers charge,
A little I'le difpenfe with't, for his loue ;
Commend me to thy Mafter, tell him from me,
On Munday night (then will my leafure ferue)
I will by Heauens afsiftance vifit him.

   Clo. On Munday Sir :
That's as I remember, iuft the day before Tuefday.

   Y. Ger. But 'twill be midnight firft, at which late
    houre,
Pleafe him to let the Garden doore ftand ope,
At that I'le enter ; But conditionally,
That neither Wife, Friend, Seruant, no third foule
Saue him, and thee to whom he trufts this meffage,
Know of my comming in, or pafsing out :
When, tell him, I will fully fatisfie him
Concerning my forct abfence.

   Clo. I am fomething obliuious ; Your meffage

would bee the truelier deliuered if it were ſet downe
in blacke and white.

    Y. Ger. I'le call for Pen and Incke,
And inſtantly diſpatch it.   *Exeunt.*

Aĉtus Quartus. Scena Prima.

Enter Reignald.

    Reig. Now impudence, but ſteele my face this once,
Although I neere bluſh after; Heere's the houſe,
Ho, whoſe within? What, no man to defend
                        Enter Mr. Ricot.
Theſe innocent gates from knocking?
    Ric. Whoſe without there?
    Reig. One Sir that euer wiſht your worſhips health;
And thoſe few houres I can find time to pray in,
I ſtill remember it.
    Ric. Gramercy Reignald,
I loue all thoſe that wiſh it: You are the men
Leade merry liues, Feaſt, Reuell, and Carowſe;
You feele no tedious houres; Time playes with you,
This is your golden age.
    Reig. It was, but now Sir,
That Gould is turned to worſe then Alcamy,
It will not ſtand the teſt; Thoſe dayes are paſt,
And now our nights come on.
    Ric. Tell me Reignald, is he return'd from Sea?
    Reig. Yes, to our griefe already, but we feare
Hereafter, it may prooue to all our coſt's.
    Ric. Suſpeĉts thy Maſter any thing?
    Reig. Not yet Sir;
Now my requeſt is, that your worſhip being
So neere a Neighbour, therefore moſt diſturb'd,
Would not be firſt to peach vs.
    Ric. Take my word;

With other Neighbours make what peace you can,
I'le not be your accufer.

Reig. Worfhipfull Sir ;
I fhall be ftill your Beads-man ; Now the bufineffe
That I was fent about, the Old Man my Mafter
Claiming fome intereft in acquaintance paft,
Defires (might it be no way troublefome)
To take free view of all your Houfe within.

Ric. View of my Houfe ? Why 'tis not fet to Sale,
Nor bill vpon the doore ; Looke well vpon't :
View of my Houfe ?

Reig. Nay, be not angry Sir,
Hee no way doth difable your eftate ;
As farre to buy, as you are loath to fell ;
Some alterations in his owne hee'd make,
And hearing yours by worke-men much commended,
Hee would make that his Prefident.

Ric. What fancies
Should at this age poffeffe him ; Knowing the coft,
That hee fhould dreame of Building.

Reig. 'Tis fuppos'd,
He hath late found a Wife out for his Sonne ;
Now Sir, to haue him neere him, and that neereneffe
Too, without trouble, though beneath one roofe,
Yet parted in two Families ; Hee would build
And make what's pickt, a perfit quadrangle,
Proportioned iuft with yours, were you fo pleafed,
To make it his example.

Rio. Willingly ; I will but order fome few things
within,
And then attend his comming.   *Exit.*

Reig. Moft kind cox-combe,
Great *Alexander*, and *Agathocles*,
Cæfar, and others, haue bin Fam'd, they fay,
And magnified for high Facinerous deeds ;
Why claime not I, an equall place with them ?
Or rather a prefedent : Thefe commanded
Their Subiects, and their feruants ; I my Mafter,
And euery way his equalls, where I pleafe,

Lead by the nofe along ; They plac'd their burdens
On Horfes, Mules, and Camels ; I, old Men
Of ftrength and wit, loade with my knauerie,

Enter Old Lionell.

Till both their backs and braines ake ; Yet poore
    animalls,
They neere complaine of waight ; Oh are you come
    Sir ?
   Old Lio. I made what hafte I could.
   Reig. And brought the warrant ?
   Old Lio. See heere, I hau 't.
   Reig. 'Tis well done, but fpeake, runs it
Both without Baile and Maineprize ?
   Old Lio. Nay, it carries both forme and power.
   Reig. Then I fhall warrant him ;
I haue bin yonder Sir.
   Old Lio. And what fayes hee ?
   Reig. Like one that offers you
Free ingreffe, view and regreffe, at your pleafure ;
As to his worthy Land-lord.
   Old Lio. Was that all ?
   Reig. Hee fpake to me, that I would fpeake to you,
To fpeake vnto your Sonne ; And then againe,
To fpeake to him, that he would fpeake to you ;
You would releafe his Bargaine.
   Old Lio. By no meanes,
Men muft aduife before they part with Land,
Not after to repent it ; 'Tis moft iuft,
That fuch as hazzard, and disburfe their Stockes,
Should take all gaines and profits that accrew,

Enter Mr. Ricot *againe walking before the gate.*

As well in Sale of Houfes, as in Barter,
And Traficke of all other Merchandize.
   Reig. See, in acknowledgement of a Tenants duty.
Hee attends you at the gate ; Salute him Sir.

Old Lio. My worthy Friend.

Ric. Now as I liue, all my beft thoughts and
wifhes
Impart with yours, in your fo fafe returne ;
Your feruant tels me, you haue great defire
To take furuiew of this my houfe within.

Old Lio. Bee 't Sir, no trouble to you.

Ric. None, enter bouldly ;
With as much freedome, as it were your owne.

Old Lio. As it were mine ; Why Reignald, is it
not ?

Reig. Lord Sir, that in extremity of griefe,
You'le adde vnto vexation ; See you not
How fad hee's on the fuddaine,

Old Lio. I obferue it.

Reig. To part with that which he hath kept fo
long ;
Efpecially his Inheritance ; Now as you loue
Goodneffe, and Honefty, torment him not
With the leaft word of Purchafe.

Old Lio. Councell'd well ;
Thou teacheft me Humanitie.

Ric. Will you enter ?
Or fhall I call a feruant, to conduct you
Through euery Roome and Chamber ?

Old Lio. By no means ;
I feare wee are too much troublefome of our felues.

Reig. See what a goodly Gate ?

Old Lio. It likes me well.

Reig. What braue caru'd poafts ; Who knowes but
heere,
In time Sir, you may keepe your Shreualtie ;
And I be one oth' Seriants.

Old Lio. They are well Caru'd.

Ric. And coft me a good price Sir ; Take your
pleafure,
I haue bufineffe in the Towne.   *Exit.*

Reig. Poore man, I pittie him ;
H 'ath not the heart to ftay and fee you come,

As 'twere, to take Poffefsion ; Looke that way Sir,
What goodly faire Baye windowes ?   *Bayes.*

    Old Lio. Wondrous ftately.

    Reig. And what a Gallerie, How coftly Seeled ;
What painting round about ?

    Old Lio. Euery frefh objeƈt to good, adds better-
neffe.

    Reig. Tarraft aboue, and how below fupported;
doe they pleafe you ?

    Old Lio. All things beyond opinion ; Truft me
Reignald,

I'le not forgoe the Bargaine, for more gaine
Then halfe the price it coft me.

    Reig. If you would ? I fhould not fuffer you ; Was
not the

Money due to the Vfurer, tooke vpon good ground,
That prou'd well built vpon ?   Wee were no fooles
That knew not what wee did.

    Old Lio. It fhall be fatisfied.

    Reig. Pleafe you to truft me with 't, I'le fee 't dif-
charged.

    Old Lio. Hee hath my promife, and I'le doo 't
my felfe :

Neuer could Sonne haue better pleas'd a Father,
Then in this Purchafe : Hie thee inftantly
Vnto my houfe ith' Countrey, giue him notice
Of my arriue, and bid him with all fpeede
Poafte hither.

    Reig. Ere I fee the warrant feru'd ?

    Old Lio. It fhall be thy firft bufineffe ; For my
Soule

Is not at peace, till face to face, I approoue
His Husbandrie, and much commend his Thrift ;
Nay, without paufe, be gone.

    Reig. But a fhort iourney ;

For hee's not farre, that I am fent to feeke :
I haue got the ftart, the beft part of the Race
Is runne already, what remaines, is fmall,
And tyre now, I fhould but forfeit all.

Old Lio. Make hafte, I doe intreat thee. *Exeunt.*

Enter the Clowne.

Clo. This is the Garden gate ; And heere am I fet to ftand Centinell, and to attend the comming of Young Mafter Geraldine : Mafter Dalauill's gone to his Chamber ; My Miftreffe to hers ; 'Tis now about Mid-night ; A Banquet prepared, bottles of Wine in readineffe, all the whole Houfhold at their reft ; And no creature by this, honeftly ftirring, fauing I and my Old Mafter ; Hee in a bye Chamber, prepared of purpofe for their priuate Meeting ; And I heere to play the Watchman, againft my will ; Chauelah,

Enter Young Geraldine.

Stand ; Who goes there ?

Y. Ger. A Friend.

Clo. The Word ?

Y. Ger. Honeft Roger.

Clo. That's the Word indeed ; You haue leaue to paffe freely
Without calling my Corporall.

Y. Ger. How goe the affaires within ?

Clo. According to promife, the bufineffe is compofed, and the feruants difpofed, my young Miftris repofed, my old Mafter according as you propofed, attends you if you bee expofed to giue him meeting ; Nothing in the way being interpofed, to tranfpofe you to the leaft danger : And this I dare be depofed, if you will not take my word, as I am honeft Roger.

Y. Ger. Thy word fhall be my warrant, but fecur'd Moft in thy Mafters promife, on which building ;
By this knowne way I enter.

Clo. Nay, by your leaue,
I that was late but a plaine Centinell will now be your Captaine conducter : Follow me. *Exeunt.*

Table and Stooles fet out ; Lights : a Banquet, Wine.

Enter Mafter Wincott.

Winc.   I wonder whence this ftrangeneffe fhould
    proceed,
Or wherein I, or any of my houfe,
Should be th' occafion of the leaft diftafte ;
Now, as I wifh him well, it troubles me ;

Enter Clow. *and* Y. Ger.

But now the time growes on, from his owne mouth
To be refolu'd ; And I hope fatisfied :
Sir, as I liue, of all my friends to me
Moft wifhedly, you are welcome : Take that Chaire,
I this : Nay, I intreat no complement ;
Attend——Fill wine.
    Clo.   Till the mouthes of the bottles yawne directly
vpon the floore, and the bottomes turne their tayles
vp to the feeling ; Whil'ft there's any blood in their
bellies, I'le not leaue them.
    Winc.   I firft falute you thus.
    Y. Ger.   It could not come
From one whom I more honour ; Sir, I thanke you.
    Clo.   Nay, fince my Mafter begun it, I'le fee 't goe
    round
To all three.
    Winc.   Now giue vs leaue.
    Clo.   Talke you by your felues, whileft I find fome-
thing to fay to this : I haue a tale to tell him fhall
make his ftony heart relent.   *Exit.*
    Y. Ger.   Now, firft Sir, your attention I intreat :
Next, your beliefe, that what I fpeake is iuft,
Maugre all contradiction.
    Winc.   Both are granted.
    Y. Ger.   Then I proceed ; With due acknowledge-
    ment

Of all your more then many curtefies :
Y'aue bin my fecond father, and your wife,
My noble and chafte Miftris ; All your feruants
At my command ; And this your bounteous Table,
As free and common as my Fathers houfe ;
Neither 'gainft any, or the leaft of thefe,
Can I commence iuft quarrell.

 Winc. What might then be
The caufe of this conftraint, in thus abfenting
Your felfe from fuch as loue you ?

 Y. Ger. Out of many,
I will propofe fome few : The care I haue
Of your (as yet vnblemifhed) renowne ;
The vntoucht honour of your vertuous wife ;
And (which I value leaft, yet dearely too)
My owne faire reputation.

 Winc. How can thefe,
In any way be queftioned ?

 Y. Ger. Oh deare Sir,
Bad tongues haue bin too bufie with vs all ;
Of which I neuer yet had time to thinke,
But with fad thoughts and griefes vnfpeakeable :
It hath bin whifper'd by fome wicked ones,
But loudly thunder'd in my fathers eares,
By fome that haue malign'd our happineffe ;
(Heauen, if it can brooke flander, pardon them)
That this my cuftomary comming hither,
Hath bin to bafe and forded purpofes :
To wrong your bed ; Iniure her chaftity ;
And be mine owne vndoer : Which, how falfe ?

 Wenc. As Heauen is true, I know 't.

 Y. Ger. Now this Calumny
Ariuing firft vnto my fathers eares,
His eafie nature was induc'd to thinke,
That thefe things might perhaps be pofsible :
I anfwer'd him, as I would doe to Heauen :
And cleer'd my felfe in his fufpitious thoughts,
As truely, as the high all-knowing Iudge
Shall of thefe ftaines acquit me ; which are meerely

Afperfions and vntruthes : The good old man
Poffeft with my fincerity, and yet carefull
Of your renowne, her honour, and my fame ;
To ftop the worft that fcandall could inflict ;
And to preuent falfe rumours, charges me,
The caufe remoou'd, to take away the effect ;
Which onely could be, to forbeare your houfe
And this vpon his blefsing : You heare all.

   Winc.   And I of all acquit you : This your ab-
     fence,
With which my loue moft cauell'd ; Orators
In your behalfe.   Had fuch things paft betwixt
     you,
Not threats nor chidings could haue driuen you
     hence :
It pleads in your behalfe, and fpeakes in hers ;
And armes me with a double confidence,
Both of your friendfhip, and her loyalty :
I am happy in you both, and onely doubtfull
Which of you two doth moft impart my loue :
You fhall not hence to night.

   Y. Ger.   Pray pardon Sir.

   Winc.   You are in your lodging.

   Y. Ger.   But my fathers charge.

   Winc.   My coniuration fhall difpence with that ;
You may be vp as early as you pleafe ;
But hence to night you fhall not.

   Y. Ger.   You are powerfull.

   Winc.   This night, of purpofe, I haue parted
     beds,
Faining my felfe not well, to giue you meeting ;
Nor can be ought fufpected by my Wife,
I haue kept all fo priuate : Now 'tis late,
I'le fteale vp to my reft ; But howfoeuer,
Let 's not be ftrange in our writing, that way
     dayly
We may conferre without the leaft fufpect,
In fpight of all fuch bafe calumnious tongues

So, Now good-night fweet friend.   *Exit.*
  Y. Ger. May he that made you
So iuft and good, ftill guard you.   Not to bed,
So I perhaps might ouer-fleepe my felfe,
And then my tardy wakeing might betray me
To the more early houfhold ; Thus as I am,
I'le reft me on this Pallat ; But in vaine,
I finde no fleepe can faften on mine eyes,
There are in this difturbed braine of mine
So many mutinous fancies : This, to me,
Will be a tedious night ; How fhall I fpend it ?
No Booke that I can fpie ? no company ?
A little let me recollect my felfe ;
Oh, what more wifht company can I find,
Suiting the apt occafion, time and place ;
Then the fweet contemplation of her Beauty ;
And the fruition too, time may produce,
Of what is yet lent out ? 'Tis a fweet Lady,
And euery way accomplifht : Hath meere accident
Brought me thus neere, and I not vifit her ?
Should it ariue her eare, perhaps might breed
Our lafting feparation ; For 'twixt Louers,
No quarrell's to vnkindneffe, Sweet opportunity
Offers preuention, and inuites me too't :
The houfe is knowne to me, the ftaires and roomes ;
The way vnto her chamber frequently
Trodden by me at mid-night, and all houres :
How ioyfull to her would a meeting be,
So ftrange and vnexpected ; Shadowed too
Beneath the vaile of night ; I am refolu'd
To giue her vifitation, in that place
Where we haue paft deepe vowes, her bed-cham-
    ber :
My fiery loue this darkeneffe makes feeme bright,
And this the path that leades to my delight.
    He goes in at one doore, and comes out at another.
And this the gate vntoo't ; I'le liften firft,
Before too rudely I difturbe her reft :
And gentle breathing ; Ha ? fhee's fure awake,

For in the bed two whifper, and their voyces
Appeare to me vnequall ;——One a womans——
And hers ;——Th' other fhould be no maids tongue,
It beares too big a tone ; And harke, they laugh ;
(Damnation) But lift further ; 'Tother founds——
Like——'Tis the fame falfe periur'd traitor, Dalauill,
To friend and goodnefle : Vnchaft impious woman,
Falfe to all faith, and true coniugall loue ;
There's met, a Serpent and a Crockadell ;
A Synon and a Circe : Oh, to what
May I compare you ?——But my Sword,
I'le act a noble execution,
On two vnmatcht for fordid villanie :——
I left it in my Chamber, And thankes Heauen
That I did fo ; It hath preuented me
From playing a bafe Hang-man ; Sinne fecurely,
Whilft I, although for many, yet leffe faults,
Striue hourely to repent me ; I once loved her,
And was to him intir'd ; Although I pardon,
Heauen will find time to punifh, I'le not ftretch
My iuft reuenge fo farre, as once by blabbing,
To make your brazen Impudence to blufh ;
Damne on, reuenge too great ; And to fuppreffe
Your Soules yet lower, without hope to rife,
Heape Offa vpon Pelion ; You haue made mee
To hate my very Countrey, becaufe heere bred :
Neere two fuch monfters ; Firft I'le leaue this Houfe,
And then my Fathers ; Next I'le take my leaue,
Both of this Clime and Nation, Trauell till
Age fnow vpon this Head : My pafsions now,
Are vnexpreffable, I'le end them thus ;
Ill man, bad Woman, your vnheard of trecherie,
This vniuft cenfure, on a Iuft man giue,
To feeke out place, where no two fuch can liue.

Exit.

Enter Dalauill *in a Night-gowne* : Wife *in a night-
tyre, as comming from Bed.*

Dal. A happy Morning now betide you Lady,

To equall the content of a fweet Night.

Wife. It hath bin to my wifh, and your defire;
And this your comming by pretended loue
Vnto my Sifter Pru. cuts off fufpition
Of any fuch conuerfe 'twixt you and mee.

Dal. It hath bin wifely carried.

Wife. One thing troubles me.

Dal. What's that my Deareft?

Wife. Why your Friend Geraldine,
Should on the fudden thus abfent himfelfe?
Has he had thinke you no intelligence,
Of thefe our priuate meetings.

Dal. No, on my Soule,
For therein hath my braine exceeded yours;
I ftuddying to engroffe you to my felfe,
Of his continued abfence haue bin caufe;
Yet hee of your affection no way iealous,
Or of my Friendfhip——How the plot was caft,
You at our better leafure fhall partake;
The aire growes cold, haue care vnto your health,
Sufpitious eyes are ore vs, that yet fleepe,
But with the dawne, will open; Sweet retire you
To your warme Sheets; I now to fill my owne,
That haue this Night bin empty.

Wife. You aduife well;
Oh might this Kiffe dwell euer on thy Lips,
In my remembrance.

Dal. Doubt it not I pray,
Whileft Day frights Night, and Night purfues the day:
Good morrow. *Exeunt.*

Enter Reignald, Y. Lionell, Blanda, Scapha, Rioter,
and two Gallants, Reig. *with a Key in his hand.*

Reig. Now is the Goale deliuerie; Through this
backe gate
Shift for your felues, I heere vnprifon all.

Y. Lio. But tell me, how fhall we difpofe our
felues?

Wee are as farre to feeke now, as at the firft ;
What is it to repreeue vs for few houres,
And now to fuffer, better had it bin
At firft, to haue ftood the triall, fo by this,
Wee might haue paft our Pennance.

 Bla. Sweet Reignald.

 Y. Lio. Honeft rogue.

 Rio. If now thou faileft vs, then we are loft for
 euer,

 Reig. This fame fweete Reignald, and this honeft
 rogue,
Hath bin the Burgeffe, vnder whofe protection
You all this while haue liu'd, free from Arrefts,
But now, the Sefsions of my power's broake vp,
And you expos'd to Actions, Warrants, Writs ;
For all the hellifh rabble are broke loofe,
Of Seriants, Sheriffes, and Baliffes.

 Omn. Guard vs Heauen.

 Reig. I tell you as it is ; Nay, I my felfe
That haue bin your Protector, now as fubiect
To euery varlots Peftle, for you know
How I am engag'd with you——At whofe fuit fir.

 Omn. Why didft thou Start.   *All Start.*

 Reig. I was afraid fome Catchpole ftood behind
 me,
To clap me on the Shoulder.

 Rio. No fuch thing ;
Yet I proteft thy feare did fright vs all.

 Reig. I knew your guilty confciences.

 Y. Lio. No Braine left ?

 Bla. No crotchet for my fake ?

 Reig. One kiffe then Sweete,
Thus fhall my crotchets, and your kiffes meete.

 R. Lio. Nay, tell vs what to truft too.

 Reig. Lodge your felues
In the next Tauerne, ther's the Cafh that's left,
Goe, health it freely for my good fucceffe ;
Nay, Drowne it all, let not a Teafter fcape
To be confum'd in rot-gut ; I haue begun,

And I will ſtand the period.

 Y. Lio. Brauely ſpoke.

 Reig. Or periſh in the conflict.

 Rio. Worthy Reignald.

 Reig. Well, if he now come off well, Fox you all ;

Goe, call for Wine ; For ſinglie of my ſelfe

I will oppoſe all danger ; But I charge you,

When I ſhall faint or find my ſelfe diſtreſt ;

If I like braue *Orlando*, winde my Horne,

Make haſte vnto my reſcew.

 Y. Lio. And die in't.

 Reig. Well haſt thou ſpoke my noble Charlemaine,

With theſe thy Peeres about thee.

 Y. Lio. May good Speede

Attend thee ſtill.

 Reig. The end ſtill crownes the deede. *Exeunt.*

Enter Old Lionell, *and the firſt Owner of the Houſe.*

 Own. Sir ſir, your threats nor warrants, can fright me ;

My honeſtie and innocency's knowne

Alwayes to haue bin vnblemiſht ; Would you could

As well approue your owne Integrity,

As I ſhall doubtleſſe acquit my ſelfe

Of this ſurmiſed murder.

 Old Lio. Rather Surrender

The price I paid, and take into thy hands

This haunted manſion, or I'le proſecute

My wrong, euen to the vtmoſt of the Law,

Which is no leſſe then death.

 Own. I'le anſwere all

Old Lionell, both to thy ſhame and ſcorne ;

This for thy Menaces.

Enter the Clowne.

 Clo. This is the Houſe, but where's the noyſe that

was wont to be in't ? I am fent hither, to deliuer a
Noate, to two young Gentlemen that heere keepe
Reuell-rout ; I remember it, fince the laft Maflacre of
Meat that was made in't ; But it feemes, that the great
Storme that was raifed then, is chaft now; I haue
other Noates to deliuer, one to Mafter Rycott——and
——I fhall thinke on them all in order; My Old
Mafter makes a great Feaft, for the parting of young
Mafter Geraldine, who is prefently vpon his departure
for Trauell, and the better to grace it, hath inuited
many of his Neighbours and Friends ; Where will be
Old Mafter Geraldine——his Sonne, and I cannot tell
how many ; But this is ftrange, the Gates fhut vp at
this time a day, belike they are all Drunke and laid to
fleepe, if they be, I'le wake them, with a Murraine.

Knockes.

Old Lio.   What defperate fellowe's this, that ignorant

Of his owne danger, thunders at thefe Gates ?

Clo.   Ho, Reignald, Riotous Reignald, Reuelling
Reignald.

Old Lio.   What madneffe doth poffeffe thee, honeft
Friend,

To touch that Hammers handle ?

Clo.   What madneffe doth poffeffe thee, honeft
Friend,

To afke me fuch a queftion ?

Old Lio.   Nay, ftirre not you ?

Own.   Not I ; The game begins.

Old Lio.   How doeft thou, art thou well ?

Clo.   Yes very well, I thanke you, how doe you
Sir ?

Old Lio.   No alteration ; What change about thee ?

Clo.   Not fo much change about me at this time,
As to change you a Shilling into two Teafters.

Old Lio.   Yet I aduife thee Fellow, for thy good,
Stand further from the Gate.

Clo.   And I aduife thee Friend, for thine owne
good, ftand not betwixt mee and the Gate, but giue

me leaue to deliuer my errant; Hoe, Reignald, you
mad Rafcall.

Old Lio. In vaine thou thunder'ft at thefe filent
    Doores,
Where no man dwels to anfwere, fauing Ghofts,
Furies, and Sprights.

Clo. Ghofts; Indeed there has bin much walking,
in and about the Houfe after Mid-night.

Old Lio. Strange noyfe oft heard.

Clo. Yes, terrible noife, that none of the neighbours could take any reft for it, I haue heard it my
felfe.

Old Lio. You heare this; Heere's more witneffe.

Own. Very well Sir.

Old Lio. Which you fhall dearely anfwere——
whooping.

Clo. And hollowing.

Old Lio. And fhouting.

Clo. And crying out, till the whole houfe rung
againe.

Old Lio. Which thou haft heard?

Clo. Oftner then I haue toes and fingers.

Old Lio. Thou wilt be depos'd of this?

Clo. I'le be fworne too't, and that's as good.

Old Lio. Very good ftill; Yet you are in-
    nocent:
Shall I intreat thee friend, to auouch as much
Heere by, to the next Iuftice.

Clo. I'le take my fouldiers oath on't.

Old Lio. A fouldiers oath, What's that?

Clo. My corporall oath; And you know Sir, a
Corporall is an office belonging to a fouldier.

Old Lio. Yet you are cleere?
Murder will come to light.

Enter Robin, *the old feruing-man.*

Own. So will your gullery too.

Rob. They fay my old Mafter's come home; I'le

fee if hee will turne me out of doores, as the young
man has done ; I haue laid rods in piffe for fome-
body, fcape Reignald as hee can, and with more freedome then I durft late, I bouldly now dare knocke.

Robin knocks.

Old Lio.   More mad-men yet; I thinke fince my
    laft voyage,
Halfe of the world's turn'd franticke : What do'ft
    meane,
Or long'ft thou to be blafted ?

Rob.   Oh Sir, you are welcome home ; 'Twas time
    to come
Ere all was gone to hauocke.

Old Lio.   My old feruant? before I fhall demand
    of further bufines,
Refolue me why thou thunder'ft at thefe doores,
Where thou know'ft none inhabits ?

Rob.   Are they gone Sir ?
'Twas well they haue left the houfe behind ;
For all the furniture, to a bare bench,
I am fure is fpent and wafted.

Old Lio.   Where's my fonne,
That Reignald poafting for him with fuch fpeed,
Brings him not from the Countrey ?

Rob.   Countrey Sir ?
'Tis a thing they know not ; Heere they Feaft,
Dice, Drinke, and Drab ; The company they keepe,
Cheaters and Roaring-Ladds, and thefe attended
By Bawdes and Queanes : Your fonne hath got a
    Strumpet,
On whom he fpends all that your fparing left,
And heere they keepe court ; To whofe damn'd
    abufes,
Reignald giues all encouragement.

Old Lio.   But ftay ftay ;
No liuing foule hath for thefe fixe moneths fpace
Heere enter'd, but the houfe ftood defolate.

Rob.   Laft weeke I am fure, fo late, and th' other
    day,

Such Reuells were here kept.

Old Lio.   And by my fonne ?

Rob.   Yes, and his fervant Reignald.

Old Lio.   And this houfe at all not haunted ?

Rob.   Saue Sir with fuch Sprights.

Enter Mafter Ricott.

Own.   This Murder will come out.

Old Lio.   But fee, in happy time heere comes my
  Neighbour

Of whom he bought this manfion ; He, I am fure

More amply can refolue me : I pray Sir,

What fummes of moneys haue you late receiued

Of my young fonne ?

Ric.   Of him ? None I affure you.

Old Lio.   What of my feruant Reignald ?

Ric.   But deuife

What to call leffe then nothing, and that fumme

I will confeffe receiu'd.

Old Lio.   Pray Sir, be ferious ;

I doe confeffe my felfe indebted to you,

A hundred pound.

Ric.   You may doe well to pay't then, for heere's
  witneffe

Sufficient of your words.

Old Lio.   I fpeake no more

Then what I purpofe ; Iuft fo much I owe you,

And ere I fleepe will tender.

Ric.   I fhall be

As ready to receiue it, and as willing,

As you can bee to pay't.

Old Lio.   But prouided,

You will confeffe feuen hundred pounds receiued

Before hand of my fonne ?

Ric.   But by your fauour ;

Why fhould I yeeld feuen hundred [pounds] receiu'd

Of them I neuer dealt with ? Why ? For what ?

What reafon ? What condition ? Where or when
Should fuch a fumme be paid mee ?

    Old Lio. Why ? For this bargaine : And for what ?
    This houfe :

Reafon ? Becaufe you fold it : The conditions ?
    Such

As were agreed betweene you : Where and When ?
That onely hath efcapt me.

    Ric. Madneffe all.

    Old Lio. Was I not brought to take free view
    thereof,

As of mine owne poffefsion ?

    Ric. I confeffe ;

Your feruant told me you had found out a wife
Fit for your fonne, and that you meant to build ;
Defir'd to take a friendly view of mine,
To make it your example : But for felling,
I tell you Sir, my wants be not fo great,
To change my houfe to Coyne.

    Old Lio. Spare Sir your anger,

And turne it into pity ; Neighbours and friends,
I am quite loft, was neuer man fo fool'd,
And by a wicked feruant ; Shame and blufhing
Will not permit to tell the manner how,
Left I be made ridiculous to all :
My feares are to inherit what's yet left ;
He hath made my fonne away.

    Rob. That's my feare too.

    Old Lio. Friends, as you would commiferate a
    man

Depriu'd at once, both of his wealth and fonne ;
And in his age, by one I euer tender'd
More like a fonne then feruant : By imagining
My cafe were yours, haue feeling of my griefes
And helpe to apprehend him ; Furnifh me
With Cords and Fetters, I will lay him fafe
In Prifon within Prifon.

    Ric. Weel affift you.

Rob. And I.

Clo. And all ;

But not to doe the leaft hurt to my old friend Reignald.

Old Lio. His Leggs will be as nimble as his Braine,

And 'twill be difficult to feaze the flaue,

    Enter Reignald *with a Horne in his pocket* : *they withdraw behind the Arras.*

Yet your endeauours, pray peace, heere hee comes.

Reig. My heart mif-giues, for 'tis not pofsible

But that in all thefe windings and indents

I fhall be found at laft : I'le take that courfe

That men both troubled and affrighted doe,

Heape doubt on doubt, and as combuftions rife,

Try if from many I can make my peace,

And worke mine owne atonement.

Old Lio. Stand you clofe,

Be not yet feene, but at your beft aduantage

Hand him, and bind him faft : Whil'ft I diffemble

As if I yet knew nothing.

Reig. I fufpeĉt

And find there's trouble in my Mafters lookes ;

Therefore I muft not truft my felfe too farre

Within his fingers.

Old Lio. Reignald ?

Reig. Worfhipfull Sir.

Old Lio. What fayes my fonne ith' Countrey ?

Reig. That to morrow,

Early ith' morning, heele attend your pleafure,

And doe as all fuch dutious children ought ;

Demand your blefsing Sir.

Old Lio. Well, 'tis well.

Reig. I doe not like his countenance.

Old Lio. But Reignald ? I fufpeĉt the honefty

And the good meaning of my neighbour heere,

Old mafter Ricott ; Meeting him but now,

And hauing fome difcourfe about the houfe,

He makes all ftrange, and tells me in plaine termes,

Hee knowes of no fuch matter.

    Reig.   Tell mee that Sir ?

    Old Lio.   I tell thee as it is : Nor that fuch moneys,

Tooke vp at vfe, were euer tender'd him

On any fuch conditions.

    Reig.   I cannot blame your worfhip to bee pleafant,

Knowing at what an vnder-rate we bought it, but you euer

Were a moft merry Gentleman.

    R. Lio.   (Impudent flaue)

But Reignald, hee not onely doth denie it,

But offers to depofe Himfelfe and Seruants,

No fuch thing euer was.

    Reig.   Now Heauen, to fee to what this world's growne too.

I will make him——

    Old Lio.   Nay more, this man will not confeffe the Murder.

    Reig.   Which both fhall deerely anfwere ; You haue warrant

For him already ; But for the other Sir,

If hee denie it, he had better——

    Old Lio.   Appeare Gentlemen,   *Softly.*

'Tis a fit time to take him.

    Reig.   I difcouer the Ambufh that's laid for me.

    Old Lio.   Come neerer Reignald.

    Reig.   Firft fir refolue me one thing, amongft other Merchandize

Bought in your abfence by your Sonne and me,

Wee ingroft a great comoditie of Combes,

And how many forts thinke you ?

    Old Lio.   You might buy

Some of the bones of Fifhes, fome of Beafts,

Box-combes, and Iuory-combes.

    Reig.   But befides thefe, we haue for Horfes Sir,

Mayne-combes, and Curry-combes ; Now Sir for men,

Wee haue Head-combes, Beard-combes, I and Cox-combes too ;

Take view of them at your pleafure, whil'ft for my
part,
I thus beſtow my felfe.

They all appeare with Cords and Shackels,
Whileſt hee gets vp.

Clo. Well faid Reignald, nobly put off Reignald,
Looke to thy felfe Reignald.
Old Lio. Why doſt thou climbe thus ?
Reig. Onely to practice
The nimbleneſſe of my Armes and Legges,
Ere they prooue your Cords and Fetters.
Old Lio. Why to that place ?
Reig. Why ? becauſe Sir 'tis your owne Houſe ; It
hath bin my Harbour long, and now it muſt bee my
Sanctuary ; Diſpute now, and I'le anfwere.
Own. Villaine, what deuiliſh meaning had'ſt thou
in't,
To challenge me of Murder ?
Reig. Oh fir, the man you kil'd is aliue at this
preſent to iuſtifie it :
I am, quoth he, a Tranf-marine by birth——
Ric. Why, challenge me receipt of Moneys, and to
giue abroad,
That I had fold my Houſe ?
Reig. Why ? becauſe fir,
Could I haue purchaſt Houſes at that rate,
I had meant to haue bought all London.
Clo. Yes, and Middlefex too, and I would haue
bin thy halfe Reignald.
Old Lio. Yours are great,
My wrongs infufferable ; As firſt, to fright mee
From mine owne dwelling, till they had confumed
The whole remainder of the little left ;
Befides, out of my late ſtocke got at Sea,
Difcharge the clamorous Vfurer ; Make me accufe
This man of Murder ; Be at charge of warrants ;
And challenging this my worthy Neighbour of

Forfwearing Summes hee neuer yet receiued ;
Foole mee, to thinke my Sonne that had fpent all,
Had by his thrift bought Land ; I and him too,
To open all the fecrets of his Houfe
To mee, a Stranger ; Oh thou infolent villaine,
What to all thefe canft anfwere ?

 Reig. Guiltie, guiltie.

 Old Lio. But to my Sonnes death, what thou
  flaue ?

 Reig. Not Guiltie.

 Old Lio. Produce him then ; Ith' meane time,
  and——

Honeft Friends, get Ladders.

 Reig. Yes, and come downe in your owne Ropes.

 Own. I'le fetch a Peece and fhoote him.

 Reig. So the warrant in my Mafters pocket, will
ferue for my Murder ; And euer after fhall my Ghoft
haunt this Houfe.

 Clo. And I will fay like Reignald,
This Ghoft and I am Friends.

 Old Lio. Bring faggots, I'le fet fire vpon the
  Houfe,
Rather then this indure.

 Reig. To burne Houfes is Fellony, and I'le
  not out
Till I be fir'd out ; But finee I am Befieged thus,
I'le fummon fupplies vnto my Refcue.

Hee windes a Horne. Enter Young Lionell, Rioter,
  two Gallants Blanda, &c.

 Y. Lio. Before you chide, firft heere mee, next
  your Blefsing,
That on my knees I begge ; I haue but done
Like mif-fpent youth, which after wit deere bought,
Turnes his Eyes inward, forrie and afhamed ;
Thefe things in which I haue offended moft,
Had I not prooued, I fhould haue thought them ftill

Eſſential things, delights perdureable ;
Which now I find meere Shaddowes, Toyes and
    Dreames,
Now hated more then earſt I doated on ;
Beſt Natures, are ſooneſt wrought on ; Such was
    mine ;
As I the offences, So the offendors throw
Heere at your feete, to puniſh as you pleaſe ;
You haue but paid ſo much as I haue waſted,
To purchaſe to your ſelfe a thrifty Sonne ;
Which I from hencefoorth, Vow.
    Old Lio. See what Fathers are,
That can three yeeres offences, fowle ones too,
Thus in a Minute pardon ; And thy faults
Vpon my ſelfe chaſtife, in theſe my Teares ;
Ere this Submiſsion, I had caſt thee off ;
Riſe in my new Adoption : But for theſe——
    Clo. The one you haue nothing to doe withall,
here's his Ticket for his diſcharge ; Another for you
Sir, to Summon you to my Maſters Feaſt, For you,
and you, where I charge you all to appeare, vpon his
diſpleaſure, and your owne apperils.
    Y. Lio. This is my Friend, the other one I
    loued,
Onely becauſe they haue bin deere to him
That now will ſtriue to be more deere to you ;
Vouchſafe their pardon.
    Old Lio. All deere, to me indeed, for I haue payd
    for't ſoundly,
Yet for thy ſake, I am atton'd with all ; Onely that
    wanton,
Her, and her Company, abandon quite ;
So doing, wee are friends.
    Y. Lio. A iuſt Condition, and willingly ſub-
    ſcrib'd to.
    Old Lio. But for that Villaine ; I am now de-
    uiſing
What ſhame, what puniſhment remarkable,

To inflict on him.

Reig. Why Mafter? Haue I laboured,
Plotted, Contriued, and all this while for you,
And will you leaue me to the Whip and Stockes;
Not mediate my peace.

Old Lio. Sirra, come downe.

Reig. Not till my Pardon 's fealed, I'le rather ftand
   heere
Like a Statue, in, in the Fore-front of your houfe
For euer ; Like the picture of Dame Fortune
Before the Fortune Play-houfe.

Y. Lio. If I haue heere
But any Friend amongft you, ioyne with mee
In this petition.

Clo. Good Sir, for my fake, I refolued you truly
Concerning Whooping, the Noyfe, the Walking, and
   the Sprights,
And for a need, can fhew you a Ticket for him too.

Own. I impute my wrongs rather to knauifh Cunning,
Then leaft pretended Malice.

Ric. What he did,
Was but for his Young Mafter, I allow it
Rather as fports of Wit, then iniuries ;
No other pray efteeme them.

Old Lio. Euen as freely,
As you forget my quarells made with you ;
Rais'd from the Errours firft begot by him ;
I heere remit all free ; I now am Calme,
But had I feaz'd vpon him in my Spleene——

Reig. I knew that, therefore this was my In-
   uention,
For Pollicie 's the art ftill of Preuention.

Clo. Come downe then Reignald, firft on your
hands and feete, and then on your knees to your
Mafter ; Now Gentlemen, what doe you fay to your
inuiting to my Mafters Feaft.

Ric. Wee will attend him.

Old Lio. Nor doe I loue to breake good company;
For Mafter Wincott is my worthy Friend,

Enter Reignald.

And old acquaintance ; Oh thou crafty Wag-ftring,
And could'ft thou thus delude me ? But we are
Friends ;
Nor Gentlemen, let not what's heere to paft,
In your leaft thoughts difable my Eftate ;
This my laft Voyage hath made all things good,
With furplus too ; Be that your comfort Sonne :
Well Reignald——But no more.
Reig. I was the Fox,
But I from hencefoorth, will no more the Cox——
Combe, put vpon your pate.
Old Lio. Let's walke Gentlemen.

Exeunt Omnes.

A&tus Quintus. Scena Prima.

Enter Old Geraldine, *and* Young Geraldine.

Old Ger. Sonne, let me tell you, you are ill ad-
uifed ;
And doubly to be blam'd, by vndertaking
Vnneceffary trauell ; Grounding no reafon
For fuch a rafh and giddy enterprife :
What profit aime you at, you haue not reapt ;
What Nouelty affoords the Chriftian world,
Of which your view hath not participated
In a full meafure ; Can you either better
Your language or experience ? Your felfe-will
Hath onely purpofe to depriue a father

Of a loued ſonne, and many noble friends,
Of your much wiſht acquaintance.

    Y. Ger.   Oh, deare Sir,
Doe not, I doe intreat you, now repent you
Of your free grant ; Which with ſuch care and
    ſtuddy,
I haue ſo long, ſo often laboured for.

    Old Ger.   Say that may be diſpens'd with, ſhew
    me reaſon
Why you deſire to ſteale out of your Countrey,
Like ſome Malefaƈtor that had forfeited
His life and freedome ; Heere's a worthy Gentle-
    man
Hath for your ſake inuited many gueſts,
To his great charge, onely to take of you
A parting leaue : You ſend him word you cannot,
After, you may not come : Had not my vrgence,
Almoſt compulſion, driuen you to his houſe,
Th' vnkindneſſe might haue forfeited your loue,
And raced you from his will ; In which he hath
    giuen you
A faire and large eſtate ; Yet you of all this ſtrange-
    neſſe,
Show no ſufficient ground.

    Y. Ger.   Then vnderſtand ;
The ground thereof tooke his firſt birth from you ;
'Twas you firſt charg'd me to forbeare the houſe,
And that vpon your bleſſing : Let it not then
Offend you Sir, if I ſo great a charge
Haue ſtriu'd to keepe ſo ſtriƈtly.

    Old Ger.   Mee perhaps,
You may appeaſe, and with ſmall difficulty,
Becauſe a Father ; But how ſatisfie
Their deare, and on your part, vnmerited loue ?
But this your laſt obedience may ſalue all :
Wee now grow neere the houſe.

    Y. Ger.   Whoſe doores, to mee,
Appeare as horrid as the gates of Hell :
Where ſhall I borrow patience, or from whence ?

Enter Wincott, Wife, Ricott, *the two* Lionells, Owner,
Dalauill, Prudentilla, Reignald, Rioter.

To giue a meeting to this viperous brood,
Of Friend and Miftris.

    Winc. Y'aue entertain'd me with a ftrange dif-
    courfe
Of your mans knauifh wit, but I reioyce,
That in your fafe returne, all ends fo well :
Moft welcome you, and you, and indeed all ;
To whom I am bound, that at fo fhort a warning,
Thus friendly, you will deigne to vifit me.

    Old Lio. It feemes my abfence hath begot fome
    fport,
Thanke my kinde feruant heere.

    Reig. Not fo much worth Sir.

    Old Lio. But though their riots tript at my eftate,
They haue not quite ore-throwne it.

    Winc. But fee Gentlemen,
Thefe whom we moft expected, come at length ;
This I proclaime the mafter of the Feaft,
In which to expreffe the bounty of my loue,
I'le fhew my felfe no niggard.

    Y. Ger. Your choife fauours
I ftill tafte in abundance.

    Wife. Methinks it would not mif-become me Sir,
To chide your abfence ; That haue made your felfe,
To vs, fo long a ftranger.

    Hee turnes away fad, as not being minded.

    Y. Ger. Pardon mee Sir,
That haue not yet, fince your returne from Sea,
Voted the leaft fit opportunity,
To entertaine you with a kind falute.

    Old Lio. Moft kindly Sir I thanke you.

    Dal. Methinks friend,

You fhould expect greene rufhes to be ftrow'd,
After fuch difcontinuance.

    Y. Ger. Miftris Pru,
I haue not feene you long, but greet you thus,
May you be Lady of a better husband
Then I expect a wife.

    Winc. I like that greeting :
Nay, enter Gentlemen ; Dinner perhaps
Is not yet ready, but the time we ftay,
Weele find fome frefh difcourfe to fpend away.

                             Exeunt.

Manet Dalauill.

    Dal. Not fpeake to me ? nor once vouchfafe an
        anfwere,
But fleight me with a poore and bafe neglect ?
No, nor fo much as caft an eye on her,
Or leaft regard, though in a feeming fhew
Shee courted a reply ? 'twixt him and her,
Nay him and mee, this was not wont to be ;
If fhe haue braine to apprehend as much

Enter Young Geraldine *and* Wife.

As I haue done, fheele quickly find it out :
Now as I liue, as our affections meete,
So our conceits, and fhee hath fingled him
To fome fuch purpofe : I'le retire my felfe,
Not interrupt their conference.   *Exit.*

    Wife. You are fad Sir.

    Y. Ger. I know no caufe.

    Wife. Then can I fhew you fome ;
Who could be otherwayes, to leaue a Father
So carefull, and each way fo prouident ?
To leaue fo many, and fuch worthy Friends ?
To abandon your owne countrey ? Thefe are fome,
Nor doe I thinke you can be much the merrier
For my fake ?

Y. Ger. Now your tongue fpeakes Oracles;
For all the reft are nothing, 'tis for you,
Onely for you I cannot.
　Wife. So I thought;
Why then haue you bin all this while fo ftrange ?
Why will you trauell ? fuing a diuorce
Betwixt vs, of a loue infeperable ;
For heere fhall I be left as defolate
Vnto a frozen, almoft widdowed bed ;
Warm'd onely in that future, ftor'd in you ;
For who can in your abfence comfort me ?
　Y. Ger. Shall my oppreffed fufferance yet breake
　　foorth
Into impatience, or endure her more ?
　Wife. But fince by no perfwafion, no intreats,
Your fetled obftinacy can be fwai'd,
Though you feeme defperate of your owne deare
　　life,
Haue care of mine, for it exifts in you.
Oh Sir, fhould you mifcarry I were loft,
Loft and forfaken ; Then by our paft vowes,
And by this hand once giuen mee, by thefe teares,
Which are but fprings begetting greater floods,
I doe befeech thee, my deere Geraldine,
Looke to thy fafety, and preferue thy health ;
Haue care into what company you fall ;
Trauell not late, and croffe no dangerous Seas ;
For till Heauens bleffe me in thy fafe returne,
How will this poore heart fuffer ?
　Y. Ger. I had thought
Long fince the Syrens had bin all deftroy'd ;
But one of them I find furuiues in her ;
Shee almoft makes me queftion what I know,
An Hereticke vnto my owne beliefe :
Oh thou mankinds feducer.
　Wife. What ? no anfwere ?
　Y. Ger. Yes, thou haft fpoke to me in Showres,
I will reply in Thunder ; Thou Adulfreffe,
That haft more poyfon in thee then the Serpent,

Who was the firft that did corrupt thy fex,
The Deuill.

    Wife. To whom fpeakes the man ?

    Y. Ger. To thee,
Falfeft of all that euer man term'd faire ;
Hath Impudence fo fteel'd thy fmooth foft skin,
It cannot blufh ? Or finne fo obdur'd thy heart,
It doth not quake and tremble ? Search thy con-
    fcience,
There thou fhalt find a thoufand clamorous tongues
To fpeake as loud as mine doth.

    Wife. Saue from yours,
I heare no noife at all.

    Y. Ger. I'le play the Doctor
To open thy deafe eares ; Munday the Ninth
Of the laft Moneth ; Canft thou remember that ?
That Night more blacke in thy abhorred finne,
Then in the gloomie darkneffe ; That the time.

    Wife. Munday ?

    Y. Ger. Wouldeft thou the place know ? Thy pol-
    luted Chamber,
So often witneffe of my fin-leffe vowes ;
Wouldeft thou the Perfon ? One not worthy Name,
Yet to torment thy guilty Soule the more,
I'le tell him thee, That Monfter Dalauill ;
Wouldeft thou your Bawd know ? Mid-night, that the
    houre :
The very words thou fpake ; Now what would Geral-
    dine
Say, if he faw vs heere ? To which was anfwered,
Tufh hee's a Cox-combe, fit to be fo fool'd :
No blufh ? What, no faint Feauer on thee yet ?
How hath thy blacke fins chang'd thee ? Thou
    Medufa,
Thofe Haires that late appeared like golden Wyers,
Now crawle with Snakes and Adders ; Thou art
    vgly.

    Wife. And yet my glaffe, till now, neere told me
    fo ;

Who gaue you this intelligence ?

Y. Ger.   Onely hee,
That pittying fuch an Innocencie as mine,
Should by two fuch delinquents bee betray'd,
Hee brought me to that place by mirracle ;
And made me an eare witneffe of all this.

Wife.   I am vndone.

Y. Ger.   But thinke what thou haft loft
To forfeit mee ; I not withftanding thefe,
(So fixt was my loue and vnutterable)
I kept this from thy Husband, nay all eares,
With thy tranfgrefsions fmothering mine owne wrongs,
In hope of thy Repentance.

Wife.   Which begins
Thus low vpon my knees.

Y. Ger.   Tufh, bow to Heauen,
Which thou haft moft offended ; I alas,
Saue in fuch (Scarce vnheard of) Treacherie,
Moft finfull like thy felfe ; Wherein, Oh wherein,
Hath my vnfpotted and vnbounded Loue
Deferu'd the leaft of thefe ? Sworne to be made a
    ftale
For terme of life ; And all this for my goodneffe ;
Die, and die foone, acquit me of my Oath,
But prethee die repentant ; Farewell euer,
'Tis thou, and onely thou haft Banifht mee,
Both from my Friends and Countrey.

Wife.   Oh, I am loft.   *Sinkes downe.*

Enter Dalauill *meeting* Young Geraldine *going out.*

Dal.   Why how now, what's the bufineffe ?

Y. Ger.   Goe take her Vp, whom thou haft oft
    throwne Downe,
Villaine.

Dal.   That was no language from a Friend,
It had too harfh an accent ; But how's this ?
My Miftreffe thus low caft vpon the earth
Grauelling and breathleffe, Miftreffe, Lady, Sweet——

Wife. Oh tell me if thy name be Geraldine,
Thy very lookes will kill mee?
  Dal. View me well,
I am no fuch man ; See, I am Dalauill.
  Wife. Th'art then a Deuill, that prefents before
    mee
My horrid fins; perfwades me to difpaire ;
When hee like a good Angel fent from Heauen,
Befought me of repentance ; Swell ficke Heart,
Euen till thou burft the ribs that bound thee in ;
So, there's one ftring crackt, flow, and flow high,
Euen till thy blood diftill out of mine eyes,
To witneffe my great forrow.
  Dal. Faint againe,
Some helpe within there, no attendant neere?
Thus to expire, in this I am more wretched,
Then all the fweet fruition of her loue
Before could make me happy.

Enter Wincott, Old Geraldine, Young Geraldine, *the*
    two Lionells, Ricott, Owner, Prudentilla, Reig-
    nald, Clowne.

  Winc. What was hee
Clamor'd fo lowd, to mingle with our mirth
This terrour and affright?
  Dal. See Sir, your Wife in thefe my armes ex-
    piring.
  Winc. How?
  Prud. My fifter?
  Winc. Support her, and by all meanes pofsible
Prouide for her deere fafety.
  Old Ger. See, fhee recouers.
  Winc. Woman, looke vp.
  Wife. Oh Sir, your pardon ;
Conuey me to my Chamber, I am ficke,
Sicke euen to death, away thou Sycophant,
Out of my fight, I haue befides thy felfe,

Too many finnes about mee.
 Clo. My fweet Miftreffe.
 Dal. The ftorme's comming, I muft prouide for
  harbour.   *Exit.*
 Old Lio. What ftrange and fudden alteration's
  this,
How quickly is this cleere day ouercaft ;
But fuch and fo vncertaine are all things,
That dwell beneath the Moone.
 Y. Lio. A Womans qualme,
Frailties that are inherent to her fex,
Soone ficke, and foone recouer'd.
 Winc. If fhee misfare,
I am a man more wretched in her loffe,
Then had I forfeited life and eftate ;
Shee was fo good a creature.
 Old Ger. I the like
Suffer'd, when I my Wife brought vnto her graue ;
So you, when you were firft a widower ;
Come arme your felfe with patience.
 Ric. Thefe are cafualties
That are not new, but common.
 Reig. Burying of Wiues,
As ftale as fhifting fhirts, or for fome feruants,
To flout and gull their Mafters.
 Own. Beft to fend
And fee how her fit holds her.

    Enter Prudentilla *and* Clowne.

 Prud. Sir, my Sifter
In thefe few Lines commends her laft to you,
For fhe is now no more ; What's therein writ,
Saue Heauen and you, none knowes ; This fhe de-
  fir'd
You would take view of ; and with thefe words
  expired.
 Winc. Dead ?

Y. Ger. She hath made me then a free releafe,
Of all the debts I owed her.

Winc. My feare is beyond pardon, Dalauill
Hath plaid the villaine, but for Geraldine,
Hee hath bin each way Noble——Loue him ftill,
My peace already I haue made with Heauen ;
Oh be not you at warre with me ; My Honour
Is in your hands to punifh, or preferue ;
I am now Confeft, and only Geraldine
Hath wrought on mee this vnexpected good ;
The Inke I write with, I wifh had bin my blood,
To witneffe my Repentance——Dalauill ?
Where's hee ? Goe feeke him out.

  Clo. I fhall, I fhall Sir.   *Exit.*

  Winc. The Wills of Dead folke fhould be ftill
  obeyed ;
How euer falfe to mee, I'le not reueale't ;
Where Heauen forgiues, I pardon Gentlemen,
I know you all commiferate my loffe ;
I little thought this Feaft fhould haue bin turn'd

Enter Clowne.

Into a Funerall ; What's the newes of him ?

  Clo. Hee went prefently to the Stable, put the
Sadle vpon his Horfe, put his Foote into the Stirrup,
clapt his Spurres into his fides, and away hee's Gallopt,
as if hee were to ride a Race for a Wager.

  Winc. All our ill lucks goe with him, farewell hee ;
But all my beft of wifhes wait on you,
As my chiefe Friend ; This meeting that was made
Onely to take of you a parting leaue,
Shall now be made a Marriage of our Loue,
Which none faue onely Death fhall feparate.

  Y. Ger. It calles me from all Trauell, and from
  hencefoorth,
With my Countrey I am Friends.

  Winc. The Lands that I haue left,

You lend mee for the fhort fpace of my life;
As foone as Heauen calles mee, they call you Lord;
Firft feaft, and after Mourne; Wee'le like fome Gal-
    lants
That Bury thrifty Fathers, think't no finne,
To weare Blacks without, but other Thoughts within.

Exeunt omnes.

F I N I S.

A Pleasant Comedy, called

A

MAYDEN-HEAD WELL LOST.

As it hath beene publickly Acted at the *Cocke-pit*
in Drury-lane, with much Applause :
By her Maiesties *Seruants.*

Written by THOMAS HEYVVOOD.

Aut prodesse solent, aut delectare.

LONDON,
Printed by *Nicholas Okes* for *Iohn Iackson* and
Francis Church, and are to be sold at the
Kings Armes in *Cheape-side.* 1634.

To the Reader.

Ourteous Reader, (*of what ſexe ſo-
ever*) *let not the Title of this Play
any way deterre thee from the
peruſall thereof*: *For there is nothing herein
contained, which doth deuiate either from*
Modeſty, *or good* Manners. *For though
the Argument be drawne from a* Mayden-
head *loſt, yet to be well loſt, cleares it from
all aſperſion. Neither can this be drawne
within the Criticall cenſure of that moſt
horrible* Hiſtriomaſtix, *whoſe vncharitable
doome having damned all ſuch to the flames
of Hell, hath it ſelfe already ſuffered a moſt
remarkeable fire here vpon Earth. This
hath beene frequently, and publickly Aſted
without exception, and I preſume may be
freely read without diſtaſte ; and of all in*

generall: excepting ſuch, whoſe prepared palats, diſguſting all Poems *of this nature, are poyſoned with the bitter iuice of that* Coloquintida *and* Hemlocke, *which can neither reliſh the peace of the* Church *nor* Common-weale. *Nothing remaineth further to be ſaid, but read charitably, and then cen-ſure without preiudice.*

By him who hath beene euer ſtudious of thy fauour,

Thomas Heywood.

Dramatis Personæ.

The Duke of *Florence.*
The Prince of *Florence.*
Mounsieur, the Tutor to the Prince.
The Widdow of the Generall.
Sforsa.
Their Daughter *Lauretta.*
The Clowne their Seruant.
A Huntsman.
A Lord of *Florence.*

The Duke of *Millaine.*
The Prince of *Parma.*
Julia Daughter to *Millain.*
Stroza Secretary to the Duke.
A Souldier of *Sforza'es.*
Three maimed Souldiers.
A Lord of *Millaine.*
Attendants.
Other Lords, *&c.*

The Prologue.

PRologues to Playes in vſe, and common are,
  As Vſhers to Great Ladies ; Both walke bare,
And comely both ; conducting Beauty they
And wee appeare, to vſher in our Play.
Yet, be their faces foule, or featur'd well,
Be they hard-fauoured, or in lookes excell,
Yet being Vſher, he owes no leſſe duty
Vnto the moſt deformed, then the choiſe Beautie.
It is our caſe ; we vſher Acts and Scenes,
Some honeſt, and yet ſome may proue like Queanes.
(Looſe and baſe ſtuſſe) yet that is not our fault,
We walke before, but not like Panders hault
Before ſuch cripled ware : Th' Acts we preſent
We hope are Virgins, drawne for your content
Vnto this Stage : Maides gratefull are to Men,
Our Scenes being ſuch, (like ſuch) accept them then.

A
MAYDEN-HEAD
WELL LOST.

Actus primus, Scena prima.

Enter Iulia and Stroza.

Iulia.

Hat fhee fhould doo't ?
  Stroza. Shee ?
  Iul. May we build vpon't ?
  St. As on a bafe of Marble ; I have
feene
Strange paffages of loue, loofe enterchanges
Of hands and eyes betwixt her and the Prince,
Madame looke too't.
 Iul. What hope hath he in one
So meanly bred ? or fhee t'obtaine a Prince
Of fuch difcent and linnage ?
 Str. What but this
That you muft vndergoe the name of wife,
And fhe to intercept the fweetes of loue
Due to your bed.
 Iul. To be his ftrumpet *Stroza* ?
 Str. Madame a woman may gueffe vnhappily.

Iul.   Thou fhouldft be honeft *Stroza.*

Str.   Yes, many fhould

Be what they are not : but I alwayes was,

And euer will be one, (that's ftill my felfe.)

Iul.   The Generall *Sforfaes* daughter ? is't not fhe ?

Str.   Is that yet queftioned ? as if the chafte Court

Had faue her felfe one fo degenerate,

So diffolutely wanton, fo profufe

In proftitution too, fo impudent

And blufhleffe in her proud ambitious aime,

As if no man could her intemperance pleafe,

Saue him whom Heaven hath deftin'd to your bed.

Iul.   I never faw them yet familiar.

Str.   Ha, ha, as if they'd fend for you to fee't,

To witneffe what they moft ftriue to conceale,

Be guld ? be branded : 'las to me, all's nothing,

I fhall ne're fmart for't, what is't to me ?

If being a Bride, you haue a widdowed fortune ;

If being married, you muft throw your felfe

Vpon a defolate bed, and in your armes,

Clafpe nought but Ayre, whilft his armes full of pleafure

Borrow'd from a ftolne beauty, fhall this grieue

Or trouble me ? breake my fleepes ? make me ftarte

At midnight vp, and fill the houfe with clamours ?

Shall this bring ftrange brats to be bred and brought

Vp at my fire, and call me Dad ? No : this

Concernes not me more then my loue to you

To your high Soueraignty.

Iul.   I now repent

Too late, fince I too lauifhly haue giuen him

The vtmoft he could aske, and ftretcht my honour

Beyond all lawfull bounds of modefty.

Hee's couetous of others, and neglects

His owne ; but I will part thofe their ftolne
   pleafures,
And croffe thofe luftfull fports they haue in chafe,
Not be the pillow to my owne difgrace.   *Exit.*

   Str. The game's on foote, and there's an eafie
   path
To my reuenge ; this beauteous *Millanois*
Vnto th' Duke fole heire, ftill courted, crau'd,
And by the *Parma* Prince follicited,
Which I ftill ftudy how to breake, and caft
Afperfions betwixt both of ftrange diflike ;
But wherein hath the other innocent Mayde
So iniur'd me, that I fhould fcandall her ?
Her Father is the Generall to the Duke :
For when I ftuddied to be rais'd by Armes,
And purchafe me high eminence in Campe,
He croft my fortunes, and return'd me home
A Cafhierd Captaine ; for which iniury
I fcandall all his meanes vnto the Duke,
And to the Princeffe all his daughters vertues
I labour to inuert, and bring them both
Into difgracefull hatred.

Enter Prince Parma.

   Par. *Storza ?*
   Str. My Lord ?
   Par. Saw you the Princeffe ?
   Str. *Iulia* ?
   Par. She ?
   Str. I haue my Lord of late no eare of hers,
Nor fhe a tongue of mine ; the time hath bin
Till foothing Sycophants and Court Parafites
Supplanted me.
   Par. I haue the power with her
To bring thee into grace.
   Str. Haue you the power
To keepe your felfe in ? doe you fmile my Lord ?

Par. I tell thee *Stroza*, I haue that intereſt
In *Iulias* boſome, that the proudeſt Prince
In *Italy* cannot ſupplant me thence.

Str. Sir,
I no way queſtion it : but haue I not knowne
A Prince hath bin repulſt, and meaneſt perſons
Boſom'd ? the Prince would once have lookt vpon
   me,
When ſmall intreaty would haue gain'd an eye,
An eare, a tongue, to ſpeake yea, and a heart,
To thinke I could be ſecret.

Par. What meanes *Stroza ?*

Str. But 'tis the fate of all mortality :
Man cannot long be happy ; but my paſſion
Will make me turne blab, I ſhall out with all.

Par. Whence comes this ? 'tis ſuſpicious, and I
   muſt be
Inquiſitiue to know't.

Str. A Ieſt my Lord,
I'le tell you a good Ieſt.

Par. Prithee let's heare it.

Str. What will you ſay, if at your meeting next
With this faire Princeſſe ? ſhee begins to raue,
To raile vpon you, to exclaime on your
Inconſtancy, and call the innocent name
Of ſome chaſte Maide in queſtion, whom perhaps
You neuer ey'd my Lord.

Par. What of all this ?

Str. What but to excuſe her owne : (I'le not ſay
   what)
Put off the purpos'd Contract : and my Lord
Come, come, I know you haue a pregnant wit.

Par. We parted laſt with all the kindeſt greeting
Louers could adde fare-well with : but ſhould this
   change
Suite thy report, I ſhould be forc't to thinke
That, which euen Oracles themſelues could neuer
Force me to that ſhe is.

Str. All women are not
Sincerely conftant, but obferue my Lord.

Enter Iulia, *the Generals Wife, and* Lauretta
her Daughter.

Iul. Minion is'ft you? there's for you, know your
owne.
Iulia meets her and ftrikes her, then fpeakes.
Str. Obferu'd you that my Lord?
Lau. Why did you ftrike me Madame?
Iul. Strumpet, why?
Dare you conteft with vs?
Lau. Who dare with Princeffe? fubjects muft
forbeare
Each ftep I treade I'le water with a teare.
Exeunt Mother and Lauretta *weeping.*
Str. I fpy a ftorme a comming, Ile to fhelter.
Exit Stro.
Par. Your meaning Madame?
Iul. Did it Sir with yours
But correfpond, it would be bad indeede.
Par. Why did you ftrike that Lady?
Iul. Caufe you fhould pitty her.
Par. Small caufe for blowes.
Iul. I ftrucke her publickly.
You give her blowes in priuate.
Par. *Stroza* ftill?
Iul. Go periurd and difpofe thy falfe allure-
ments
'Mongft them that will beleeue thee, thou haft loft
Thy credit here for euer.
Par. I fhall finde
Faith elfe-where then.
Iul. Eye fpread thy fnares
To catch poore innocent Maides: and hauing tane
them
In the like pit-fall, with their fhipwrackt honours,
Make feafure of their liues.

Par. Iniurious Lady,
All thou canft touch my Honour with, I caft
On thee, and henceforth I will flye thee as
A Bafaliske. I haue found the change of luft,
Your loofe inconftancy, which is as plaine
To me, as were it writ vpon thy brow,
You fhall not caft me off: I hate thy fight,
And from this houre I will abiure thee quite.

Exit Parma.

Iul. Ile call him backe : if *Stroza* be no villaine,
He is not worth my clamour. What was that
Startled within me ? Oh I am difhonoured
Perpetually ; for he hath left behinde
That pledge of his acquaintance, that will for euer
Cleaue to my blood in fcandall, I muft now
Sue, fend, and craue, and what before I fcorn'd
By prayers to grant, fubmiffiuely implore. *Exit Iulia.*

A flourifh. Enter the Duke *of Millenie, the Generals
wife, and deliuers a petition with* Stroza, Lauretta,
and attendants.

Duke. Lady your fuite ?
Wife. So pleafe your Grace perufe it,
It is included there.
Duk. Our generals Wife ?
We know you Lady, and your beauteous Daughter,
Nay you fhall fpare your knee.
Str. More plot for mee ;
My brain's in labour, and muft be deliuered
Of fome new mifcheife ?
Duk. You petition heere
For Men and Money ! making a free relation
Of all your Husbands fortunes, how fupplyes
Haue beene delay'd, and what extremities
He hath indurd at *Naples* dreadfull Seige ;
Wee know them all, and withall doe acknowledge
All plentious bleffings by the power of Heauen,
By him wee doe obtaine, and by his valour

Lady we greue he hath beene ſo negleᶜted.

Wife. O Roiall Sir, you ſtill were Gratious,
But twixt your Vertues and his Merits there
Hath beene ſome interception, that hath ſtopt
The current of your fauours.

Duk. All which ſhal bee remou'd, and hee
  appeare
Henceforth a bright ſtarre in our courtly ſpheare.

Str. But no ſuch Comet here ſhall daze my ſight,
Whilſt I a Cloud am to Eclips that light. *Exit Stroza.*

Duk. We ſent out our Commiſſions two Monthes
  ſince
For Men and Money, nor was't our intent
It ſhould bee thus delayd : though we are Prince,
We onely can command, to execute
Tis not in vs but in our Officers,
We vnderſtand that by their negligence
He has beene put to much extremity
Of Dearth and Famine, many a ſtormy night
Beene forc'd to roofe himſelfe i'th open field,
Nay more then this, much of his owne reuenue
He hath expended, all to pay his Souldiers :
Yet Reuerend Madame, but forget what's paſt,
Though late, weele quit his merit at the laſt.

Enter Iulia and Stroza whiſpering.

Wife. Your Highneſſe is moſt Royall ?

Stro. Her Father ſhall be in the Campe releiu'd,
She grac'd in Court, how will ſhe braue you then ?
If ſuffer this take all ? why the meaneſt Lady
Would neuer brooke an equall ? you a Princeſſe ?
And can you brooke a baſe competitor ?

Iulia. It ſhall not, we are fixt and ſtand immou'd,
And will be ſwaid by no hand.

Duk. Iulia ?

Iulia. A Sutor to that Lady Royall Father,
Before ſhe be a widdow that you are
So priuate in diſcourſe ?

Duk.   O you miſtake,
For ſhee the ſutor is, and hath obtain'd.
    Iulia.   I am glad I haue found you in the giuing
        vaine,
Will you grant me one boone to ?
    Duk.   Queſtion not,
To haſt your Marriage with the former Prince,
Or at the leaſt the contraƈt, is't not that ?
    Iulia.   Say twere my Lord ?
    Duk.   It could not be denide.
But ſpeake ? thy ſuite ?
    Iulia.   To haue this modeſt Gentlewoman
Baniſht the Court.
    Wife.   My Daughter Royall princeſſe,
Show vs ſome cauſe I beg it ?
    Iulia.   Lady though
You be i'th begging vaine, I am not now
In the giuing, will you leaue vs ?
    Lauretta.   Wherein O Heauen
Haue I deſeru'd your wrath, that you ſhould thus
Perſue me ? I haue ſearcht, indeed beyond
My vnderſtanding, but yet cannot finde ?
Wherein I haue offended by my chaſtity.
    Iulia.   How chaſtity ?
A thing long ſought 'mongſt Captains wiues and
        daughters,
Yet hardly can bee found.
    Duk.   Faire Lady yeild
Vnto my daughters ſpleen her rage blowne 'ore,
Feare not, Ile make your peace, as for your ſuite
Touching your husband, that will I ſecure.
    Iul.   Haſte *Stroza*, vnto the Prince his chamber,
Giue him this letter, it concernes my honor,
My ſtate, my life, all that I can call good
Depends vpon the ſafe deliuery
Of theſe few broken Letters.
    Str.   Maddam, tis done———   *Exit.*
    Iul.   What ſtayes ſhe to out-face me ?
    Lau.   Madam, I yeeld

Way to your ſpleene, not knowing whence it growes,
Bearing your words more heauy then your blowes.
    Wife. Small hope there is to ſee the Father
    righted
When the child is thus wrong'd.

Enter a Souldier and Stroza.

    Soul. Muſt ſpeake with the Duke.
    Str. Muſt fellow ? ſtay your howre, and dance at-
    tendance
Vntill the Duke's at leiſure.
    Soul. Ile doe neither,
I come in haſte with newes.
    Str. Why then keepe out ſir.
    Soul. Ha Milkſop ? know perculliſt gates
Though kept with Pikes & Muskets, could nere kepe
    me out
And doſt thou thinke to ſhut me out with Wainſcot ?
    Duk. What's he ?
    Soul. A Souldier.
    Duk. Whence ?
    Soul. The Campe.
    Duk. The newes ?
    Soul. A mighty loſſe ; a glorious victory.
    Duke. But which the greater ?
    Soul. Tis vncertaine ſir :
But will you heare the beſt or bad newes firſt ?
    Duke. Cheere me with conqueſt firſt, that being
    arm'd
With thy beſt newes, we better may endure
What ſounds more fatall.
    Soul. Heare me then my Lord,
We ſack't the Citty after nine Moneths ſiege,
Furniſht with ſtore of all warres furniture,
Our (neuer to be praiſd enough) braue Generall
Fought in the Cannons face, their number ſtill
Increaſt, but ours diminiſht ; their ſouldiers pay
Doubled, and ours kept backe : but we (braue ſpirits)

The leffe we had of Coyne, the more we tooke
Vnto our felues of Courage, but when all
Our furniture was fpent euen to one day,
And that to morrow we muft be inforc't
To raife a fhameful fiege, then ftood our General
(Our valiant General) vp, and breath'd vpon vs
His owne vndaunted fpirit, which fpred through
The Campe, return'd it doubly arm'd againe :
For he did meane to lay vpon one fhott
His ftate and fortune, and then inftantly
He bad vs arme and follow : On then he went,
We after him ; oh ! 'twas a glorious fight,
Fit for a Theater of Gods to fee,
How we made vp and mauger all oppofure,
Made way through raging ftormes of fhowring bullets ;
At laft we came to hooke our ladders, and
By them to skale.   The firft that mounted, was
Our bold couragious Generall : after him
Ten thoufand, fo we inftantly were made
Lords of the Citty, purchas'd in two houres
After a nine Moneths fiege : all by the valour
Of our approued Generall.
 Duke. I neuer heard a brauer victory,
But what's our loffe ?
 Soul. Oh that, which ten fuch Conquefts
Cannot make good, your worthy Generall.
 Wife. My Lord and husband ? fpare me paffion,
I muft with-draw to death.   *Exit.*
 Duke. How perifh't he ?
What dy'de he by the fword ?
 Soul. Sword ?   No alas,
No fword durft byte vpon his noble flefh,
Nor bullet raze his skinne : he whom War feared,
The Cannon fpar'd, no fteele durft venture on.
No Duke, 'twas thy vnkinde ingratitude
Hath flaine braue *Sforza.*
 Duke. Speake the caufe ?
 Soul. I fhall :
This Citty feaz'd, his purpofe was the fpoyle

To giue his Souldiers ; but when his feal'd Commiffion
He had vnript, and faw expreffe command,
To deale no farther then to victory,
And that his great Authority was curb'd,
And giuen to others, that refpect their profit
More then the worth of fouldiers : euen for griefe,
That he could neither furnifh vs with pay
Which was kept back, nor guerdon vs with fpoile,
What was about him he diftributed,
Euen to the beft deferuers, as his garments,
His Armes, and Tent, then fome few words fpake,
And fo oppreft with griefe, his great heart brake.

 Str. There's one gone then.
 Duke. Attend for thy reward,
So leaue vs.
 Soul. Pray on whom fhall I attend ?
Who is't muft pay me ?
 Str. I fir.
 Soul. You fir ? tell me,
Will it not coft me more the waiting for,
Then the fumme comes to when it is receiu'd ?
I doe but aske the queftion.
 Str. You are a bold
And faucy fouldier.
 Soul. You are a cunning flaue,
And cowardly Courtier.
 Duke. See all things be difpatcht
Touching conditions of attoned peace
'Twixt vs and *Naples* : fee that fouldier to
Haue his reward.
 Soul. Come will you pay me fir ? *Exit Soul.*
 Str. Sir, will you walke : as for your faucineffe
I'le teach you a Court-tricke : you fhal be taught
How to attend.
 Duke. But that our General's loft :
 Str. Is't not now peace, what fhould a Generall
  doe ?
Had he return'd, he would haue lookt for honours,
This fuite and that for fuch a follower :

Now Royall fir, that debt is quite difcharg'd.

Duke.   But for his wife, we muſt be mindefull of her,
And fee we doe fo.   *Exit Duke.*

Iul.   Speake, will he come?

Str.   Madam, I found him ready to depart
The Court with expedition : but at my vrgence
He promiſt you a parley.

Iul.   It is well :
If prayers or teares can moue him, Ile make way
To faue my owne fhame, and enforce his ſtay.
                                               Exeunt.

Enter three fouldiers : one without an arme.

1 *Soul.*   Come fellow fouldiers, doe you know the reafon
That we are fummon'd thus vnto the houfe
Of our dead Generall ?

2 *Soul.*   Sure 'tis about
Our pay.

3 *Soul.*   But ſtand afide, here comes the Lady.

Enter the Mother, Lauretta, *and Clowne.*

Wife.   Are all thefe Gentlemen fummond together,
That were my Husbands followers, and whofe fortunes
Expir'd in him ?

Clo.   They are if pleafe your Ladiſhip : though I
was neuer Tawny-coate, I haue playd the fummoners
part, and the reſt are already paide, onely thefe three
attend your Ladiſhips remuneration.

Wife.   Welcome Gentlemen,
My Husband led you on to many dangers
Two yeares, and laſt to pouerty : His reuenewes
Before hand he fold to maintaine his Army,
When the Dukes pay ſtill fail'd, you know you were
Stor'd euer from his Coffers.

2 *Soul.* He was a right
And worthy Generall.

2. *Soul.* He was no leſſe.

Clo. He was no leſſe ; and all you know hee was
no more, well, had he liu'd, I had beene plac't in ſome
houſe of office or other ere this time.

Wife. It was his will, which to my vtmoſt power
I will make good, to ſatisfie his ſouldiers
To the vtmoſt farthing. All his Gold and Iewels
I haue already added, yet are we ſtill
To ſcore to ſouldiery ? what is your ſumme ?

1 *Soul.* Pay for three Moneths.

Wife. There's double that in Gold.

1. *Soul.* I thanke your Ladiſhip.

Wife. What yours ?

2. *Soul.* Why Madam,
For foure Moneths pay.

Wife. This Iewell ſurmounts that.

2. *Soul.* I am treble ſatisfied.

Wife. You are behinde hand too.

Clo. Ey but Madam, I thinke he be no true
ſouldier.

Wife. No true Souldier ? your reaſon ?

Clo. Marry becauſe he walkes without his Armes.

Wife. The Dukes Treaſure
Cannot make good that loſſe, yet are we rich
In one thing :
Nothing we haue that were of nothing made,
Nothing we owe, my Husbands debts are payd.
Morrow Gentlemen.

All. Madam, Hearts, Swords and hands, reſt ſtill
At your command.

Wife. Gentlemen I'me ſorry that I cannot pay you
better,
Vnto my wiſhes and your owne deſert,
'Tis plainely ſeene great Perſons oft times fall,
And the moſt Rich cannot giue more then all.
Good morrow Gentlemen.

All. May you be euer happy.

Exeunt Souldiers.

Clo. I but Madam, this is a hard cafe being truly confidered, to giue away all, why your Shoe-maker, though he hath many other Tooles to worke with, he will not giue away his All.

Wife. All ours was his alone, it came by him, And for his Honour it was paid againe.

Clo. Why, fay I had a peece of Meate I had a mind to, I might perhaps giue away a Modicum, a Morcell, a Fragment or fo, but to giue away and bee a hungry my felfe, I durft not doo't for my Guts, or fay I fhould meete with a friend that had but one Penny in his Purfe, that fhould giue mee a Pot of Ale, that fhould drinke to me, and drinke vp all, I'le ftand too't there's no Confcience in't.

Lau. What hath beene done was for my Fathers Honor.

Clo. Shee might haue giuen away a little, and a little, but when all is gone, what's left for me ?

Wife. Wee will leaue *Millaine* and to *Florence* ftraight, Though wee are poore, yet where we liue vn-knowne 'Tis the leffe griefe, firrah, will you confort With vs, and beare a part in our misfortunes ?

Clo. Troth Madam, I could find in my heart to goe with you but for one thing.

Wife. What's that ?

Clow. Becaufe you are too liberall a Miftreffe : and that's a fault feldome found among Ladies : For looke, you vfe to giue away all, and I am all that is left ; and I am affraide when you come into a ftrange Countrey, you'le giue away me too, fo that I fhall neuer liue to be my owne man.

Wife. Tufh, feare it not.

Clo. Why then I'le goe with you in fpite of your teeth.

Wife. Leaue *Milleine* then, to *Florence* be our
   guide,
Heauen when man failes, muſt for our helpe prouide.
                                        Exeunt.

Aĉtus Secundus, Scena prima.

Enter Parma *reading a Letter*: *after him* Julia.

Par. This Letter came from you, 'tis your
   Charaĉter.
Iul. That hand in Contraĉt you ſo long haue had,
Should not ſeeme ſtrange to you now.
Par. You are with - childe,
So doth your Letter ſay : what change your face ?
Iu. My bluſhes muſt ſpeake for me.
Par. And this Childe
You would beſtow on me : y'are very liberall Lady,
You giue me more then I did meane to aske.
Iu. And yet but what's your owne Sir, I am
   ſerious,
And it will ill become your Oathes and Vowes
To ieſt at my vndoeing.
Par. You would ſay
Rather your doing.
Iu. In doing thus, you ſhould vndoe me quite.
Par. What doe you weepe, that late did rayle in
   clamor ?
Your thunders turnd to ſhowres ? It is moſt ſtrange.
Iu. You haue diſhonoured me, and by your
   flattery
Haue rob'd me of my chaſte Virginity :
Yet ere I yeelded, we were man and wife,
Sauing the Churches outward Ceremony.
Par. But Lady, you that would be wonne by me

To fuch an act of luft, would foone confent
Vnto another.
    Iu. Can this be found in man?
    Par. This *Strozas* language moues me, and I
        intend
To try what patience, conftancy, and loue
There can be found in woman: why do you weepe?
You are not hungry, for your bellie's full;
Lady, be rul'd by me: take the aduice
A Doctor gaue a Gentleman of late,
That fent to him to know, whether Tobacco
Were good for him or no: My friend quoth he,
If thou didft neuer loue it, neuer take it;
If thou didft euer loue it, neuer leaue it;
So I to thee; if thou wert as thou haft
Beene alwayes honeft, I could wifh thee ftill
So to continue; but being a broken Lady,
Your onely way's to make vfe of your Talent,
Farewell, I'le to my Countrey.   *Exit Parma.*
    Iu. Oh miferable,
Let me but reckon vp ten thoufand ills
My loofeneffe hath committed, the afperfion
And fcandalous reputation of my Childe,
My Father too, 'tmuft come vnto his eare,
Oh——

Enter Milleine.

    Duke. Iulia.
    Iu. Away.
    Duke. Come hither, but one word.
    Iu. That all thofe blacke occurrents fhould con-
        fpire,
And end in my difgrace.
    Duke. Ha! what's the bufineffe?
    Iu. If all men were fuch,
I fhould be forry that a man begot me,
Although he were my father.
    Duke. Iulia, how's that?

Iul. Oh Sir, you come to know whether Tobacco
be good for you or no; Ile tell you, if you neuer
tooke it, neuer take it then, or if you euer vs'd it, take
it ſtill; Nay, I'me an excellent Phiſitian growne of
late I tell you.

Duke. What meane theſe ſtrange Anagrams?
I am thy Father and I loue thee ſweete.

Iul. Loue me thou doſt not.

Duke. Why thou doeſt know I doe.

Iul. I ſay thou doeſt not : lay no wager with me,
For if thou doſt, there will be two to one
On my ſide againſt thee.

Duke. Ha ! I am thy Father,
Why *Iulia*?

Iu. How my Father! then doe one thing
For me your Daughter.

Duke. One thing? any thing,
Ey all things.

Iu. Inſtantly then draw your ſword,
And pierce me to the heart.

Duke. I loue thee not ſo ill,
To be the Author of thy death.

Iu. Nor I my ſelfe ſo well, as to deſire
A longer life : if you be then my Father,
Puniſh a ſinne that hath diſgrac't your Daughter,
Scandald your blood, and poyſon'd it with mud.

Duke. Be plaine with vs.

Iu. See, I am ſtrumpeted,
A baſtard iſſue growes within my wombe.

Duke. Whoſe faſt?

Iu. Prince *Parmaes.*

Duke. Stroza.

Str. My Lord.

Duke. Search out
Prince *Parma,* bring the Traytour backe againe
Dead or aliue.

Str. My Lord, he is a Prince.

Duke. No matter; for his head ſhall be the
ranſome

Of this foule Treaſon.   When I ſay begon.
But as for thee baſe and degenerate——
    Iul.   Doe ſhew your ſelfe a Prince : let her no
      longer
Liue, that hath thus diſgrac't your Royall blood.
    Duk.   Nature preuailes 'boue honour : her offence
Merits my vengeance, but the name of Childe
Abates my Swords keene edge : yet Royalty
Take th' vpper hand of pitty : kill the ſtrumpet,
And be renown'd for Iuſtice.
    Iul.   Strike, I'le ſtand.
    Duke.   How eaſie could I period all my care,
Could I her kill, and yet her Infant ſpare :
A double Murder I muſt needes commit,
To ruine that which neuer offended yet.
Oh Heauen ! in this I your aſſiſtance craue,
Puniſh the faulter, and the innocent ſaue.
    Iul.   You are not true to your owne honour
      Father,
To let me longer liue.
    Duke.   Oh *Iulia*, *Iulia*,
Thou haſt ouerwhelm'd vpon my aged head
Mountaines of griefe, t'oppreſſe me to my graue.
Is *Parma* found ?
    Str.   My Lord, hee's priuately
Fled from the Court.
    Duke.   Then flye thou after villaine.
    Str.   Sir, are you madde ?
    Duke.   What's to be done ?   Alacke,
I cannot change a father and a Prince
Into a cruell Hang-man : tell me *Iulia*,
Is thy guilt yet but priuate to thy ſelfe ?
    Iul.   It is my Lord.
    Duke.   Conceale it then : wee'le ſtudy
To ſalue thy honour, and to keepe thy looſeneſſe
From all the world conceal'd, compreſſe thy griefe,
And I will ſtudy how to ſhadow mine.
Wipe from thy cheekes theſe teares : oh curſed
    Age,

When Children 'gainſt their Parents all things dare,
Yet Fathers ſtill proue Fathers in their care.   *Exeunt.*

Enter Mother, Lauretta, *and* Clowne.

Moth. Oh miſery beyond compariſon!
When ſaue the Heauens we haue no roofe at all
To ſhelter vs.
Clow. That word all ſtickes more in my ſtomacke
then my victuals can : For indeede wee can get none
to eate now : I told you, you were ſo prodigall we
ſhould pinch for't.
Wife. What place may wee call this? what Clime?
what Prouince?
Clow. Why this is the Duke-dome of *Florence*, and
this is the Forreſt where the hard-hearted Duke hunts
many a Hart : and there's no Deere ſo deare to him,
but hee'le kill it : as goodly a large place to ſtarue
in, as your Ladiſhip can deſire to ſee in a Summers
day.
Wife. Yet here, ſince no man knowes vs, no
   man can
Deride our miſery : better dye ſtaru'd,
Then baſely begge.
Clow. How better ſtarue then begge ; all the
Ladies of *Florence* ſhal neuer make me of that beleefe.
I had rather beg a thouſand times, then ſtarue once,
doe you ſcorne begging? Your betters doe not, no
Madam ; get me a Snap-ſacke, I'le to *Florence* : I'le
make all the high-wayes ring of me with for the Lords
ſake. I haue ſtudied a Prayer for him that giues, and
a Poxe take him that giues nothing : I haue one for
the Horſe-way, another for the Foote-way, and a third
for the turning-ſtile. No Madam, begging is growne
a gentleman-like Calling here in our Countrey.
Wife. I haue yet one poore piece of Gold reſeru'd,
Step to the Village by and fetch ſome Wine.
Clow. You had better keepe your Gold, and truſt

to my begging Oratory, yet this is the worſt they can
ſay to mee, that I am my Ladies Bottle-man.

Exit Clowne.

Wife. Here's a ſtrange change : we muſt be
patient,
Yet can I not but weepe thinking on thee.

Lau. Madam on me ? there is no change of
Fortune
Can puffe me or deiect me ; I am all one
In rich abundance and penurious want :
So little doe my miſeries vexe me,
Or the faire Princeſſe wrong,
That I will end my paſſions in a Song.

A Song.

Sound Hornes within.

Wife. It ſeemes the Duke is Hunting in the
Forreſt,
Here let vs reſt our ſelues, and liſten to
Their Tones, for nothing but miſhap here lies ;
Sing thou faire Childe, I'le keepe tune with my eyes.

Winde hornes. And enter the Prince of Florence
& Mounſieur.

Prince. This way the voyce was, let vs leaue the
Chace.

Moun. Behold my Lord two ſad deiected Creatures
Throwne on the humble verdure.

Prince. Here's beauty mixt with teares, that
pouerty
Was neuer bred in Cottage : I'le farther queſtion
Their ſtate and fortune.

Wife. Wee're diſcouered,
Daughter ariſe.

Prince. What are you gentle Creatures ?

Nay anſwere not in teares.
If you by caſuall loſſe, or by the hand
Of Fortune haue beene cruſht beneath theſe ſorrowes,
He demands your griefe
That hath as much will as ability
To ſuccour you, and for your owne faire ſake ;
Nay beautious Damſell, you neede not queſtion that.
 Lau. If by the front we may beleeue the heart,
Or by the out-ſide iudge the inward vertue :
You faire Sir, haue euen in your ſelfe alone
All that this world can promiſe ; for I ne're
Beheld one ſo compleate ; and were I ſure
Although you would not pitty, yet at leaſt
You would not mocke our miſery : I would relate
A Tale ſhould make you weepe.
 Prince. Sweete if the Prologue
To thy ſad paſſion mooue thus : what will the Sceane
And tragicke act it ſelfe doe ? Is that Gentlewoman
Your Mother ſweete ?
 Lau. My wretched Mother Sir.
 Prince. Pray of what Prouince ?
 Lau. Milleine.
 Prince. What fortune there ?
 Lau. My Father was a Noble Gentleman,
Rank't with the beſt in Birth, and which did adde
To all his other vertues, a bold Souldier ;
But when he dy'de——
 Prince. Nay, proceede beauteous Lady,
How was your Father ſtil'd ?
 Lau. To tell you that,
Were to exclaime vpon my Prince, my Countrey,
And their Ingratitude : For he being dead,
With him our fortunes and our hopes both fail'd ;
My Mother loath to liue ignobly baſe,
Where once ſhe flouriſht, hauing ſpent her meanes
Not looſely nor in riot, but in the honour
Of her dead Husband : left th' ingratefull Land,
Rather to ſpend her yeares in pouerty,
Mongſt thoſe that neuer knew her height of Fortune,

Then with her thankeleffe Friends and Countrey-men,
Fled here to perifh.

Prince. More then her charming beauty
Her paffion moues me : where inhabit you ?

Lau. Here, euery where.

Prince. Beneath thefe Trees ?

Lau. We haue
No other roofe then what kinde Heanen lends.

Prince. Gentle Creature,
Had you not told me that your Birth was Noble,
I fhould haue found it in your face and gefture.
Mounfieur.

Mounfieur. My Lord.

Prince. Goe winde thy Horne abroad, and call to
vs
Some of our traine : we pitty thefe two Ladies,
And we will raife their hope : Cheere you old
Madam,
You fhall receiue fome bounty from a Prince.

Enter a Huntf-man.

Who keepes the Lodge below ?

Huntf. Your Highneffe Huntf-man.

Prince. Command him to remoue, and inftantly
We giue it to thefe Ladies : befides, adde
Vnto our Gueft three thoufand pounds a yeare :
We'le fee it furnifht too with Plate and Hangings.
'Las pretty Maide, your Father's dead you fay,
We'le take you now to our owne Patronage,
And truft me Lady, while wee're Prince of *Florence,*
You fhall not want nor foode, nor harborage.

Wife. Pardon Great Sir, this our neglect of
duty
Vnto a Prince fo gracious and compleate
In vertuous indowments.

Lau. To excufe
Our former negligence, behold I caft
Me at your foote.

Prince. Ariſe ſweete, pray your name ?
Lau. *Lauretta.*
Prince. Faire *Lauretta*, you ſhall be henceforth
ours,
Oh Mounſieur ! I ne're ſaw where I could loue
Till now.
Moun. How now my Lord, remember pray,
What you are to this poore deiected Maide.
Prince. Well Mounſieur, well ; when e're I match,
pray Heauen,
We loue ſo well : but loue and toyle hath made vs
Euen ſomewhat thirſty, would we had ſome Wine.

Enter Clowne.

Clow. Nay, now I thinke I haue fitted you with a
Cup of Mipſilato.
Movn. How now ſirrah, what are you?
Clow. What am I ? Nay what art thou ?
I thinke you'le proue little better then a ſmell-
ſmocke,
That can finde out a pretty wench in ſuch a Corner.
Wife. Peace ſirrah, 'tis the Prince.
Clow. What if he be ? he may loue a Wench as
well as another man.
Prince. What haſt thou there ?
Clow. A bottle of Wine and a Manchel that my
Lady ſent me for.
Prince. Thou ne're couldſt come to vs in better
time,
Reach it vs Mounſieur.
Moun. Your bottle quickly ſirrah, come I ſay.
Clow. Yes, when ? can you tell ? doe you thinke
I am ſuch an Aſſe, to part ſo lightly with my liquor ?
Know thou my friend, before I could get this bottle
fill'd, I was glad to change a piece of gold, and call
for the reſt againe : And doe you thinke I'le looſe my
liquor, and haue no Gold nor reſt againe ? Not ſo
my Friend, not ſo.

Moun. There's Gold fir.

Clow. Madam, will you giue me a Licence to fell Wine? I could get no Plate in the Forreft but a woodden Difh.

Wife. Fill to the Prince *Lauretta.*

Lau. Will it pleafe

Your Highneffe drinke out of a woodden Mazer?

Prinee. Yes fweete with thee in any thing: you know

Wee are a Prince, and you fhall be our tafter.

Lau. Why fhould I loue this Prince? his bounteous gifts

Exalt me not, but make me much more poore,

I'me more deiected then I was before.

Wife. Sir.

Moun. Lady, thankes: I feare me he is caught,

But if he be, my Counfell muft diuert him.

Clow. The bottome of the bottle is at your feruice Sir,

Shall you and I part ftakes?

Moun. There's more Gold for you.

Clow. I had rather you had broke my pate then my draught, but harke you Sir, are you as a man fhould fay, a belonger to?

Hunt. A belonger to? what's that fir?

Clow. Oh ignorant! are you a follower?

Hunt. I feldome goe before when my betters are in place.

Clow. A Seruing-man I take it.

Hunt. Right fir.

Clow. I defire you the more complement: I haue the courtefie of the Forreft for you.

Hunt. And I haue the courtefie of the Court for you fir.

Clow. That's to bring me to Buttery hatch, and neuer make me drinke.

Prince. Sirrah, conduct thofe Ladies to the Lodge, And tell the keeper we haue ftor'd for him,

A better fortune: you fhall heare further from vs,

You vſher them.

Hunt. Come Ladies will you walke ?

Clow. How now ſawce-boxe, know your manners : was not I Gentleman vſher before you came ? Am not I hee that did the bottle bring ? Come Ladies follow me. *Exit Clowne with Ladies, with Huntſman.*

Moun. Your purpoſe Sir, is to loue this Lady, And hazard all your hopes.

Prince. Oh gentle Friend, Why was I borne high ? but to raiſe their hopes That are deiected—ſo much for my bounty.

Moun. But for your loue.

Prince. It is with no intent To make the Maide my wife, becauſe I know Her fortunes cannot equall mine.

Moun. Then 'twere more diſhonorable To ſtrumpet her.

Prince. Still thou miſtak'ſt, mine Is honourable loue, and built on vertue ; Nor would I for the Emperours Diademe Corrupt her whom I loue.

Moun. Braue Prince I'me glad That ere I kept thy company.

Prince. Come Mounſieur, night ſteales on, not many yeares Shall paſſe me, but I purpoſe to reuiſite This my new Miſtreſſe, my auſpicious fate To thee my happy loue I conſecrate. *Exeunt.*

A Dumbe ſhow. Enter the Duke *of Milleine, a Midwife with a young Childe, and after them* Stroza : *the Duke ſhewes the Childe to* Stroza, *hee takes it :* then the Duke ſweares them both to ſecrecy vpon his Sword, and exit with the Midwife : then *Stroza goes to hide it, and* Parma *dogs him : when hee hath laid the Childe in a Corner, he departs in haſte, and* Parma *takes vp the Childe and ſpeakes.*

Par. Thou ſhouldſt be mine : and durſt I for my Head

Euen in the open Court I'de challenge thee,
But I haue fo incenft th' offended Duke,
And layd fuch heauy fpots vpon her head,
I cannot doo't with fafety : methinks this Child
Doth looke me in the face, as if 'twould call
Me Father, and but this fufpeſted *Stroza*
Stuft my too credulous eares with iealoufies.
For thee fweete Babe I'le fweare, that if not all,
Part of my blood runnes in thy tender veynes,
For thofe few drops I will not fee thee perifh ;
Be it for her fake whom once I lov'd,
And fhall doe euer : Oh iniurious *Stroza !*
I now begin to feare ; for this fweete Babe
Hath in his face no baftardy, but fhewes
A Princely femblance : but *Stroza* and the Duke,
This will I keepe as charie as her honour,
The which I prize aboue the Vniuerfe.
Though fhe were forc't to be vnnaturall,
I'le take to me this Infants pupillage ;
Nor yet refolu'd, till I a way haue found
To make that perfeſt which is yet vnfound.   *Exit.*

Explicit Aſtus Secundus.

Aſtus Tertius.

Enter Milleine *with Lords and* Iulia.

Milleine.   Forbeare my Lords for a few priuate
    words :
Faire Daughter, wee'le not chide you farther now,
Nor adde vnto your blufhes by our rude reproofes :
Your faults are couered with thefe your fighes,
Since all your fire of luft is quencht in afhes.

Iul. Durſt I preſume my Lord, to know
Whither you haue ſent my ſonne ?
   Mil. I'le not haue it queſtion'd.
I ſtriue to ſalue thy honour, and thou ſeek'ſt
To publiſh thy diſgrace : my ſtudy is
Where I may picke thee out a noble Husband,
To ſhadow theſe diſhonours, and keepe thee
From the like ſcandall.
   Iul. Whom but *Parmaes* Prince.
   Mil. Oh name him not thou ſtrumpet.
   Iul. I haue done.
   Mil. There's a Prince of noble hopes and for-
     tunes,
The Prince of *Florence* : what if I ſent to him
About a ſpeedy Marriage ? for I feare,
Delay may breed ſtrange doubts.
   Iul. Since I haue loſt the name of Child,
I am a ſeruant now and muſt obey.

Enter Stroza *and Lords.*

   Mil. *Stroza.*
   Str. Your eare my Lord, 'tis done.
   Mil. Laid out ?
   Str. To ſafety as I hope.
   Mil. What, and ſuſpectleſſe ?
   Str. Vnleſſe the ſilent Groue of Trees ſhould
     blabe,
There is no feare of ſcandall, mantled cloſe,
I left the fucking Babe where the next paſſenger
Muſt finde it needes, and ſo it hapned for
Some two yeares after,
Paſſing that way to know where 'twas become,
'Twas gone, and by ſome courteous hand I hope
Remou'd to gentle foſterage.
   Mil. My excellent friend,
For this wee'le boſome thee : your counſel *Stroza*,
Our Daughter's growne to yeares, and we intend
To picke her out a Husband, in whoſe iſſue

Her name may flouriſh, and her honours liue.

All Lords.   Moſt carefully deuis'd.

Mil.   But where my Lords
May we prouide a match to equall her ?

    1. *Lord.*   *Ferrara* hath a faire and hopefull Heire.

    2. *Lord.*   And ſo hath *Mantua.*

    3. *Lord.*   How do you prize the Noble *Florentine ?*

    1. *Lord.*   In fame no whit inferior.

    2. *Lord.*   But in ſtate
Many degrees excelling : aime no further Sir,
If that may be accepted.

    Duke.   To *Florence* then wee'le ſtreight diſpatch
      Embaſſadours,
Stroza, bee't your care to mannage this high buſineſſe.
Oh to ſee
How Parents loue deſcends : and howſoe're
The Children proue vngratefull and vnkinde,
Though they deride, we weepe our poore eyes blinde.

                            Exeunt.

    Enter Clowne *gallant, and the* Huntſman.

    Clow.   Nay, nay, the caſe is alter'd with mee ſince
you ſaw me laſt : I was neuer in any hope to purchaſe any other ſuite then that I wore yeſterday ;
but now I can ſay *Ecce ſignum,* the caſe is alter'd.
Now euery begger comes vpon me with *good Gentleman, good Gentleman* : when yeſterday Gentlemen
would haue ſhun'd the way for feare I ſhould haue
begg'd of them.   Then comes another vpon mee with
good your Worſhip, good your Worſhip, then doe I
double my fyles, and caſt him a ſingle two pence.

    Hunt.   Sirrah, thou mayſt thanke the Prince for
    this.

    Clow.   Thou ſay'ſt true ; for he hath chang'd our
woodden Diſhes to Siluer Goblets : goodly large Arras
that neuer yet deſeru'd hanging, he hath caus'd to be
hang'd round about the Chamber : My Lady and
Miſtreſſe, now my Lady and Miſtreſſe lyes ouer head

and eares in Downe and Feathers : well, if they be
rul'd by me, I would haue them to keepe their
beds.

Hunt. Why wouldſt thou haue them lye a bed all
day ?

Clow. Oh dull ignorant ! I meane knowing how
hard they haue bin lodg'd in the Forreſt ; I would
not haue them fell away their beds, and lie vpon
the boords.

Hunt. Oh now I vnderſtand you ſir.

Clow. Ey, ey ; thou may'ſt get much vnderſtanding by keeping my company : But Sir, does not the
new Gowne the Prince ſent my Miſtreſſe, become
her moſt incomparably ?

Hunt. 'Tis true : 'tis ſtrange to ſee how Apparrell
makes or marres.

Clow. Right : for yeſterday thou wouldſt haue
taken me for a very Clowne, a very Clowne ; and now
to ſee, to ſee.—

Enter Mother and the young Lady gallant.

Wife. Sirrah.

Clow. Madam.

Lau. Why doſt view me thus ?

Clow. To ſee if the Tayler that made your Gowne,
hath put ne're an M. vnder your Girdle, there belongs
more to beaten Sattin then ſirrah.

Lau. What thinke you Mother of the Prince his
    bounty,
His vertue, and perfection ?

Wife. He's a mirrour, and deſerues a name
Amongſt the famous Worthies.

Lau. Heighoe.

Wife. Why ſigh you ?

Lau. Pray tell me one thing Mother : when you
    were
Of my yeares, and firſt lou'd, how did you feele
Your ſelfe ?

Wife.   Loue Daughter ?

Clow.   Shee talkes now, as if fhe fhould bc enamored of my comely fhape ; for I haue (as they fay) fuch a foolifh yong and relenting heart, I fhould neuer fay her nay, I fhould neuer weare off this.

Lau.   Stand farther off fir.

Clow.   No, I'le affure your Ladifhip 'tis beaten Sattin.

Lau.   Then take your Sattin farther.

Clow.   Your Ladifhip hath coniur'd me, and I will auoide Satan.

Lau.   Had you not fometimes mufings, fometimes extafies,
When fome delicate man 'boue other
Was prefent ?

Wife.   I aduife you curbe your fence in time,
Or you will bring your felfe into the way
Of much difhonour.

Lau.   And fpeake you by experience Mother ?
then
I doe begin to feare left that his fhape
Should tempt me, or his bounty worke aboue
My ftrength and patience ; pray Mother leaue vs neuer,
Left that without your Company, my loue
Contending with my weakeneffe, fhould in time
Get of 't the vpper hand.

Wife.   For this I loue thee.

Enter Clowne *running.*

Clow.   So hoe Miftris Madam, yonder is the Prince, and two or three Gentlemen come riding vpon the goodlieft Horfes that euer I fet my eyes vpon : and the Princes Horfe did no fooner fee me, but he weeighed and wagg'd his tayle : now I thinking he had done it to take acquaintance of me, faid againe to him, Gramercy Horfe ; fo I left them, and came to tell you Ladifhip.

Lau. Goe ſee them ſtabled, my ſoule leapt within
   me
To heare the Prince but named.

Enter Prince *and* Mounſieur.

Prince. Now my faire Friend.
Lau. Your hand-mayd mighty Prince.
Prince. Looke Mounſieur,
Can ſhe be leſſe then Noble ? nay deſerues ſhe
Thus habited, to be tearm'd leſſe then Royall,
What thinkſt thou Mounſieur ?
Moun. Faith my Lord,
I neuer loue a woman for her habite,
When Sir I loue, I'le ſee my loue ſtarke naked.
Prince. Right courteous Lady,
Our bounty is too ſparing for your worth,
Yet ſuch as 'tis accept it.
Wife. Royall ſir,
'Tis beyond hope or merit.
Prince. I prithee Mounſieur,
A little complement with that old Lady,
Whilſt I conferre with her.
Moun. I thanke you Sir :
See, you would make me a ſir Panderus,
Yet farre as I can ſee you, I will truſt you.
Hee talkes with the old Lady.
Sweete Lady, how long is't—nay keepe that hand,
Since thoſe fierce warres 'twixt *Florence* and great
   Millaine ?
Nay that hand ſtill.
Prince. And haue you ne're a loue then ?
Lau. Yes my Lord :
I ſhould belye my owne thoughts to deny,
And ſay I had none.
Prince. Pray acquaint me with him,
And for thy ſake I'le giue him ſtate and Honours,
And make him great in *Florence.* Is he of birth ?
Lau. A mighty Duke-domes Heire.

Prince. How now my *Lauretta* ?
I prithee fweete where liues he ?
   Lau. In his Countrey.
   Prince. Honour me fo much
As let me know him.
   Lau. In that your Grace muft pardon me.
   Prince. Muft ? then I will.   Is he of prefence
fweete ?
   Lau. As like your Grace as one Prince to an-
other.
   Prince. Honour me fo much then, as let me know
him.
   Lau. In that excufe me Sir.
   Prince. Thee, loue I will
In all things : wherefore ftudy you ?
   Lau. Why my Lord ?
I was euen wifhing you a mighty harme ;
But pardon me 'twas out euen vnawares.
   Prince. Harme ? there's none can come from thee
   Lauretta,
Thou art all goodneffe, nay confeffe it fweete.
   Lau. I was wifhing with my felfe that you were
   poore :
Oh pardon me my Lord, a poore, a poore man.
   Prince. Why my *Lauretta* ?
   Lau. Sir, becaufe that little
I haue, Might doe you good : I would you had
No money, nay, no meanes : but I fpeake idly,
Pray pardon me my Lord.
   Prince. By all my hopes,
I haue in *Florence*, would thou wert a Dutcheffe,
That I might court thee vpon equall tearmes ;
Or that I were of low deiected fortunes,
To ranke with thee in Birth : for to enioy
Thy beauty, were a greater Dowre then *Florence*
Great Duke-dome.

         Enter Clowne.

   Clow. Oh my Lord, my Lord,

Are you clofe at it ? and you too crabbed Age,
And you—there's Rods in piffe for fome of you.
    Prince. Now fir, the newes?
    Clow. Oh my Lord, there's a Nobleman come
from the Court to fpeake with you.
    Prince. Mounfieur,
Vpon my life 'tis fome Embaffadour.
    Moun. Good Sir make hafte, left I be challeng'd
for you.
    Prince. No worthy Friend, for me thou fhalt not
      fuffer,
At our beft leafur'd houres we meane to vifite you ;
Now giue me leaue to take a fhort fare-well.
               Exeunt Prince *and* Mounfieur.
    Lau. Your pleafure is your owne,
To part from him I am rent quite afunder.
    Clow. And you can but keepe your leggs clofe,
Let him rend any thing elfe and fpare not.   *Exeunt.*

Enter Florence *and* Lords *with* Stroza Embaffadour.

    Flo. Speake the true Tenor of your Embaffie.
    Str. If *Florence* prize the Duke of *Millaines*
      loue,
His indear'd Amity : If he haue minde
To mixe with him in confanguinity,
To ftrengthen both your Realmes : he makes this pro-
      iect
To your faire Treaty, that your hopefull Heire
Shall with the Princeffe *Iulia* his faire Daughter,
Be ioyn'd in Marriage ; her large Dowre fhall be
A fpacious Duke-dome after his deceafe.
But which my Lord counts moft, is a faire League
'Twixt your diuided Duke-domes.
    Florence. We doe conceite you :
But for the Dowre you craue ?
    Str. Ten thoufand Crownes
By th'yeare.

Flo. 'Tis granted : onely our Sonnes confent
Is wanting : but fee here, he wifht for comes.

Enter Prince and Mounfieur.

Prince. Mounfieur, what are thofe ?
Moun. Embaffadours my Lord.
Prince. Whence are thefe Lords ?
Dake. From *Millaine.*
Prince. Their bufineffe Royall Sir ?
Flo. About a match,
Which if you 't pleafe, we highly fhall applaud.
They offer you a faire and vertuous Princeffe
Vnto your bed.
Prince. Vnto my bed my Lord ?
I am not fo affraide of fpirits Sir,
But I can lye alone without a bed-fellow.
Flo. 'Tis the faire Princeffe *Iulia* you muft marry.
Prince. Marry my Lord ?
Flo. I marry muft you Sir,
Or you diuorce your felfe from our deare loue.
Prince. But is fhe faire ?
Stro. As euer *Hellen* was.
Prince. What, and as Chafte ?
Stroza. It were not Princely in you, Royall Sir,
To queftion fuch a Princeffe Chaftity :
I could haue inftanc'd *Lucrece.*
Prince. Would you had,
For both were rauifht.
Moun. How's this my Lord ?
They offer loue and beauty, which being both
So freely offer'd, doe deferue acceptance.
Stroza. Your anfwere Sir ?
Prince. That I am yours : the States ;
And if you pleafe fo to difpofe me, hers,
What ere fhe be : come friend, I muft impart
My Loue this newes, or it will rend my heart.
                                        Exit Prince.

Stroza. I fhall returne this anfwere.

Flo. Faithfully
As we intend it : But you firft fhall tafte
The bounty of our Court, with royall Prefents
Both to the Duke your mafter, and the Princeffe ;
It done, prepare we for this great folemnity,
Of Hymeneall Iubilies. Fixt is the day,
Wherein rich *Florens* fhall her pompe difplay.

Exeunt.

Enter Parma *and a Lord of* Millaine.

Parm. Onely to you, of all the *Millaine* Peeres,
I dare expofe my fafety.

Lord. In thefe armes
My Lord, you are Sanctuared.

Parm. I doe not doubt it :
But I pray you tell me, fince I left the Court,
How is my abfence taken ?

Lord. Of the Duke,
With much diftafte.

Parm. But of the Princeffe *Iulia ?*

Lord. Full two Moneths
Shee kept her Chamber, grieuoufly diftracted,
They fay, meere griefe for your departure hence.

Parm. Brauely manag'd,
The Duke I fee was more kind to her fame,
Then to his prettie grand-childe ; well Ile falt it all,
But what thinke you if after all I fhould
Send Letters to her, or Ambaffadors ?
I fhould not win her, for I know
They haue her heart in bondage.

Lord. Why worthy Prince,
Haue you not heard the newes : Shee hath beene
    offered
Vnto the Florentine, the match accepted,
And the Nuptiall day the tenth of the next Moneth.

Parm. No more : Pray leaue mee Sir.

Lord. I will : Pray Sir

Regard your fafety.   Exit *Lord.*

Parm. To bee married, *Ruimus in veftitum fem-per,*
I did neglect her, but being deni'd,
I doate upon her beautie : Methinkes 'tis fit,
If I begot the Child ? I wed the Mother :
The Prince, I pitie hee fhould bee fo wrong'd,
And I the Inftrument : Now helpe mee braine,
That neare was wont to fayle mee : 'Tis decreed
Something to Plot, although I fayle to fpeede.
                                        Exit *Parma.*

Enter Clowne, Mother, *and* Lauretta.

Clowne. I wonder you fhould bee fo fad and melan-
chollie, Ile lay a yeeres wages before hand Ile tell your
difeafe, as well as any Doctor in *Florence,* and let me
but feele your pulfe.

Lauret. Away, you are a foole, and trouble vs.

Clowne. That's no matter whether I bee a foole
or a phifitian, if I loofe, Ile pay, that's certain.

Wife. Try the fooles counfell daughter, but bee
fure
To forfit, and to pay.

Lauret. Now fir, your skill.

Clowne. Nay I muft feele your pulfe firft, for if a
Womans pulfe bee neere a place, I know there's few
heere of my yeeres but would bee glad to turne
Doctors.

Lauret. Now fir, you fee I doe not fmile.

Clawne. Nay, if it bee nothing elfe, Ile fetch that
will cure you prefently.   Exit *Clowne.*

Wife. Child I muft chide you, you giue too much
way
Vnto this humour : It alters much your beautie.

Enter the Clowne.

Clowne. Oh young Miftris, where are you, the
Prince,

The Prince.

   Lauret. Oh Mother, doe you heare the newes, the
     Prince,
The Prince is comming : Where is hee, oh where ?

   Clowne. Where is hee ? Why at the Court ; where
ſhould hee bee ? I did but doo't to make you ſmile :
Nay, Ile tickle you for a Doctor : Madam I haue a
yeeres wages before hand.

   Lauret. Is hee not come then ?

   Clowne. No marrie is hee not.

   Lauret. My ſoule did leape within, to heare the
     Prince
But nam'd : It ſtarted every ioynt.

   Clowne. Nay Madam, the Prince is come.

   Wife. Away, your foolerie's vnſeaſonable,
Weele not beleeve you.

      Enter the Prince *and* Mounſieur.

   Clowne. If you will not belieue mee, will you
     beleeue theſe ?

   Lauret. Welcome my Lord : And wherefore doe
     you ſigh ?

   Prince. I ſigh *Lauretta,* cauſe I cannot chuſe.

   Lauret. Nor could I chuſe, ſhould you but ſigh
     againe.

   Prince. Ile tell thee Loue, ſtrange newes : I muſt
     be married.

   Lauret. Married my Lord !

   Prince. Why doe you weepe ? You blam'd mee now
     for ſighing :
Why doe you melt in teares ? Sweet what's the
     cauſe ?

   Lauret. Nay, nothing.

   Prince. And as I told thee Sweete ; I muſt bee
     married,
My Father and the State will haue it ſo ;
And I came inſtantly to tell the newes

To thee *Lauretta* ; As to one, from whom
I nothing can conceale.

 Lauret. Why fhould you grieue
For that? For I, my Lord, muft haue a Husband
  too.

 Prince. Muft you? But when's the day?

 Lauret. When's yours my Lord?

 Prince. The tenth of the next moneth.

 Lauret. The felfe fame day,
And felfe fame houre that you inioy your loue,
My Princely Husband I muft then inioy.

 Prince. But doe you loue him?

 Lauret. Not my felfe more deere.

 Prince. How happie are you aboue mee faire
  friend,
That muft inioy where you affect? When I
Am tide to others fancies : It was your promife
That I fhould know him further.

 Lauret. You fhall fee him
That day, as richly habited as the great
Heire of *Florence :* But royall Sir, what's fhee
That you muft bed then?

 Prince. 'Tis *Iulia*,
The Duke of *Millaines* daughter : Why change your
  Face?   *Lauretta fpeakes to her felfe.*

 Lauret. That fhee that hates mee moft fhould liue
  to inioy
Him I affect beft : O my ominous fate,
I thought to haue hid mee from thee in thefe
  defarts,
But thou doft dogg mee euery where.

        Shee Swounes.

 Prince. Looke to her fafety, not for the Crowne
Of *Florence* I would haue her perifh.

 Wife. Helpe to fupport her.

      Exit with Mother and Clowne.

 Prince. Oh Friend, that I fhould change my
  Royaltie

To weakneffe now : I doe thinke this lodge
A Pallace, and this Beautious Mayden-head
Of greater worth then *Iulia.*
Moun. Come my Lord,
Lay by thefe idle thoughts, and make you ready
To entertaine your Bride.

Enter Parma *difguifed.*

Parm. The Prince, the Prince,
I come to feeke the Prince, and was directed
Vnto this place.
Prince. Thy newes.
Parm. A Letter.
Prince. Whence ?
Parm. Reade, the Contents will fhew you ; their
eyes are from mee, and I muft hence. Exit *Parma.*

The Prince *reades.*

Prince. The *Millaine* Princeffe is betroathed ; de-
flowred,
Not worthy of your loue, beleeue this true
Vpon a Prince his word ; when you fhall bed
her,
And find her flawd in her Virginitie,
You fhall haue caufe to thinke vpon his loue
From whom you had this caution ;
But doe it with that Princely management,
Her honour bee not flandered : Hee that loues,
Admires, and honours you :
Where's hee that brought this Letter ?
Moun. Fled my Lord.
Prince. Poaft after ; bring him backe,
Could hee not fet his hand to't——
How now, the newes ?
Moun. Hee's fled vpon a milke white Gennet
Sir,
Seeming t' outftrip the winde, and I—loft him.

Prince. Thou haſt loſt mee quite.

Moun. What meanes this paſsion Sir?

Prince. Mounfieur reade there,
What will confound thee: Oh if ſhee bee vnchaſt!
Could they find none but mee to worke vpon.

Moun. It confounds mee my Lord.

Prince. If ſhee bee Chaſt,
How ſhall I wrong her, to queſtion her faire Vertues?

Moun. Right.

Prince. But if ſhee bee not right? I wrong my
Honor,
Which after marriage, how ſhall I recall?

Moun. 'Tis certaine.

Prince. Yes: Oh how am I perplext!
Come, Ile to Court,
Ile not bee ſway'd : Were ſhee a Potent Queene,
Where Counſell fayles mee, Ile once truſt to ſpleene.

Exeunt.

Enter the Clowne *with his Table-bookes.*

Clowne. Let me fee, the *Prince* is to bee married
to morrow, and my young Miſtris meanes to keepe a
Feaſt in the Forreſt, in honour of his wedding at the
Court: Now am I ſent as Caterer into the City to
prouide them with victualls, which they charg'd
me to buy; no ordinary fare, no more it ſhall,
and therefore I haue caſt it thus ; Firſt and foremoſt,
wee will haue—(yes downe it ſhall) we will haue a
Gammon of Bacon roaſted, and ſtufft with Oyſters ;
And fixe Black-Puddings to bee ſerued vp in Sorrell-
ſops ; A pickell'd ſhoulder of Mutton, and a furloyne
of Beefe in White-broth, ſo much for the firſt courſe.
Now for the ſecond, we will haue a Cherry-Tart cut
into Raſhers and broyled ; A Cuſtard Carbonado'd on
the coales ; A liue Eele ſwimming in clowted Creame ;
And fixe Sheepes-heads baked, with the hornes peer-
ing out of the paſty-cruſt. The morrall is, becauſe it
is a wedding-dinner.

Enter Stroza *with another Lord.*

Stro. The ioyfull day's to morrow.   Paffe this plunge
And we are made for euer.

Clowne. What, my old Polititian? hee that vnder-min'd my old Lady and my yong Miftris? now that I could find but one ftratagem to blow him vp; I would toffe him, I would blanket him i' th Ayre, and make him cut an Italian caper in the Clouds : Thefe Politicians can doe more execution with a pen, in their ftudies, then a good Souldier with his fword in the field, but he hath fpi'd mee.

Stro. Thee friend I fhould haue knowne?

Clowne. And you too, I fhould haue knowne, but whether for a friend, or no, ther's the queftion?

Stro. Thou feru'ft the Generall *Sforza.*

Clow. I confeffe it ; but whether you haue feru'd him well, or no, there hangs a Tale.

Stro. How doth thy noble Lady, faire *Lauretta*? They have left *Millaine* long, refide they here
Neere to the City *Florence* ?

Clow. Some three miles off, here in the Forreft, not halfe an houres riding.

Stro. I pray thee recommend me to them both,
And fay, It fhall goe hard with mine affaires
But Ile find feafon'd houres to vifit them.

Clow. You fhall not want directions to find the place, come when you will, you fhall be moft heartily ——poyfon'd.

Stro. Tell them, The newes that they are well
Is wondrous pleafing to me, and that power
I haue in *Millaine* is referu'd for them,
To worke them into grace : I can but fmile,
To fee how clofe I haue plotted their exile.
Now bufineffe calls me hence : farewell.   *Exit.*

Clow. And be hang'd, Mounfieur *Stroza*, whofe defcription my *Mufe* hath included in thefe few lines ;

Stroza, *Thy Head is of a comely Block,*
And would ſhew well, crown'd with the combe of Cock :
His Face an Inne, his Brow a ſluttiſh Roome,
His Noſe the Chamberlaine, his Beard the Broome,
Or like New-market Heath, that makes theeues rich,
In which his Mouth ſtands iuſt like Deuills-ditch.
And ſo farewell to your worſhip, graue Mounſieur
Stroza, for I muſt about my market.   *Exeunt.*

Actus Quartus.

A Dumbe ſhew. *Enter at one doore, the Duke oſ*
  Millaine, Iulia, Stroza, *and a* Biſhop : *At the*
  other doore, the Duke of Florens, *the* Prince *and*
  Mounſieur, *with attendants : Then the* Biſhop
  takes their hands and makes ſignes to marry them,
  and then the Prince *ſpeakes.*

  Prince. Stay till we be reſolu'd.
  Florens. What meanes our ſonne ?
  Princ. Not to be gull'd by the beſt Prince in
    Europe;
Much leſſe by *Millaine.*
  Millaine. Sir, be plaine with vs.
  Prin. I much ſuſpect that Ladies Chaſtity.
  Millaine. Hers.
  Prin. I haue ſaid.
  Stroza. Ther's Worme-wood.
  Millaine. I came in termes of Honour,
Brought with me, all my comforts here on earth,
My daughter ; to beſtow her on thy ſon :
Poore Lady, innocently comming, forſaking all,
Father and Countrey, to betake her ſelfe

Vnto his boſome ; and is ſhe for all this,
Branded with ſhame ?

    Stro. Who can accuſe her, ſpeake ? what proba-
        bilities ?
What ground ? the place ? the meanes ? the ſeaſon how
Shee did become corrupt ?

    Prince. Sir, ſo we haue heard.

    Stro. Produce the witneſſe ; and behould, I ſtand
The Champion for her honour, and will auerre
Her Chaſte, aboue degree ; infinitely honeſt :
Oh Prince ! what, can you ground ſuch iniury
Vpon vaine heare-ſay ? Speake for your ſelfe, take
        ſpirit.

    Iulia. Came we thus farre, to be thus wrong'd ?
                          Apart to herſelfe.

    Stro. Was the ſlaue neuer Chriſten'd, hath hee no
        name ?

    Iulia. Haue you ſent for me, to accuſe me heere
In this ſtrange Clime ? It is not Princely done.

    Prince. O Heauen, how am I perplext !

    Floren. Sonne, Sonne, you wrong
Your ſelfe and me too, to accuſe a Lady
Of ſuch high birth and fame ; vnleſſe you confeſſe
You ſelfe to haue err'd, you needs muſt forfeit vs.

    Moun. My Lord, yeeld to your father, leſt you draw
His wrath vpon you.

    Prince. Well, ſince I muſt, I will :
Your pardon, Royall Father : Yours faire Princeſſe :
And yours great Duke ;
If I ſhall find my ſelfe truely to haue err'd,
I ſhall confeſſe your chaſtity much iniur'd.

    Iulia. Submiſſion is to me full recompence.

    Milla. My daughters honour ?

    Stro. Doe not ſtand off my Lord,
If ſhe be wrong'd, ſhee's not much behind-hand.

    Milla. Oh let me alone *Stroza.*

    Flor. Nay, good Brother
Accept him as your Sonne.

    Milla. My hearts no cloſet for reuenge ; 'tis done.

Prin. Now heare my proteſtations : I receiue
This Ladies hand on theſe Conditions ;
If you, my Lord, her father, or her ſelfe,
Know her ſelfe faulty, Oh confeſſe it here,
Before the Ceremonies faſten on me : for if hereafter
I find you once corrupted ? by this right hand,
My future hopes, my Fathers royalty,
And all the honours due vnto our houſe,
Ile haue as many liues and heads for it,
As he hath Manners, Caſtles, Liues and Towres ;
It ſhall be worthy to be lockt in Chronicles
Of all ſtrange tongues : And therefore beautious
        Lady,
As you eſteeme a Prince his name or honour,
That youd be a *Mecænas* vnto vertue ;
If in the leaſt of theſe you guilty be,
Pull backe your hand.
        Stro. What if you find her chaſte ?
        Prin. If chaſte, ſhe ſhall be dearer farre to me
Then my owne foule : I will reſpeɔt her honour,
Equall with that of my great Anceſtours ;
All this I vow, as I am Prince and vertuous.
        Stro. Then ioyne their hands.
        Prin. Shee's mine : Set forwards then.
                        Exeunt all but Stroza.
        Stro. All goes not well, This iugling will be
        found,
Then where am I ? would I were ſafe in *Millaine.*
Here Matchiuell thou waſt hatcht : Could not the
        ſame
Planet inſpire this pate of mine with ſome
Rare ſtratagem, worthy a laſting Charaɔter :
No, 'twill not be ; my braine is at a non plus,
For I am dull.

                Enter Millaine.

Milla. Stroza.
Stro. My Lord.

Milla. Oh now, or neuer *Stroza*!

Stro. I am turn'd Foole, Affe, Iddeot; Are they
    married?

Milla. Yes, and the Prince after the Ceremonie,
Imbrac'd her louingly.

Stro. But the hell is
That they muſt lie together, ther's the Deuill.

Milla. And then——

Stro. And then we are difgrac'd and ſham'd.

Milla. Canſt thou not help't man?

Stro. Why you would make
A man—midwife, woo'd you? I haue no skill.

Milla. Stroza, awake, th'art drowſie.

Stro. Peace, interrupt me not,
I ha'te : ſo to reuenge mee vpon her
Whom moſt I hate. To Strumpet her 'twere braue.

Milla. Counfell aduife me.

Stro. Youle make me mad my Lord :
And in this ſweet reuenge, I am not onely
Pleas'd (with iuſt fatisfaction for all wrongs)
But the great Prince moſt palpably deceiu'd.

Milla. The time runs on, thinke on my honor
    Stroza.

Stro. If youle eate grapes vnripe, edge your owne
    teeth,
Ile ſtay the mellow'd feafon, doo't your felfe,
Vnleffe you giue me time for't.

Milla. But thinke with mine, on thine owne fafety
    Stroza.

Stro. Peace, giue me way my Lord, ſo ſhall the
    Prince
Bee palpably deceiu'd, Faire *Iulia's* honor
Moſt profperouſly preferu'd, The Duke my maſter,
Freed from all blame, Warre hindred, Peace con-
    firm'd,
And I fecur'd ; Oh I am fortunate
Beyond imagination!

Milla. O deare *Stroza*,
Helpe now, or neuer!

Stro.   Hee was a meere Aſſe
That rais'd Troy's Horſe : 'twas a pritty ſtructure.
Milla.   Oh mee !
Stro.   *Synon*, a foole, I can doe more
With precious Gold, then hee with whining Teares.
Milla.   Oh my tormented foule !
Stro.   Pray my Lord, giue mee
Fiue hundred crownes.
Milla.   What to doe with them man ?
Stro.   See how you ſtand on trifles ; when our
liues,
Your honour ; all our fortunes lie a bleeding ;
What ſhall I haue the Gold ?
Milla.   Thy purpoſe preethee ?
Stro.   I know a deſolate Lady, whom with Gold
I can corrupt.
Milla.   There are fiue hundred Crownes,
Stroza bethinke thee what thou vndertak'ſt,
Such an Act, would make huge *Atlas* bend his head
Vnto his heele.
Stro.   But ſay I cannot win her,
They bide the brunt of all, heere let them ſtay,
With theſe fiue hundred Crownes Ile poaſt away.
                              Exit Stroza, *and* Duke.

Enter Mother, Daughter, *and* Clowne.

Clow.   Maddam, yonder's a Gentleman comes to
ſpeake with you in all haſt.
Lauret.   Admit him in.

Enter Stroza.

Stro.   Lady bee happy, and from this bleſt houre
Euer reioyce faire Virgin, for I bring you
Gold, and Inlargement ; with a recouerie
Of all your former loſſe, and dignitie,
But for a two houres labour : Nay, that no labour
Nor toyle, but a meere pleaſure.

Lau. Your words like mufick, pleafe me with de-
light,
Beyond imagination : Offered to vs ?
Being exil'd our Countrey, and our friends,
Therefore good fir, delay not with long comple-
ment ;
But tell thefe hopes more plaine.
   Stro. Haue wee not heere
Too many eares ?
   Lauret. Wee would bee priuate firra,
And therefore leaue vs.   Exit *Clowne.*
   Stro. You haue feene the Prince of *Florence* ?
   Lauret. Yes I haue.
   Stro. Is he not for his Feature, Beauty, Good-
neffe,
The moft Compleate ? So abfolute in all things.
   Lauret. All this is granted.
   Stro. How happy doe you thinke that Lady then
That fhall Inioy him ?   Nay, that fhall bee the firft
To prooue him, and exchange Virginitie,
Were't not bright Lady a great happineffe ?
   Lauret. I wifh that happineffe were mine alone,
Oh my faint heart : Paffion ouer-fwayes me quite,
But hide thy griefe *Lauretta* : Sir, you'le make
Me fall in loue with him : Were I his equall,
I then fhould iudge him worthy of no leffe.
   Stro. Loue him : What's fhe doth not, if fhee haue
eyes ?
Were I my felfe a Woman : I would lay
My felfe a proftitute vnto the Prince :
Shee is not wife that would refufe him Lady.
   Lauret. Good Sir bee briefe :
To what pray tends thefe fpeeches ?
   Stro. To thee fweete Lady : I offer all thefe plea-
fures,
Oh happie fate that hath felefted mee
To be your raifer : Lady take this gold,
But that's not all : For there are greater honours

Prepared for you ; the Duke of *Millaine* doth
Commend him to you : *Iulia* his daughter
Hath in her honour late miſcarried,
Now't lies in you to falue and make all good.

 Wife. Who ? Lies this in my daughter.

 Stro. Yes, in her,
Shee hath the power to make the Duke her friend,
Iulia her ſiſter, and all *Millaine* bound
To offer vp for her their Orriſons.

 Lauret. Good Sir bee plaine.

 Stro. This night lie with the Prince
In *Iulia's* ſtead : There's way made for you,
Who would not woo, for what you are wooed too ?

 Lauret. Doe you not bluſh, when you deliuer
this
Pray tell the Duke, all Women are not *Iulia*,
And though wee bee deiected, thus much tell him,
Wee hold our honour at too high a price,
For Gold to buy.

 Stro. Nay Lady, heare mee out ;
You ſhall preſerue her honour, gaine the Duke,
Redeeme your fortunes : Strengthen you in friends,
You ſhall haue many Townes and Turrets ſtanding,
Which future Warre may ruine : Thinke on that.

 Wife. Lauretta, oh behold thy mothers teares !
Thinke on thy Father, and his honour wonne,
And call to mind our exile : All the wrongs
Wee haue indured by her, to whom wee gaue
No cauſe, and now are plundg'd in a deepe ſtreame,
Which not reſiſted, will for euer blemiſh
The name of *Sforſa* thy great Anceſtors,
Thou'lt waken thy dead Father from his graue,
And cauſe his honour'd wounds which hee receiu'd
From that vnthankfull Duke, to bleede afreſh,
Powring out new blood from his griſly wounds,
If thou conſenteſt to this abhorred fact,
Thy Mothers curſe will ſeaze on thee for euer :
Oh child, behold me on my knees : Ile follow thee ;

Oh doe not leaue me thus, and pull on thee
An euerlafting ftaine, to fcandall all
Thy former Vertues, for the momentarie
Short pleafures of one night.

Stro.   She doth not councell well ; 'tis foolifh rafh-
nes,
Womanifh Indifcretion.

Lauret.   Sir bee anfwered,
If *Iulia* bee difloyall : Let her bee found
So by the Prince fhe wedds : Let her be branded
With the vile name of ftrumpet : Shee difgrac'd
Mee, that nere thought her harme ; publikely ftrucke
mee,
Nay in the Court : And after that, procur'd
My banifhment : Thefe Injuries I reap't
By her alone, then let it light on her.

Stro.   Now fee your errour,
What better, fafer, or more fweete reuenge,
Then with the Husband ? what more could woman
aske ?

Lauret.   My blood rebells againft my reafon, and
I no way can withftand it : 'Tis not the Gold
Mooues mee, but that deere loue I beare the Prince,
Makes me negleCt the credit and the honour
Of my deare Fathers houfe : Sir, what the Duke defires
I am refolued to doe his vtmoft will.

Wife.   Oh my deare daughter.

Lauret.   Good Mother fpeake not, for my word is
paft,
And cannot bee recall'd, Sir will you away ?
I am refolute.

Stro.   Shee yeeldes vnto her fhame ; which makes
me bleft,
Let Millions fall, fo I bee crown'd with reft.

Wife.   Oh mee, vnhappie, that nere knew griefe
till now.   *Exeunt.*

Muficke.   A Dumbe Show. *Enter* Millaine, *to
him* Stroza, *and brings in* Lauretta *masked,*

the Duke takes her and puts her into the Bed, and Exit.

Enter both the Duke *and* Iulia, *they make ſignes to her and* Exit: Stroza *hides* Iulia *in a corner, and ſtands before ber.*

Enter againe with the Prince *to bring him to bed. They cheere him on, and others ſnatch his Pointes, and ſo* Exit. *The* Dukes *Imbrace, and Exeunt.*

Aɛtus Quintus.

Enter Millaine *to* Stroza.

Milla.   Thou art our truſty Counſellor ; if this paſſe currant
We're paſt all feare :   What is ſhe preethee ?   What ?
   Stro.   What's that to you, bee ſhee what ere ſhe can,
All's one to vs, ſo ſhe be found a Virgin ;
I haue hyred her, and ſhee's pleas'd.
   Milla.   But gaue you charge
Aſſoone as ere the Prince was faſt aſleepe,
That ſhee ſhould riſe and giue place to our daughter ?
   Stro.   Doubt you not that ; what, iealous already ?
   Milla.   How long ſhe ſtayes, I faine would be a bed ;
Pray heauen ſhee doe not fall
By him aſleepe, and ſo forget her ſelfe.
   Stro.   Heer's in my heart, a violent Feauer ſtill ;

Nor fhall I find my felfe in my true temper,
Vntill this brunt bee paft.
   Milla. What, not yet ?
Had fhe with *Parma* beene a bed fo long,
It would haue more perplext mee.

Enter Lauretta.

   Stro. See, here fhee is ;
The newes ?
   Lauret. The Prince is faft, all done.
   Milla. Step in her place ;
Nay when ? and counterfeit fleepe prefently.
   Stro, Away to bed my Lord : You to the For-
   reft,
I'le to my Coach, all's well.
Exeunt Stroza *and the* Duke.
   Lauret. And for my part, it was not much amifle,
Becaufe my Lord the Prince had fuch content
Which caus'd him giue his Charter to my hand,
The full affurance of faire *Iulia's* dowre :
Day gins to breake, and I muft to the Lodge.
Oh what a griefe it was to leaue the Prince !
But leaue thofe thoughts : Thefe Gifts to me affign'd,
Are nothing worth the Iem I left behind.   *Exit.*

Enter Prince *and* Mounfieur *with a Torch.*

   Moun. What doe you not like your bed-fellow, my
   Lord,
That you are vp fo foone ?
   Prin. Oh friend, was neuer man bleft with a
   Bride
So chaft ! I'me fcarce my felfe, till this be knowne
To my faire Forreft friend : Lett's mount away,
The nights quite fpent : and now begins the day.

Enter Mother *and* Clowne.

   Wife. And what was it you faid firra ?

Clow.   Marry, I would intreat your Lady-ſhip to
turne away my fellow *Ierom,* for I thinke hee's no true
man.

Wife.   No true man, Why?

Clo.   Marry, we were both in the Tauerne together
tother day——

Wife.   And hee ſtole ſome Plate?

Clo.   No Madam, but there ſtood at our elbow a
pottle Pot——

Wife.   And hee ſtole the Pot?

Clo.   No Madam, but he ſtole the wine in the Pot,
and drunke it off,

And made himſelfe ſo drunke hee be-piſt himſelfe:

Your Ladyſhip could not be better be-piſt in a Sum-
mers-day.

Enter Prince *and* Mounſieur.

Prin.   Good morrow Lady: Wher's your daughter
pray?

Wife.   She tooke ſo little reſt laſt night, my Lord,
I thinke ſhee is ſcarce well.

Prin.   Pray may wee ſee her?

Wife.   My Lord, you may.

Shee's drawne out vpon a Bed.

Song.

H*Ence with Paſsion, Sighes and Teares,*
   Defaſters, Sorrowes, Cares and Feares.
See, my Loue (my Loue) appeares,
   That thought himſelfe exil'd.
Whence might all theſe loud Ioyes grow?
Whence might Myrth, and Banquet's flow?
But that hee's come (hee's come) I know.
   Faire Fortune thou haſt ſmil'd.

2.

Giue to theſe blind windowes, Eyes;
Daze the Stars, and mocke the Skies,

And let vs two (vs two) deviſe,
    To laviſh our beſt Treaſures
Crowne our Wiſhes with Content,
Meete our Soules in ſweet conſent,
And let this night (this night) bee ſpent
    In all aboundant pleaſvres.

Prince.   Oh good morrow Lady,
I come to tell you newes !
    Lauret.   They are wellcome to me my Lord.
    Prin.   You know the Princeſſe *Iulia* was ſuppos'd
To bee adulterate――――
    Lauret.   So we haue heard it rumor'd.
    Prin.   Oh but faire friend, ſhe was indeed bely'd !
And I this morning roſe from her chaſt bed :
But wherefore ſweet caſt you that bluſhing ſmile ?
But you haue broak promiſe with me : For you told me
That the ſame day and houre I tooke my Bride,
You ſhould Inioy a Princely Husband.
    Lauret.   Trew
My Lord, I did.
    Prin.   And are you married then ?
    Lauret.   And lay with him laſt night.
    Prin.   Is hee off fortunes ?
    Lauret.   That you may ſoone conieƈture by this gift.
    Prin.   What haue you then, ſome tokens that were his ?
    Lauret.   Some few my Lord, amongſt the reſt, this diamond
Hee put vpon my finger.
    Prin.   You amaze mee !
Yet Rings may bee alike : If then your husband
Bee of ſuch ſtate and fortunes, What dowre are you allotted.
    Lauret.   Sir, ten thouſand crownes by th' yeere.
    Prin.   I gaue no more vnto my *Iulia.*
But where is the ſecurity you haue

For the performance of it ?

    Lauret.   See here, My Lord,
Sir, Is not that fufficient for a dowry ?

    Prin.   This is the Indenture that I gaue to *Iulia*;
Preethee *Lauretta*, but refolue me true,
How came you by this Charter ?

    Lauret.   Pardon great Prince ; for all that loue you
       fpake
To *Iulia*, you whifper'd in my eare :
Shee is vnchaft ; which, left you fhould haue found,
Her father fent mee here, fiue hundred crownes
By *Stroza* ; but neither his gold, nor all
His fly temptations, could one whit mooue mee ;
Onely the loue I euer bare your honour,
Made me not prife my owne.   No luftfull appetite
Made me attempt fuch an ambitious practife,
As to afpire vnto your bed my Lord.

    Prin.   Rife, doe not weepe, Oh I am ftrangely
      rapt
Into deepe ftrange confufion ?

    Moun.   *Millaine* fhould know, were it my cafe my
      Lord,
A better Prince then hee fhould not wrong me.

    Prin.   I haue bethought already how to beare
      mee ;
This Charter and this Ring, faire Loue, keepe you ;
And when I fend for you, you fhall repaire
Vnto the Court : This all I fhall inioyne you.

    Lauret.   Great Sir, I fhall.

    Prin.   Come *Mounfieur*, now 'tis caft,
Reuenge neere rules, fo it be found at laft.

                          Exeunt omnes.

       Enter the two Dukes with Iulia, Stroza *and
                 attendants.*

    Milla.   Who faw the Prince laft ? Is't a cuftome
      with him
To rife thus early ?

Floren. Sir, hee neuer fleepes
Longer then th' day, nor keepes his bed by Sunne :
'Tis not the loue of the faireft Lady liues,
Can make him leaue his morning exercife.
  Iulia. He neuer exercis'd with me, I'm fure ;
I might haue layne as fafe, free, and vntoucht,
By any Lady liuing.

Enter the Prince *and* Mounfi.

  Prince. Pardon Lords,
I haue ftay'd you long, your blefsing royall Father.
My cuftome is, euer to rife before
A womans houre : Now heare me fpeake my Lords,
I'm married to a Lady, whofe chafte honour,
Reports and falfe Suggeftions, did inforce me
To call in publike queftion ; but that we leaue
Vnto our laft nights reft.
  Stro. True my good Lord ;
But did you find me faulty ?
  Prin. I doe proteft, my Lords, I bofom'd with
As true and chafte a Virgin, as ere lodg'd
Within a Princes armes ; All this I vow
As I am Royall.
  Stro. All's well my Lord ?
  Milla. All's excellent *Stroza.*
  Princ. Now for amends and publike fatisfaction,
For the foule wrong I did her, queftioning
Her Vertue, Ile confirme her dowre, and that
Before I eate : Sweet Lady, reach the Charter
I gaue you laft night, 'fore you were full mine ?
  Iulia. I receiu'd none Sir.
  Prin. Sweet, will you tell mee that ?
With which you did receiue a Ring the Duke
My father gaue me.
  Iulia. When ?
  Prince. Laft night.
  Iulia. Where ?
  Prince. In your Bed.

Iulir. 'Twas in my dreame then.

Prince. Being broad awake.

Stro. I like not this : I ſmell a Rat.

Milla. *Stroza*, I feare too.

Stro. Brazen fore-head, Wilt
Thou leaue me now : 'Tis true my Lord.   You did
Receiue them both, Haue you forgot ſweet Lady,
This very morning, that you gaue them both
To me ? The Princeſſe ieaſted, to ſee how
You woo'd but take it.

Moun. Excellent Villaine !

Prince. 'Twas well put off :
'Tis ſtrange ſhee's ſo forgetfull : I prethee *Stroza*
Where are they ?

Stroza. Where are they ? they are——

Prince. Where ?
Why ſtuddy you ?

Stro. They are there——

Prince. Where man ?

Stro. I poaſted them
To *Millaine*, ſent them ſafe, dare you not truſt my
    word.

Prince. Not till I ſee my deeds.

Stro. By one oth' Princes Traine.

Prince. See which of the Traine is wanting.

Moun. I ſhall my Lord.

Stro. I would I were in *Turkey*.

Milla. Would I were on horſe-backe.

Prin. Nay, looke not you deiected beautious
    Bride,
For this is done onely to honour you.

Enter a Seruing-man with a child in a couered Diſh.

Gent. The Prince, my Maſter, hearing your ſo-
    lemnities,
Hath ſent this diſh, to adde a preſent to
Your royall Feaſts, wiſhing himſelfe therein
To be a wellcome gueſt.

Prince. Your Mafters name ?

Gent. Prince *Parma.*

Prince. Giue this Gentleman

A 100. crownes : This will much grace our banquet.

Flo. Ther's in that difh, fome Morrall.

Milla. Comming from him,

Meethinks it fhould be feafon'd with fome ftrange

And dangerous poyfon : Touch't not, my Lord.

Flo. There fhould be more in't, then a feafting
   difh ;

What's here, a Child ?

Iulia. O my perplexed heart !

Pri. Upon his breft ther's fomething writ, Ile
   read it.

> *'Tis fit, if Iuftice bee not quite exil'd*
> *That he that wedds the mother, keepe the child.*

This Child was fent to me.

Stro. From whom ? whom, *Parma* ? breake the
   baftards necke,

As I would doe the Fathers, were hee here.

Prin. Sure fpare't for the Mothers fake ; t'was
   fent to vs :   *Enter* Mounfieur.

Which of the trayne is wanting ?

Moun. None my Lord.

Prin. *Stroza*, where is this Charter and the
   Ring ?

Stro. I know of none.

Moun. Why, t'was confeft.

Stro. Right, I confeft it ; but your grace muft
   know,

'Twas but to pleafe your humour, which began

To grow into fome violence.

Moun. I can forbeare no longer ; Impudent
   Stroza,

Thou art a Villaine, periur'd, and forfworne :

That Duke difhonourable ; and fhee vnchaft :

Befides, thou hyredft a Virgin in her roome ;

(Slaue as thou art) to bofome with the Prince ;

Gau'ſt her fiue hundred Crownes.   That this is true,
I will maintaine by combat.

   Stro.   That I did this? Hee lies below his en-
    trayles,
That dares to braue mee with ſuch a proud affront:
And in the honour of my Prince and Countrey
I will approoue thee recreant.

   Prin.   A ſtrife, that nought ſaue combat can
    deſide,
The cauſe ſo full of doubts, and intricate.
See, they are both arm'd, and euenly, without odds,
Saue what the iuſtice of the cauſe can yeeld.

                Exit Mounſieur *and* Stroza.

           Enter Prince Parma.

   Par.   Bee't no intruſion held, if a ſtrange Prince
(Setting behind, all complementall leaue)
Amongſt ſtrange Princes enters: Let me know
Which is the Prince of *Florence?*

   Prince.   Wee are hee.

   Parm.   And *Parma?*

   Iuli.   *Parma?*

   Prince.   Excuſe mee Sir,
I know him not: But if I much miſtake not,
Wee are late indebted to you for a preſent.

   Parm.   It was a gift, I ſhould bee loath to part
    with,
But vpon good conditions.   Am I then
To all a ſtranger: Doe you not know mee Lady?

   Milla.   Heare him not ſpeake, I charge thee by
    thine honor?

   Prince.   *Parma* ſpeake, and if thy ſpeech was bent
    to mee?

   Parm.   Ere I proceede, let mee behold this babe;
Nere a Nurſe heere?   Pray hand it you ſweete Lady,
Till I find out a Mother.

   Milla.   Touch it not,
I charge thee on my bleſsing.

Iulia. Pardon Sir,
It well becomes my handling.
    Prince. *Parma* proceede.
    Parm. Then *Florence* know, thou haft wrong'd me
        beyond thought ;
Shipwrackt my Honour, and my Fame ; nay ftrumpeted
Her, whom I tearme my Bride.
    Prince. 'Tis falfe, I neuer faue with one imbrac'd,
And her, I found to be moft truely chaft.
    Parm. Then It maintaine : Haft thou a Wife
        heere ?
    Prince. Yes.
    Parm. Then Ile approue her to bee none of
        thine,
That thou haft fetch't her from anothers armes.
Nay more, that fhee's vnchaft ?
    Prin. Know *Parma*, thou haft kindled fuch a
        Flame,
That all the Oceans billowes fcarce can quench :
Bee that our quarrells ground.
    Florence. Princes, forbeare :
Firft fee the Iffue of the former Combat,
Before more blood you hazard.
    Prince. Wee are pleafed.
    Parm. And wee content.

    Enter Stroza *and the* Mounfieur, *they fight, and*
           Stroza *is ouercome.*

    Moun. Yeeld thy felfe recreant villaine, or thou
        dy'ft.
    Stro. Saue mee, I will confeffe ; Is *Parma* heere ?
    Parm. Yes, heere we are.
    Stro. I falfely ftuft thy head with Iealoufies,
And for fome priuate ends of my reuenge,
Difgrac'd the Generall, and fet odds betwixt
Lauretta and the Princeffe : All thefe mifchiefes
Proceede from my fuggeftions.
    Milla. Damne him for it.

Stro. Is that your kindneffe? giue me leaue to
liue,
Bee't but to taynt his honour.
Prince. Tell mee *Stroza,*
Was *Iulia* chafte?
Str. No.
Prince. Did her Father know it?
Str. Yes, and more too: I had the Gold from
him,
To bribe the Generalls daughter.
Florence. Iniuries,
Beyond the thought of man.
Milla. Which wee'le no longer ftriue with, fince
the heauens
Haue laid that ope moft plaine and palpable,
Which moft wee thought to conceale.
Prince. Will *Parma* fight?
Parm. Refolue mee firft? Was *Iulia* found chaft?
Priece. I heere proteft, wee parted both, as cleere,
As at our firft encounter.
Parm. Then I accept her,
If you my Lord bee pleaf'd fo to part with her.
Prince. Willingly.
Iulia. Now haue I my defires: Had I withall,
The Princely babe I boare.
Parm. See *Iulia,*
Whom thy hard-hearted Father doom'd to death,
My care hath ftill conferued, Imbrace it Lady;
Nay, tis thy owne nere feare it.
Prince. Then Prince *Parma,*
With your words Ile proceed.
  'Tis fit all Iuftice bee not quite exil'd,
  That hee that wedds the Mother keepe the child.
Florence. But Peeres, the Virgin that this *Stroza*
hired
To Iuftifie thefe wrongs?
Prince. At hand my Lord:
Mounfieur conduct them hither?
Moun. I fhall Sir.

Milla. The Generalls Wife and Daughter.

Enter Lauretta, Wife, *and* Clowne.

Clow. Yes and their man too; all that's left of
him.

Prince. This the Maide,
To whom I am fo bound ?

Lauret. Oh let me lie
As proftrate at your foot in Vaffallage,
As I was at your pleafure.

Prince. Sweete arife.

Clow. Your Lordfhip hath bin vp already, when
fhee was downe : I hope if the thing you wott of goe
no worfe forward then it hath begun, and that you
take charge of my young Lady, you neede not bee
altogether vnmindfull of her Gentleman-Vfher.

Florence. Of what birth is that Lady ?

Milla. Euen the leaft
Enuy can fpeake, Shee is a Souldiers Daughter,
Defcended from a noble parentage.

Wife. Who with her mother,
Thus kneeles to him, as to their Soueraigne.
Intreating grace and pittie.

Milla. You haue both :
Sure, fure, the heauens for our Ingratitude,
To noble *Sforza,* our braue generall,
Hath thus croft our proceedings ; which to recom-
pence,
Wee'le take you vnto our beft patronage.

Wife. *Millaine* is honorable.

Prince. But by your fauour Sir,
This muft bee our owne charge.

Florence. With which we are pleas'd.

Iulia. *Stroza* was caufe of all, but his fubmiffion
Hath fau'd him from our hate, arife in grace.
Whil'ft we thus greete *Lauretta.*

Lauret. Royall Princeffe,
I ftill fhall be your hand-maide.

Stroza. Who would ftriue,
To bee a villaine, when the good thus thriue ?
   Prince, You crowne me with your wifhes, Royall
     father;
My Miftris firft, and next my bed-fellow,
And now my Bride moft welcome. Excellent Sir,
Imbrace the *Millaine* Duke, whil'ft I change hand
With Princely *Parma*; *Iulia,* once my Wife ?
Backe to your husband I returne you chaft :
Mounfieur, bee ftill our friend : You our kind Mother:
And let fucceeding Ages, thus much fay :
Neuer was Maiden-head better giuen away.

                               Exeunt omnes.

F I N I S.

The Epilogue.

Ew Playes, are like new Fashions; If they
 take?
Followed and worne: And happy's hee can make
First into'th Garbe: But when they once haue past
Censure, and proue not well, they seldome last.
Our Play is new, but whether shaped well
In Act or Seane, Iudge you, you best can tell:
Wee hope the best, and 'tis our least of feare,
That any thing but comely should shew heere;
  However Gentlemen, 'tis in your powers,
   To make it last; or weare out, in two houres.

The late Lancashire
VVITCHES.

A well received Comedy, lately
Acted at the *Globe* on the *Banke-fide*,
by the Kings Majefties
Actors.

WRITTEN,

By T H O M. H E Y V V O O D,

AND

R I C H A R D B R O O M E.

Aut prodeffe folent, aut delectare.

LONDON,

Printed by *Thomas Harper* for *Benjamin Fifher*,
and are to be fold at his Shop at the Signe of the
Talbot, without *Alderfgate*.
1634.

THE PROLOGVE.

COrrantoes *failing, and no foot poſt late*
  Poſſeſſing us with Newes of forraine State,
No accidents abroad worthy Relation
Arriving here, we are forc'd from our owne Nation
To ground the Scene that's now in agitation.
The Projeƈt unto many here well knowne ;
Thoſe Witches the fat Iaylor brought to Towne,
An Argument ſo thin, perſons ſo low
Can neither yeeld much matter, nor great ſhow.
Expeƈt no more than can from ſuch be rais'd,
So may the Scene paſſe pardon'd, though not prais'd.

ACTVS, I.   SCENA, I.

Enter Maſter Arthur, *Mr.* Shakſtone, *Mr.* Bantam :
(*as from hunting.*)

Arthur.

As ever ſport of expectation
Thus croſt in th' height.
    Shak. Tuſh theſe are accidents all game
    is ſubject to.
  Arth. So you may call them
Chances, or croſſes, or what elſe you pleaſe,
But for my part, Ile hold them prodigies,
As things tranſcending Nature.
    Bantam. O you ſpeake this,
Becauſe a Hare hath croſt you.
    Arth. A Hare ? a Witch, or rather a Divell I
    think.
For tell me Gentlemen, was't poſſible
In ſuch a faire courſe, and no covert neere,
We in purſuit, and ſhe in conſtant view,
Our eyes not wandring but all bent that way,
The Dogs in chaſe, ſhe ready to be ceas'd,
And at the inſtant, when I durſt have layd
My life to gage, my Dog had pincht her, then
To vaniſh into nothing !
    Shak. Somewhat ſtrange,
But not as you inforce it.
    Arth: Make it plaine
That I am in an error, ſure I am

That I about me have no borrow'd eyes.
They are mine owne, and Matches.
    Bant.   She might find
Some Muſe as then not viſible to us,
And eſcape that way.
    Shak.   Perhaps ſome Foxe had earth'd there,
And though it be not common, for I ſeldome
Have knowne or heard the like, there ſquat her ſelfe,
And ſo her ſcape appeare but Naturall,
Which you proclaime a Wonder.
    Arth.   Well well Gentlemen,
Be you of your own faith, but what I ſee
And is to me apparent, being in ſence,
My wits about me, no way toſt nor troubled,
To that will I give credit.
    Bant.   Come, come, all men
Were never of one minde, nor I of yours.
    Shak.   To leave this argument, are you reſolv'd
Where we ſhall dine to day?
    Arth.   Yes where we purpos'd.
    Bant.   That was with Maſter *Generous.*
    Arth.   True, the ſame.
And where a loving welcome is preſum'd,
Whoſe liberall Table's never unprepar'd,
Nor he of gueſts unfurniſht, of his meanes,
There's none can beare it with a braver port,
And keepe his ſtate unſhaken, one who ſels not
Nor covets he to purchaſe, holds his owne
Without oppreſſing others, alwayes preſt
To indeere to him any knowne Gentleman
In whom he finds good parts.
    Bant.   A Character not common in this age.
    Brth.   I cannot wind him up
Vnto the leaſt part of his noble worth.
Tis far above my ſtrength.

              Enter Whetſtone.

    Shak.   See who comes yonder,

A fourth, to make us a full Meſſe of gueſts
At Maſter *Generous* Table.

    Arth. Tuſh let him paſſe,
He is not worth our luring, a meere Coxcombe,
It is a way to call our wits in queſtion,
To have him ſeene amongſt us.

    Baut. He hath ſpy'd us,
There is no way to evade him.

    Arth. That's my griefe ;
A moſt notorious lyar, out upon him,

    Shak. Let's ſet the beſt face on't.

    Whet. What Gentlemen ? all mine old acquaint-
ance ?
A whole triplicity of friends together ? nay then
'Tis three to one we ſhall not ſoone part Company.

    Shak. Sweet Mr. *Whetſtone.*

    Bant. Dainty Mr. *Whetſtone.*

    Arth. Delicate Maſter *Whetſtone.*

    Whet. You ſay right, Mr. *Whetſtone* I have bin,
Mr. *Whetſtone* I am, and Mr. *Whetſtone* I ſhall be,
and thoſe that know me, know withall that I have not
my name for nothing, I am hee whom all the brave
Blades of the Country uſe to whet their wits upon ;
ſweet Mr. *Shakton*, dainty Mr. *Bantham*, and dainty
Mr. *Arthur*, and how, and how, what all luſtick, all
froligozone ? I know, you are going to my Vncles to
dinner, and ſo am I too, What ſhall we all make one
randevous there, you need not doubt of your welcome.

    Shak. No doubt at all kind Mr. *Whetſtone*; but
we have not ſeene you of late, you are growne a great
ſtranger amongſt us, I deſire ſometimes to give you a
viſit ; I pray where do you lye ?

    Whet. Where doe I lye? why ſometimes in one
place, and then againe in another, I love to ſhift
lodgings ; but moſt conſtantly, wherefoere I dine or
ſup, there doe I lye ?

    Arth. I never heard that word proceed from him
I durſt call truth till now.

Whet. But where ſo ever I lye 'tis no matter for that,
I pray you ſay, and ſay truth, are not you three now
Going to dinner to my Vncles ?

Bant. I thinke you are a Witch Maſter *Whetſtone.*

Whet. How ? A Witch Gentlemen ? I hope you
doe not meane to abuſe me, though at this time (if
report be true) there are too many of them here in our
Country, but I am ſure I look like no ſuch ugly
Creature.

Shak. It ſeemes then you are of opinion that
there are Witches, for mine own part, I can hardly be
induc'd to think there is any ſuch kinde of people.

Whet. No ſuch kinde of people ! I pray you tell
me Gentlemen, did never any one of you know my
Mother ?

Arth. Why was your Mother a Witch ?

Whet. I doe not ſay as Witches goe now a dayes,
for they for the moſt part are ugly old Beldams, but
ſhe was a luſty young Laſſe, and by her owne report,
by her beauty and faire lookes bewitcht my Father.

Bant. It ſeemes then your Mother was rather a
yong wanton wench, than an old wither'd witch.

Whet. You ſay right, and know withall I come of
two ancient Families, for as I am a *Whetſtone* by the
Mother-ſide, ſo I am a *By-blow* by the Fathers.

Arth. It appeares then by your diſcourſe, that you
came in at the window.

Whet. I would have you thinke I ſcorne like my
Granams Cat to leape over the Hatch.

Shak. He hath confeſt himſelfe to be a Baſtard.

Arth. And I beleeve't as a notorious truth.

Whet. Howſoever I was begot, here you ſee I am,
And if my Parents went to it without feare or wit,
What can I helpe it.

Arth. Very probable, for as he was got without feare,
So it is apparent he was borne without wit.

Whet. Gentlemen, it ſeemes you have ſome private

bufineffe amongft your felves, which I am not willing
to interrupt, I know not how the day goes with you,
but for mine owne part, my ftomacke is now much
upon 12. You know what houre my Vncle keepes,
and I love ever to bee fet before the firft grace, I am
going before, fpeake, fhall I acquaint him with your
comming after ?

Shak.   We meane this day to fee what fare he
keepes.

Whet.   And you know it is his cuftome to fare well,
And in that refpeٮ I think I may be his kinfman,
And fo farewell Gentlemen, Ile be your fore-runner,
To give him notice of your vifite.

Bant.   And fo intyre us to you.

Shak.   Sweet Mr. *Whetftone.*

Arth.   Kind Mr. *Byblow.*

Whet.   I fee you are perfeٮ both in my name &
firname ; I have bin ever bound unto you, for which
I will at this time be your *Noverint,* and give him
notice that you *Vniverfi* will bee with him *per præ-
fentes,* and that I take to be prefently.   *Exit.*

Arth.   Farewell *As in præfenti.*

Shak.   It feemes hee's peece of a Scholler.

Arth.   What becaufe he hath read a little Scriveners
Latine, hee never proceeded farther in his Accidence
than to *Mentiri non eft meum;* and that was fuch a
hard Leffon to learne, that he ftucke at *mentiri* ; and
cu'd never reach to *non eft meum* : fince, a meere
Ignaro, and not worth acknowledgement.

Bant.   Are thefe then the beft parts he can boaft
of ?

Arth.   As you fee him now, fo fhall you finde him
ever : all in one ftrain, there is one only thing which
I wonder he left out.

Shak.   And what might that be.

Arth.   Of the fame affinity with the reft. At every
fecond word, he is commonly boafting either of his
Aunt or his Vncle.

Enter Mr. Generous.

Bant. You name him in good time, ſee where he comes.

Gener. Gentlemen, Welcome, t'is a word I uſe,
From me expect no further complement :
Nor do I name it often at one meeting,
Once ſpoke (to thoſe that underſtand me beſt,
And know I alwaies purpoſe as I ſpeake)
Hath ever yet ſuffiz'd : ſo let it you ;
Nor doe I love that common phraſe of gueſts,
As we make bold, or we are troubleſome,
Wee take you unprovided, and the like ;
I know you underſtanding Gentlemen,
And knowing me, cannot perſuade your ſelves
With me you ſhall be troubleſome or bold,
But ſtill provided for my worthy friends,
Amongſt whom you are lifted.
   Arth. Noble ſir,
You generouſly inſtruct us, and to expreſſe
We can be your apt ſchollers : in a word
Wee come to dine with you.
   Gener. And Gentlemen,
Such plainneſſe doth beſt pleaſe me, I had notice
Of ſo much by my kinſman, and to ſhow
How lovingly I tooke it, inſtantly
Roſe from my chayre to meet you at the gate,
And be my ſelfe your uſher ; nor ſhall you finde
Being ſet to meat, that i'le excuſe your fare,
Or ſay, I am ſory it falls out ſo poore ;
And had I knowne your comming wee'd have had
Such things and ſuch, nor blame my Cooke, to ſay
This diſh or that hath not bin ſauc'ſt with care :
Words, fitting beſt a common Hoſteſſe mouth,
When ther's perhaps ſome juſt cauſe of diſlike,
But not the table of a Gentleman ;
Nor is it my wives cuſtome ; in a word,
Take what you find, & ſo————

Arth. Sir without flattery
You may be call'd the ſole ſurviving ſonne
Of long ſince baniſht Hoſpitality.
 Gener. In that you pleaſe me not : But Gentle-
  men
I hope to be beholden unto you all,
Which if I proove, Ile be a gratefull debtor.
 Bant. Wherein good ſir.
 Gener. I ever ſtudied plaineneſſe, and truth
  withall.
 Shak. I pray expreſſe your ſelfe.
 Gener. In few I ſhall. I know this youth to
  whom my wife is Aunt
Is (as you needs muſt finde him) weake and ſhallow :
Dull, as his name, and what for kindred ſake
We note not, or at leaſt, are loath to ſee,
Is unto ſuch well-knowing Gentlemen
Moſt groſſely viſible : If for my ſake
You will but ſeeme to winke at theſe his wants,
At leaſt at table before us his friends,
I ſhall receive it as a courteſie
Not ſoone to be forgot.
 Arth. Preſume it ſir.
 Gener. Now when you pleaſe pray Enter Gentle-
  men.
 Arth. Would theſe my friends prepare the way
  before,
To be reſolved of one thing before dinner
Would ſomething adde unto mine appetite,
Shall I intreat you ſo much.
 Bant. O ſir you may command us.
 Gener. I'th meane time
Prepare your ſtomackes with a bowle of Sacke.
       Exit Bant. & Shak.
My Cellar can affoord it ; now Mr. *Arthur*
Pray freely ſpeake your thoughts.
 Arth. I come not ſir
To preſſe a promiſe from you, tak't not ſo,
Rather to prompt your memory in a motion

Made to you not long ſince.

    Gener. Waſt not about
A Mannor, the beſt part of your eſtate,
Morgag'd to one ſlips no advantages
Which you would have redeem'd.

    Arth. True ſir the ſame.

    Gener. And as I thinke, I promiſt at that time
To become bound with you, or if the uſurer
(A baſe, yet the beſt title I can give him)
Perhaps ſhould queſtion that ſecurity,
To have the money ready. Waſt not ſo?

    Arth. It was to that purpoſe wee diſcourſt.

    Gener. Provided, to have the Writings in my
      cuſtody.
Elſe how ſhould I ſecure mine owne eſtate.

    Arth. To denie that, I ſhould appeare to th'
      World
Stupid, and of no braine.

    Gener. Your monie's ready.

    Arth. And I remaine a man oblig'd to you.
Beyond all utterance.

    Gener. Make then your word good
By ſpeaking it no further, onely this,
It ſeemes your Vncle you truſted in ſo far
Hath failed your expectation.

    Arth. Sir he hath, not that he is unwilling or
      unable,
But at this time unfit to be ſolicited ;
For to the Countries wonder, and my ſorrow,
Hee is much to be pitied.

    Gener. Why I intreat you.

    Arth. Becauſe hee's late become the ſole diſ-
      courſe
Of all the countrey ; for of a man reſpected
For his diſcretion and knowne gravitie,
As maſter of a govern'd Family,
The houſe (as if the ridge were fixt below,
And groundſils lifted up to make the roofe)
All now turn'd topſie turvy.

Gener.   Strange, but how?

Arth.   In fuch a retrograde & prepofterous way
As feldome hath bin heard of.   I thinke never.

Gener.   Can you difcourfe the manner?

Arth.   The good man,
In all obedience kneeles vnto his fon,
Hee with an auftere brow commands his father.
The wife prefumes not in the daughters fight
Without a prepared courtefie.   The girle, fhee
Expects it as a dutie; chides her mother
Who quakes and trembles at each word fhe fpeaks,
And what's as ftrange, the Maid fhe dominiers
O're her yong miftris, who is aw'd by her.
The fon to whom the Father creeps and bends,
Stands in as much feare of the groome his man.
All in fuch rare diforder, that in fome
As it breeds pitty, and in others wonder;
So in the moft part laughter.

Gener.   How thinke you might this come.

Arth.   T'is thought by Witchcraft.

Gener.   They that thinke fo dreame,
For my beliefe is, no fuch thing can be,
A madneffe you may call it: Dinner ftayes,
That done, the beft part of the afternoone
Wee'le fpend about your bufineffe.   *Exeunt.*

Enter old Seely and Doughty.

Seely.   Nay but underftand me neighbor *Doughty.*

Doughty.   Good mafter *Seely* I do underftand
you, and over and over underftand you fo much,
that I could e'ene blufh at your fondneffe; and had I
a fonne to ferve mee fo, I would coniure a divell out
of him.

See.   Alas he is my childe.

Dough.   No, you are his childe to live in feare of
him, indeed they fay oldmen become children againe,
but before I would become my childes childe, and

make my foot my head, I would ſtand upon my head,
and kick my heels at the skies.

Enter Gregory.

See.   You do not know what an only ſon is, O ſee,
he comes now if you can appeaſe his anger towrad
me, you ſhall doe an act of timely charity.

Dou.   It is an office that I am but weakly
          verſd in
To plead to a ſonne in the fathers behalfe,
Bleſſe me what lookes the deviliſh young Raſcall
Frights the poore man withall !

Greg.   I wonder at your confidence, and how you
dare appeare before me.

Doug.   A brave beginning.

See.   O ſonne be patient.

Greg.   It is right reverend councell, I thanke you
for it, I ſhall ſtudy patience ſhall I, while you practice
waies to begger mee, ſhall I ?

Dough.   Very handſome.

See.   If ever I tranſgreſſe in the like againe—

Greg.   I have taken your word too often ſir and
neither can nor will forbeare you longer.

Dough.   What not your Father Mr. *Gregory* ?

Greg.   Whats that to you ſir ?

Dough.   Pray tell me then ſir, how many yeares has
hee to ſerve you.

Gre.   What do you bring your ſpokeſman now,
          your advocat,
What fee goes out of my eſtate now, for his Ora-
          tory ?

Dou.   Come I muſt tell you, you forget your
          ſelfe,
And in this foule unnaturall ſtrife wherein
You trample on your father.   You are falne
Below humanitie.   Y'are ſo beneath
The title of a ſonne, you cannot clayme

'To be a man, and let me tell you were you mine
Thou fhouldft not eat but on thy knees before me.
    See. O this is not the way.
This is to raife Impatience into fury.
I do not feek his quiet for my eafe,
I can beare all his chidings and his threats,
And take them well, very exceeding well,
And finde they do me good on my owne part,
Indeed they do reclaim me from thofe errors
That might impeach his fortunes, but I feare
Th' unquiet ftrife within him hurts himfelfe,
And waftes or weakens Nature by the breach
Of moderate fleepe and dyet ; and I can
No leffe than grieve to finde my weakneffes
To be the caufe of his affliction,
And fee the danger of his health and being.
    Dou. Alas poore man ? Can you ftand open
        ey'd
Or dry ey'd either at this now in a Father ?
    Greg. Why, if it grieve you, you may look of
        ont,
I have feen more than this twice twenty times,
And have as often bin deceiv'd by his diffimu-
        lations
I can fee nothing mended.
    Dou. He is a happy fire that has brought vp his
        fon to this.
    See. All fhall be mended fon content your felfe,
But this time forget but this laft fault.
    Greg. Yes, for a new one to morrow.
    Dou. Pray Mr. *Gregory* forget it, you fee how
Submiffive your poore penitent is, forget it,
Forget it, put it out o' your head, knocke it
Out of your braines. I proteft, if my Father,
Nay if my fathers dogge fhould haue fayd
As much to me, I fhould have embrac't him.
What was the trefpaffe ? It c'ud not be fo hainous.
    Greg. Wel Sir, you now fhall be a Iudge for all
        your jeering.

Was it a fatherly part thinke you having a fonne
To offer to enter in bonds for his nephew, fo to in-
      danger
My eftate to redeeme his morgage.
   See.   But I did it not fonne ?
   Gre.   I know it very well, but your dotage had
      done it,
If my care had not prevented it.
   Dou.   Is that the bufineffe : why if he had done it,
had hee not bin fufficiently fecur'd in having the mor-
gage made over to himfelfe.
   Greg.   He does nothing but practice waies to undo
himfelfe, and me : a very fpendthrift, a prodigall fire,
hee was at the Ale club but tother day, and fpent a
foure-penny.
   See.   'Tis gone and paft fonne.
   Greg.   Can you hold your peace fir ? And not long
ago at the wine he fpent his teafter, and two pence
to the piper, that was brave was it not ?
   See.   Truely we were civily merry. But I have
      left it.
   Greg.   Your civility have you not ? For no longer
agoe than laft holiday evening he gam'd away eight
double ring'd tokens on a rubbers at bowles with the
Curate, and fome of his idle companions.
   Dou.   Fie Mr. *Gregory Seely* is this feemely in a
      fonne.
You'le have a rod for the childe your father fhortly I
      feare.
Alaffe did hee make it cry ?   Give me a ftroke and Ile
      beat him,
Bleffe me, they make me almoft as mad as them-
      felves.
   Greg.   'Twere good you would meddle with your
own matters fir.
   See.   Sonne, fonne.
   Greg.   Sir, Sir, as I am not beholden to you for
houfe or Land, for it has ftood in the name of my an-

ceftry the *Seelyes* above two hundred yeares, fo will I
look you leave all as you found it.

Enter Lawrence.

Law.   What is the matter con yeow tell ?
Greg.   O *Lawrence*, welcom, Thou wilt make al
wel I am fure.
Law.   Yie whick way con yeow tell, but what the
foule evill doone yee, heres fick an a din.
Dou.   Art thou his man fellow ha ? that talkeft thus
to him.
Law.   Yie fir, and what ma' yoew o'that, he main-
teynes me to rule him, and i'le deu't, or ma' the heart
weary o'the weambe on him.
Dou.   This is quite upfide downe, the fonne con-
trolls the father, and the man overcrowes his mafters
coxfcombe, fure they are all bewitch'd.
Greg.   'Twas but fo, truely *Lawrence;* the peevifh
old man vex't me, for which I did my duty, in telling
him his owne, and Mr. *Doughty* here maintaines him
againft me.
Law.   I forbodden yeow to meddle with the old
carle, and let me alone with him, yet yeow ftill be at
him, hee ferv'd yeow but weell to baft ye for't, ant he
were ftronk enough, but an I faw foule with yee an
I fwaddle yee not favorly may my girts braft.
See.   Prethee good *Lawrence* be gentle and do not
fright thy Mafter fo.
Law.   Yie, at your command anon.
See.   Enough good *Lawrence*, you have faid
enough.
Law.   How trow yeou that ?   A fine World when
a man cannot be whyet at heame for bufie brain'd
neighpors.
Dou.   I know not what to fay to any thing here,
This cannot be but witchcraft.

Enter Ioane and Winny.

Win.　I cannot indure it nor I will not indure it.

Dou.　Hey day! the daughter upon the mother too.

Win.　One of us two, chuſe you which, muſt leave the houſe, wee are not to live together I ſee that, but I will know, if there be Law in *Lancaſhire* for't, which is fit firſt to depart the houſe or the World, the mother or the daughter.

Ioane.　Daughter I ſay.

Win.　Do you ſay the daughter, for that word I ſay the mother, unleſſe you can prove me the eldeſt, as my diſcretion almoſt warrant it, I ſay the mother ſhall out of the houſe or take ſuch courſes in it as ſhall ſort with ſuch a honſe and ſuch a daughter.

Joan.　Daughter I ſay, I wil take any courſe ſo thou wilt leave thy paſſion ; indeed it hurts.thee childe, I'le ſing and be merry, weare as fine clothes, and as delicate dreſſings as thou wilt have me, ſo thou wilt pacifie thy ſelfe, and be at peace with me.

Wiu.　O will you ſo, in ſo doing I may chance to looke upon you, Is this a fit habite for a handſome young Gentlewomans mother, as I hope to be a Lady, you look like one o' the Scottiſh wayward ſiſters, O my hart has got the hickup, and all lookes greene about me, a merry ſong now mother, and thou ſhalt be my white girle.

Ioan.　Ha, ha, ha! ſhe's overcome with joy at my converſion.

Dough.　She is moſt evidently bewitcht.

Song.

Joane.　*There was a deft Lad and a Laſſe fell in love,*
　with a fa la la, fa la la, Langtidowne dilly ;

With kiffing and toying this Maiden did prove,
  with a fa la la, fa la la, Langtidowne dilly ;
So wide i' th waft, and her Belly fo high,
That unto her mother the Maiden did cry,
  O Langtidowne dilly, O Langtidowne dilly,
  fa la la Langtidowne, Langtidowne dilly.

Enter Parnell.

Parn. Thus wodden yeou doone and I were dead,
but while I live yoeu fadge not on it, is this aw the
warke yeou con fine ?

Dough. Now comes the Mayd to fet her Miftreffes
to work.

Win. Nay pri'thee fweet *Parnell*, I was but chiding
the old wife for her unhandfomneffe, and would have
been at my work prefently, fhe tels me now fhe
will weare fine things, and I fhall dreffe her head as
I lift.

Dough. Here's a houfe well govern'd ?

Parn. Dreffe me no dreffings, leffen I dreffe yeou
beth, and learne a new leffon with a wainon right now,
han I bin a fervant here this halfe dozen o' yeares,
and con I fee yeou idler then my felve !

Ioa. Win. Nay prithee fweet *Parnell* content, &
hark thee—

Dough. I have knowne this, and till very lately, as
well govern'd a Family as the Country yeilds, and now
what a neft of feverall humors it is growne, and all
divellifh ones, fure all the Witches in the Country,
have their hands in this home-fpun medley ; and there
be no few 'tis thought.

Parn. Yie, yie, ye fhall ye fhall, another time, but not
naw I thonke yeou, yeou fhall as foone piffe and paddle
in't, as flap me in the mouth with an awd Petticoat, or
a new paire o fhoine, to be whyet, I cannot be whyet,
nor I wonnot be whyet, to fee ficky doings I.

Lawr. Hold thy prattle *Parnell*, aw's com'd about
as weene a had it, wotft thou what *Parnell* ? wotft
thou what ? o deare, wotft thou what ?

Parn. What's the fond wexen waild trow I.

Lawr. We han bin in love theſe three yeares, and ever wee had not enough, now is it com'd about that our love ſhall be at an end for ever, and a day, for wee mun wed may hunny, we mun wed.

Parn. What the Deowl ayles the lymmer lowne, bin thy braincs broke lowſe trow I.

Lawr. Sick a waddin was there never i' Lonco-ſhire as ween couple at on Monday newſt.

Par. Awa awaw, ſayn yeou this ſickerly, or done you but jaum me ?

Lawr. I jaum thee not nor flam thee not, 'tis all as true as booke, here's both our Maſters have con-ſented and concloyded, and our Miſtreſſes mun yeild toyt, to put aw houſe and lond and aw they have into our hands.

Parn. Awa, awaw.

Lawr. And we mun marry and be maſter and dame of aw.

Parn. Awa, awaw.

Lawr. And theyn be our Sijourners, becauſe they are weary of the world, to live in frendibleneſſe, and ſee what will come on't.

Par. Awa, awaw, agone.

Seel. & Greg. Nay 'tis true *Parnell*, here's both our hands on't, and give you joy.

Ioan & Win. And ours too, and 'twill be fine Ifackins.

Parn. Whaw, whaw, whaw, whaw !

Dou. Here's a mad buſineſſe towards.

Seel. I will beſpeake the Gueſts.

Greg. And I the meat :

Ioan. I'le dreſſe the dinner, though I drip my ſweat.

Law. My care ſhall ſumptuous parrelments pro-vide.

Win. And my beſt art ſhall trickly trim the Bride.

Parn. Whaw, whaw, whaw, whaw.

Greg. Ile get choyce muſick for the merriment.

Dough.   And I will waite with wonder the event.
Parn.   Whaw, whaw, whaw, whaw.

ACTVS, II. SCÆNA, I.

Enter 4. Witches : (*ſeverally.*)

All.   Oe ! well met, well met.
　　　　Meg.   What new deviſe, what dainty
　　　　　　　　ſtraine
　　　　More for our myrth now then our
　gaine,
Shall we in practice put.
　Meg.   Nay dame,
Before we play another game,
We muſt a little laugh and thanke
Our feat familiars for the pranck
They playd us laſt.
　Mawd.   Or they will miſſe
Vs in our next plot, if for this
They find not their reward.
　Meg.   'Tis right.
　Gil.   Therefore ſing *Mawd*, and call each ſpright.
Come away, and take thy duggy.

Enter foure Spirits.

　Meg.   Come my *Mamilion* like a Puggy.
　Mawd.   And come my puckling take thy teat,
Your travels have deſerv'd your meat.
　Meg.   Now upon the Churles ground
On which we're met, lets dance a round ;
That Cocle, Darnell, Poppia wild,
May choake his graine, and fill the field.

Gil.   Now ſpirits fly about the taske,
That we projected in our Maske.   *Exit Spirlts.*
Meg.   Now let us laugh to thinke upon
The feat which we have ſo lately done,
In the diſtraction we have ſet
In *Seelyes* houſe; which ſhall beget
Wonder and ſorrow 'mongſt our foes,
Whilſt we make laughter of their woes.
All.   Ha, ha ha!
Meg.   I can but laugh now to foreſee,
The fruits of their perplexity.
Gil.   Of *Seely's* family ?
Meg.   I, I, I, the Father to the Sonne doth cry,
The Sonne rebukes the Father old;
The Daughter at the mother Scold,
The wife the husband check and chide,
But that's no wonder, through the wide
World 'tis common.
Gil.   But to be ſhort,
The wedding muſt bring on the ſport
Betwixt the hare-brayn'd man and mayd,
Maſter and dame that over-ſway'd.
All.   Ha, ha, ha !
Meg.   Enough, enough,
Our ſides are charm'd, or elſe this ſtuffe
Would laughter-cracke them ; let's away
About the Iig : we dance to day,
To ſpoyle the Hunters ſport.
Gil.   I that,
Be now the ſubject of our chat.
Meg.   Then liſt yee well, the Hunters are
This day by vow to kill a Hare,
Or elſe the ſport they will forſweare ;
And hang their Dogs up.
Mawd.   Stay, but where
Muſt the long threatned hare be found ?
Gill.   They'l ſearch in yonder Meadow ground.
Meg.   There will I be, and like a wily Wat,
Vntill they put me up; ile ſquat.
Gill.   I and my puckling will a brace

Of Greyhounds be, fit for the race ;
And linger where we may be tane
Vp for the courfe in the by-lane ;
Then will we lead their Dogs a courfe,
And every man and every horfe ;
Vntill they breake their necks, and fay—
    All. The Divell on Dun is rid this way. Ha, ha,
    ha, ha.
    Meg. All the doubt can be but this,
That if by chance of me they miffe,
And ftart another Hare.
    Gil. Then we'll not run
But finde fome way how to be gone.
I fhal know thee *Peg*, by thy griffel'd gut.
    Meg. And I you *Gilian* by your gaunt thin gut.
But where will *Mawd* beftow her felfe to day ?
    Mawd. O' th' Steeple top ; Ile fit and fee you
    play.   *Exeunt.*

Enter Mr. Generous, Arthur, Bantam, Shakftone,
        and Whetftone.

    Gener. At meeting, and at parting Gentlemen,
I onely make ufe of that generall word,
So frequent at all feafts, and that but once ; y'are wel-
    come.
You are fo, all of you, and I intreat you
Take notice of that fpeciall bufineffe,
Betwixt this Gentleman my friend, and I.
About the Morgage, to which writings drawne,
Your hands are witneffe.
    Bant. & Shak. We acknowledge it.
    Whet. My hand is there too, for a man cannot fet
to his Marke, but it may be call'd his hand ; I am a
Gentleman both wayes, and it hath been held that it
is the part of a Gentleman, to write a fcurvie hand.
    Bant. You write Sir like your felfe.
    Gener. Pray take no notice of his ignorance,
You know what I foretold you.

Arth. 'Tis confeſt,
But for that word by you ſo ſeldome ſpoke
By us ſo freely on your part perform'd,
We hold us much ingag'd.

Gener. I pray, no complement,
It is a thing I doe not uſe my ſelfe,
Nor doe I love't in others.

Arth. For my part,
Could I at once diſſolve my ſelfe to words
And after turne them into matter ; ſuch
And of that ſtrength, as to attract the attention
Of all the curious, and moſt itching eares
Of this our Crittick age ; it cou'd not make
A theame amounting to your noble worth :
You ſeeme to me to ſuper-arrogate,
Supplying the defects of all your kindred
To innoble your own name : I now have done Sir.

Whet. Hey day, this Gentleman ſpeakes like a
Country Parſon that had tooke his text out of *Ovids*
Metamorphoſis.

Gener. Sir, you Hyperbolize ;
And I coo'd chide you for't, but whil'ſt you connive
At this my Kinſman, I ſhall winke at you ;
'Twil prove an equall match.

Gener. Your name proclaimes
To be ſuch as it ſpeakes, you, *Generous.*

Gener. Still in that ſtraine !

Arth. Sir, ſir, whilſt you perſever to be good
I muſt continue gratefull.

Gener. Gentlemen,
The greateſt part of this day you ſee is ſpent
In reading deeds, conveyances, and bonds,
With ſealing and ſubſcribing ; will you now
Take part of a bad Supper.

Arth. We are like travellers
And where ſuch bayt, they doe not uſe to Inne.
Our love and ſervice to you.

Gener. The firſt I accept,
The Laſt I entertaine not, farewell Gentlemen.

Arth.   We'l try if we can finde in our way home
When Hares come from their coverts, to reliffe,
A courfe or too.

Whet.   Say you fo Gentlemen, nay then I am for
your company ftill, 'tis fayd Hares are like ' Hermo-
phrodites, one while Male, and another Female, and
that which begets this yeare, brings young ones the next;
which fome think to be the reafon that witches take
their fhapes fo oft : Nay if I lye *Pliny* lyes too, but
come, now I have light upon you, I cannot fo lightly
leave you farewell Vnckle.

Gener.   Cozen I wifh you would confort your
    felfe,
With fuch men ever, and make them your Prefident
For a more Gentile carriage.

Arth.   Good Mafter *Generous——*

Exeunt, manet Generous.

Enter Robert.

Gen.   *Robin.*

Rob.   Sir.

Gen.   Goe call your Miftreffe hither.

Rob.   My Miftreffe Sir, I doe call her Miftreffe, as
I doe call you Mafter, but if you would have me call
my Miftreffe to my Mafter, I may call lowd enough
before fhe can heare me.

Gener.   Why fhe's not deafe I hope, I am fure fince
    Dinner
She had her hearing perfect.

Rob.   And fo fhe may have at Supper too for ought
I know, but I can affure you fhe is not now within my
call.

Gener.   Sirrah you trifle, give me the Key oth'
    Stable.
I will goe fee my Gelding ; i'th' meane time
Goe feeke her out, fay fhe fhall finde me there.

Rob.   To tell you true fir, I fhall neither finde my
Miftreffe here, nor you your Gelding there.

Gener. Ha ! how comes that to paſſe ?

Rob. Whilſt you were buſie about your writings,
ſhe came and commanded me to ſaddle your Beaſt,
and ſayd ſhe would ride abroad to take the ayre.

Gener. Which of your fellowes did ſhe take along
to wayte on her ?

Rob. None ſir.

Gener. None ! hath ſhe us'd it often ?

Rob. Oftner I am ſure then ſhe goes to Church,
and leave out Wedneſdayes and Fridayes.

Gener. And ſtill alone ?

Rob. If you call that alone, when no body rides in
her company.

Gen. But what times hath ſhe ſorted for theſe
journeyes ?

Rob. Commonly when you are abroad, aud ſometimes when you are full of buſineſſe at home.

Gener. To ride out often and alone, what ſayth
ſhe
When ſhe takes horſe, and at her backe returne ?

Rob. Onely conjures me that I ſhall keepe it from
you, then clappes me in the fiſt with ſome ſmall piece
of ſilver, and then a Fiſh cannot be more ſilent
then I.

Gen. I know her a good woman and well bred,
Of an unqueſtion'd carriage, well reputed
Amongſt her neighbors, reckon'd with the beſt
And ore me moſt indulgent ; though in many
Such things might breed a doubt and jealouſie,
Yet I hatch no ſuch phrenſie. Yet to prevent
The ſmalleſt jarre that might betwixt us happen ;
Give her no notice that I know thus much.
Beſides I charge thee, when ſhe craves him next
He be deny'd : if ſhe be vext or mov'd
Doe not thou feare, Ile interpoſe my ſelfe
Betwixt thee and her anger, as you tender
Your duty and my ſervice, ſee this done.

Rob. Now you have expreſt your minde, I know
what I have to doe ; firſt, not to tell her what I have

told you, & next to keep her fide-faddle from comming upon your Gueldings backe; but howfoever it is
like to hinder me of many a round tefter.

　Gener.　As oft as thou deny'ft her, fo oft clayme
That teafter from me, 't fhall be roundly payd.

　Rob.　You fay well in that fir, I dare take your
word, you are an honeft Gentleman, and my Mafter;
and now take mine as I am your true fervant, before
fhe fhall backe your Guelding again in your abfence,
while I have the charge of his keeping; fhe fhall ride
me, or Ile ride her.

　Gen.　So much for that.　Sirrah my Butler tels
　　me
My Seller is drunke dry, I meane thofe Bottles
Of Sack and Claret, are all empty growne
And I have guefts to morrow, my choyfe friends.
Take the gray Nag i'th' ftable, and thofe Bottles
Fill at *Lancafter*, there where you ufe to fetch it.

　Rob.　Good newes for me, I fhall fir.

　Gen.　O *Robin*, it comes fhort of that pure liquor
We drunke laft Terme in London at the *Myter*
In *Fleet-ftreet*, thou remembreft it; me thought
It was the very fpirit of the Grape,
Meere quinteffence of Wine.

　Rob.　Yes fir, I fo remember it, that moft certaine
it is I never fhal forget it, my mouth waters ever fince
when I but think on't, whilft you were at fupper
above, the drawer had me down into the Cellar below,
I know the way in againe if I fee't, but at that time to
finde the way out againe, I had the help of more eies
than mine owne: is the tafte of that *Ipfitate* ftil in
your pallat fir?

　Gener.　What then?　But vaine are wifhes, take
　　thofe bottles
And fee them fil'd where I command you fir.

　Rob.　I fhall: never c'ud I have met with fuch a
faire opportunity: for iuft in the mid way lies my
fweet-heart, as lovely a laffe as any is in *Lancafhire*,

and kiſſes as ſweetly : i'le ſee her going or comming, i'le have one ſmouch at thy lips, and bee with thee to bring *Mal Spencer*.   *Exit.*

Gen. Go haſten your return, what he hath told me

Touching my wife is ſomewhat ſtrange, no matter
Bee't as it will, it ſhall not trouble me.
Shee hath not lyen ſo long ſo neere my ſide,
That now I ſhould be jealous.

Enter 'a ſouldier.

Sold. You ſeeme ſir a Gentleman of quality, and no doubt but in your youth have beene acquainted with affaires military, in your very lookes there appeares bounty, and in your perſon humanity. Pleaſe you to vouchſafe the tender of ſome ſmall courteſie to help to beare a ſouldier into his countrey.

Gen. Though I could tax you friend, & juſtly too
For begging 'gainſt the Statute in that name,
Yet I have ever bin of that compaſſion,
Where I ſee want, rather to pittie it
Than to uſe power. Where haſt thou ſerv'd ?

Sold. With the Ruffian againſt the Polack, a heavy war, and hath brought me to this hard fate. I was tooke priſoner by the Pole, & after ſome few weeks of durance, got both my freedom and paſſe. I have it about me to ſhow, pleaſe you to vouchſafe the peruſall.

Gener. It ſhall not need. What Countreyman.

Sold. Yorkeſhire ſir. Many a ſharp battell by land, and many a ſharpe ſtorme at ſea, many a long mile, and many a ſhort meale, I have travel'd and ſuffer'd ere I c'ud reach thus far, I befeech you ſir take my poore & wretched caſe into your worſhips noble conſideration.

Gener. Perhaps thou lov'ſt this wandring life
To be an idle loitering begger, than
To eat of thine owne labour.

Sold. I ſir ! Loitering I defie ſir, I hate lazineſſe as I do leproſie : It is the next way to breed the ſcurvie, put mee to hedge, ditch, plow, threſh, dig, delve, any thing : your worſhip ſhal find that I love nothing leſſe than loitering.

Gener. Friend thou ſpeakeſt well.

Enter Miller (his hands and face ſcratcht, and bloudy.

Miller. Your Mill quoth he, if ever you take me in your mill againe, i'le give you leave to caſt my fleſh to the dogges, and grinde my bones to pouder, betwixt the Milſtones. Cats do you call them, for their hugeneſſe they might bee cat a mountaines, and for their clawes, I thinke I have it here in red and white to ſhew, I pray looke here ſir, a murreine take them, ile be ſworne they have ſcratcht, where I am ſure it itcht not.

Gener. How cam'ſt thou in this pickle ?

Mil. You ſee ſir, and what you ſee, I have felt, & am come to give you to underſtand i'le not indure ſuch another night if you would give mee your mill for nothing, they ſay we Millers are theeves : but I c'ud as ſoone bee hangd as ſteale one piece of a nap all the night long, good Landlord provide your ſelfe of a new tenant, the noiſe of ſuch catterwawling, & ſuch ſcratching and clawing, before I would indure againe, i'le bee tyed to the ſaile when the winde blowes ſharpeſt, and they flie ſwifteſt, till I be torne into as many fitters as I have toes and fingers.

Sold. I was a Miller my ſelfe before I was a ſouldier. What one of my own trade ſhould be ſo poorely ſpirited frighted with cats ?
Sir truſt me with the Mill that he forſakes.
Here is a blade that hangs upon this belt
That ſpight of all theſe Rats, Cats, Wezells, Witches
Or Dogges, or Divels, ſhall ſo coniure them
I'le quiet my poſſeſſion.

Gener. Well fpoke Souldier.
I like thy refolution. Fellow, you then
Have given the Mill quite over.

Mil. Over and over, here I utterly renounce it;
nor would I ftay in it longer, if you would give me
your whole eftate; nay if I fay it, you may take my
word Landlord.

Sold. I pray fir dare you truft your mill with me.

Gener. I dare, but I am loth, my reafons thefe.
For many moneths, fcarce any one hath lien there
But have bin ftrangely frighted in his fleepe,
Or from his warme bed drawne into the floore,
Or clawd and fcratcht, as thou feeft this poore man,
So much, that it ftood long untenanted,
Till he late undertooke it, now thine eies
Witneffe how he hath fped.

Sold. Give me the keies, ile ftand it all danger.

Gener. 'Tis a match: deliver them.

Mil. Mary withall my heart, and I am glad, I am
fo rid of em.   *Exeunt.*

Enter Boy with a fwitch.

Boy. Now I have gathered Bullies, and fild my
bellie pretty well, i'le goe fee fome fport. There are
gentlemen courfing in the medow hard by; and 'tis a
game that I love better than going to Schoole ten to
one.

*Enter an invifible fpirit. F. Adfon with a brace of
greyhounds.*

What have we here a brace of Greyhounds broke
loofe from their mafters: it muft needs be fo, for they
have both their Collers and flippes about their neckes.
Now I looke better upon them, me thinks I fhould
know them, and fo I do: thefe are Mr. *Robinfons*
dogges, that dwels fome two miles off, i'le take them
up, & lead them home to their mafter; it may be

fomthing in my way, for he is as liberall a gentleman, as
any is in our countrie.   Come *Hector*, come.   Now if
I c'ud but ftart a Hare by the way, kill her, and
carry her home to my fupper, I fhould thinke I
had made a better afternoones worke of it than
gathering of bullies.   Come poore curres along with
me.   *Exit.*

Enter Arthur, Bantam, Shakstone, and Whetftone.

Arth.   My Dog as yours.

Shak.   For what?

Arth.   A piece.

Shak.   'Tis done.

Bant.   I fay the pide dog fhall outftrip the browne.

Whe.   And ile take the brown dogs part againft
the pide.

Bant.   Yes when hee's at his lap youle take his
part.

Arth.   *Bantam* forbeare him prethee.

Bant.   He talks fo like an Affe I have not patience
to indure his non fence.

Whet.   The browne dogge for two peeces.

Bant.   Of what?

Whet.   Of what you dare ; name them from the laft
Farthings with the double rings, to the late Coy'ned
peeces which they fay are all counterfeit.

Bant.   Well fir, I take you : will you cover thefe,
give them into the hands of either of thefe two gentlemen.

Whet.   What needs that ? doe you thinke my word
and my money is not all one ?

Bant.   And weigh alike : both many graines too
light.

Shak.   Enough of that, I prefume Mr. *Whetftone*,
you are not ignorant what belongs to the fport of
hunting.

Whet.   I thinke I have reafon, for I have bin at
the death of more Hares.

Bant. More then you ſhed the laſt fall of the leafe.

Whet. More then any man here I am ſure. I ſhould be loath at theſe yeares to be ignorant of hairing or whoring. I knew a hare cloſe hunted, clime a tree.

Bant. To finde out birds neſts.

Whet. Another leap into a river, nothing appearing above water, ſave onely the tip of her noſe to take breath.

Shak. Nay that's verie likely, for no man can fiſh with an angle but his Line muſt be made of hare.

Whet. You ſay right, I knew another, who to eſcape the Dogges hath taken a houſe, and leapt in at a window.

Bant. It is thought you came into the World that way.

Whet. How meane you that?

Bant. Becauſe you are a baſtard.

Whet. Baſtard! O baſe.

Bant. And thou art baſe all over.

Arth. Needs muſt I now condemne your indiſcretion.
To ſet your wit againſt his.

Whe. Baſtard? that ſhall be tried; well Gentlemen concerning Hare-hunting you might have hard more, if he had had the grace to have ſaid leſſe, but for the word Baſtard, if I do not tell my Vncle, I and my Aunt too, either when I would ſpeake ought or goe of the skore for any thing, let me never be truſted, they are older than I, and what know I, but they might bee by when I was begot; but if thou *Bantam* do'ſt not heare of this with both thine eares, if thou haſt ſtill, and not loſt them by ſcribling, inſtead of *Whet-ſtone* call me *Grinde-ſtone*, and for *By-blow*, *Bulfinch*. Gentlemen, for two of you your companie is faire and honeſt; but for you *Bantam*, remember and take notice alſo, that I am a baſtard, and ſo much i'le teſtifie to my Aunt and Vncle.   *Exit.*

Arth. What have you done, 'twill grieve the good old Gentleman, to heare him baffled thus.

Bant. I was in a cold fweat ready to faint The time he ftaid amongft us.

Shak. But come, now the Hare is found and ftarted,

She fhall have Law, fo to our fport.   *Exit.*

Enter Boy with the Greyhounds.

A Hare, a Hare, halloe, halloe, the Divell take thefe curres, will they not ftir, halloe, halloe, there, there, there, what are they growne fo lither and fo lazie? Are Mr. *Robinfons* dogges turn'd tykes with a wanion? the Hare is yet in fight, halloe, halloe, mary hang you for a couple of mungrils (if you were worth hanging), & have you ferv'd me thus? nay then ile ferve you with the like fauce, you fhall to the next bufh, there will I tie you, and ufe you like a couple of curs as you are, & though not lafh you, yet lafh you whileft my fwitch will hold, nay fince you have left your fpeed, ile fee if I can put fpirit into you, and put you in remembrance what halloe, halloe meanes.

As he beats them, there appeares before him, Gooddy Dickifon, *and the Boy upon the dogs, going in.*

Now bleffe me heaven, one of the Greyhounds turn'd into a woman, the other into a boy! The lad I never faw before, but her I know well; it is my gammer *Dickifon.*

G. Dick. Sirah, you have ferv'd me well to fwindge me thus.

You yong rogue, you haue vs'd me like a dog.

Boy. When you had put your felf into a dogs skin, I pray how c'ud I help it; but gammer are not you a Witch? if you bee, I beg upon my knees you will not hurt me.

Dickif. Stand up my boie, for thou fhalt have no harme.

Be filent, fpeake of nothing thou haft feene.
And here's a fhilling for thee.

Boy.   Ile have none of your money gammer, becaufe you are a Witch : and now fhe is out of her
foure leg'd fhape, ile fee if with my two legs I can
out-run her.

Dickif.   Nay, firra, though you be yong, and I old,
you are not fo nimble, nor I fo lame, but I can over-
take you.

Boy.   But Gammer what do you meane to do
with me
Now you have me ?

Dickif.   To hugge thee, ftroke thee, and embrace
thee thus,
And teach thee twentie thoufand prety things.
So thou tell no tales ; and boy this night
Thou muft along with me to a brave feaft.

Boy.   Not I gammer indeedla, I dare not ftay out
late,
My father is a fell man, and if I bee out long, will
both chide and beat me.

Dickif.   Not firra, then perforce thou fhalt along,
This bridle helps me ftill at need,
And fhall provide us of a fteed.
Now firra, take your fhape and be
Prepar'd to hurrie him and me.   *Exit.*
Now looke and tell mee wher's the lad become.

Boy.   The boy is vanifht, and I can fee nothing in
his ftead
But a white horfe readie fadled and bridled.

Dickif.   And thats the horfe we muft beftride,
On which both thou and I muft ride,
Thou boy before and I behinde,
The earth we tread not, but the winde,
For we muft progreffe through the aire,
And I will bring thee to fuch fare
As thou ne're faw'ft, up and away,
For now no longer we can ftay.

                She catches him up, & turning round.   *Exit.*

Boy. Help, help.

Enter Robin and Mall.

Thanks my ſweet Mall for thy courteous entertainment, thy creame, thy cheeſe-cakes, and every good
thing, this, this, & this for all.   *kiſſe.*

Mal. But why in ſuch haſt good *Robin* ?

Robin. I confeſſe my ſtay with thee is ſweet to
mee, but I muſt ſpur Cutt the faſter for't, to be at
home in the morning, I have yet to Lancaſter to ride
to night, and this my bandileer of bottles, to fill to
night, and then halfe a ſcore mile to ride by currie-
combe time, i' the morning, or the old man chides,
Mal.

Mal. Hee ſhall not chide thee, feare it not.

Robin. Pray *Bacchus* I may pleaſe him with his
wine, which will be the hardeſt thing to do ; for ſince
hee was laſt at London and taſted the Divinitie of the
Miter, ſcarce any liquour in Lancaſhire will go downe
with him, ſure, ſure he will never be a Puritane, he
holds ſo well with the Miter.

Mal. Well *Robert*, I find your love by your haſte
from me, ile undertake you ſhal be at Lancaſter, &
twiſe as far, & yet at home time enough, and be rul'd
by me.

Rob. Thou art a witty rogue, and thinkſt to
make me believe any thing, becauſe I ſaw thee
make thy broome ſweepe the houſe without hands
t'other day.

Mal. You ſhall ſee more than that preſently, becauſe you ſhall beleeve me ; you know the houſe is all
a bed here : and I dare not be miſt in the morning.
Beſides, I muſt be at the wedding of *Lawrence* and
Parnell to morrow.

Rob. I your old ſweet heart *Lawrence* ? Old love
will not be forgotten.

Mal. I care not for the loſſe of him, but if I fit
him not hang me : but to the point, if I goe with you

to night, and help you to as good wine as your maſter
deſires, and you keepe your time with him, you will
give me a pinte for my company.

Rob.   Thy belly full wench.

Mal.   I'le but take up my milk payle and leave it
in the field, till our comming backe in the morning,
and wee'll away.

Rob.   Goe fetch it quickly then.

Mal.   No *Robert*, rather than leave your company
ſo long, it ſhall come to me.

Rob.   I would but ſee that.

The Payle goes.

Mal.   Looke yonder, what do you thinke on't.

Rob.   Light, it comes ; and I do thinke there is ſo
much of the Divell in't as will turne all the milke
ſhall come in't theſe ſeven yeares, and make it burne
too, till it ſtinke worſe than than the Proverbe of the
Biſhops foot.

Mal.   Looke you ſir, heere I have it, will you get
up and away.

Rob.   My horſe is gone, nay prithee *Mal.* thou haſt
ſet him away, leave thy Roguerie.

Mal.   Looke againe.

Rob.   There ſtands a black long-ſided jade : mine
was a truſs'd gray.

Mal.   Yours was too ſhort to carrie double ſuch a
journey. Get up I ſay, you ſhall have your owne
againe i'th morning.

Rob.   Nay but, nay but.

Mal.   Nay, and you ſtand butting now, i'le leave
you to look your horſe.   Payle on afore to the field,
and ſtaie till I come.

Rob.   Come away then, hey for *Lancaſter* : ſtand
up.   *Exeunt.*

ACTVS, III. SCENA, I.

Enter old Seely *and* Ioane *his wife.*

Seely.

Ome away wife, come away, and let us be ready to breake the Cake over the Brides head at her entrance ; we will have the honour of it, we that have playd the Steward and Cooke at home, though we loſt Church by't, and faw not Parſon *Knit-knot* doe his office, but wee ſhall ſee all the houſe rites perform'd ; and—— oh what a day of jollity and tranquility is here to-wards ?

Ioane. You are ſo frolick and ſo cranck now, upon the truce is taken amongſt us, becauſe our wrangling ſhall not wrong the Wedding, but take heed (you were beſt) how ye behave your ſelfe, leſt a day to come may pay for all.

Seel. I feare nothing, and I hope to dye in this humor.

Joan. Oh how hot am I ! rather then I would dreſſe ſuch another dinner this twelve moneth, I would wiſh Wedding quite out of this yeares Alma-nack.

Seel. Ile fetch a Cup of Sack Wife——

Ioan. How brag he is of his liberty, but the holy-day carries it.

Seel. Here, here ſweet-heart, they are long me thinks a comming, the Bels have rung out this halfe houre, harke now the wind brings the ſound of them ſweetly againe.

Ioan. They ring backwards me thinks.

Seel. Ifack they doe, ſure the greateſt fire in the Pariſh is in our Kitchin, and there's no harme done yet, no 'tis ſome merry conceit of the ſtretch-ropes the Ringers, now they have done, and now the Wedding comes, hearke, the Fidlers and all, now have I liv'd to ſee a day, come, take our ſtand, and be ready for the Bride-cake, which we will ſo cracke and crumble upon her crowne: o they come, they come.

Enter Muſitians, Lawrence, Parnell, Win. Mal. Spencer, two Country Laſſes, Doughty, Greg. Arthur, Shakton, Bantam, and Whetſtone.

All. Ioy, health, and children to the married paire.

Lawr. & Parn. We thanke you all.

Lawr. So pray come in and fare.

Parn. As well as we and taſte of every cate:

Lawr. With bonny Bridegroome and his lovely mate.

Arth. This begins bravely.

Doug. They agree better then the Bels eene now, 'slid they rung tunably till we were all out of the Church, and then they clatter'd as the divell had beene in the Bellfry: on in the name of Wedlocke, Fidlers on.

Lawr. On with your melody.

Bant. Enter the Gates with joy,

And as you enter play the ſack of *Troy*.

   The Fidlers paſſe through, and play the battle.

      The Spirit appeares.

Ioan. Welcome Bride *Parnell.*

Seel. Bridegroome *Lawrence* eke,

In you before, for we this cake muſt breake.

         Exit Lawrence.

Over the Bride——
> *As they lift up the Cake, the Spirit snatches it,*
> *and poures down bran.*

Forgi' me—what's become
O' th' Cake wife !

Ioan. It flipt out of my hand, and is falne into crums I think.

Dought. Crums? the divell of crum is here, but bran, nothing but bran, what prodigie is this?

Parn. Is my beft Brides Cake come to this? o wea warth it.

> *Exit Parn. Seely, Joane, and Maides.*

Whet. How daintily the Brides haire is powder'd with it.

Arth. My haire flands an end to fee it.

Bant. And mine.

Shak. I was never fo amaz'd !

Dough. What can it meane?

Greg. Pax, I think not on't, 'tis but fome of my Father and Mothers roguery, this is a Law-day with 'em, to doe what they lift.

Whet. I never feare any thing, fo long as my Aunt has but bidden me thinke of her, and fhe'll warrant me.

Dough. Well Gentlemen, let's follow the reft in, and feare nothing yet, the houfe fmels well of good cheere.

Seel. Gentlemen, will it pleafe you draw neere, the guefts are now all come, and the houfe almoft full, meat's taken up.

Dough. We were now comming.

Seel. But fonne *Gregory*, Nephew *Arthur*, and the reft of the young Gentlemen, I fhall take it for a favor if you will (it is an office which very good Gentlemen doe in this Country) accompane the Bride-groome in ferving the meat.

All. With all our hearts.

Seely. Nay neighbor *Doughty*, your yeares fhall excufe you.

Dough. Peugh, I am not ſo old but I can carry more meate then I can eate, if the young raſcals coo'd carry their drinke as well, the Country would be quieter——

Knock within, as at dreſſer.

Seel. Well fare your hearts,—the dreſſer calls in Gentlemen, *Exeunt Gentlemen.* 'Tis a buſie time, yet will I review the Bill of fare, for this dayes dinner——(*Reades*) for 40. people of the beſt quality, 4. meſſes of meat ; *viz.* a leg of Mutton in plum-broth, a diſh of Marrow-bones, a Capon in white-broth, a Surloyne of beefe, a Pig, a Gooſe, a Turkie, and two Pyes : for the ſecond courſe, to every meſſe 4. Chickens in a diſh, a couple of Rabbets, Cuſtard, Flawn, Florentines, and ſtewd pruines,—-all very good Country fare, and for my credit,——

Enter Muſitians playing before, Lawrence, Doughty, Arthur, Shakton, Bantam, Whetſtone, and Gregory, with diſhes : A Spirit (over the doore) does ſome action to the diſhes as they enter.

The ſervice enters, O well ſayd Muſicke, play up the meat to the Table till all be ſerv'd in, Ile ſee it paſſe in anſwer to my bill.

Dough. Hold up your head Mr. Bridegroome.

Lawr. On afore Fidlers, my doubler cewles in my honds.

Seely. Imprimus, a leg of Mutton in plum-broth, —how now Mr. Bridegroome, what carry you ?

Lawr. 'Twere hot eene now, but now it's caw'd as a ſteane.

Seel. A ſtone, 'tis horne man.

Lawr. Aw—— *Exit Fidlers.*

Seely. It was Mutton, but now 'tis the horns on't.

Lawr. Aw where's my Bride—— *Exit.*

Dough. 'Zookes, I brought as good a Surloyne of Beefe from the Dreſſer as Knife coo'd be put to, and ſee——Ile ſtay i' this houſe no longer.

Arth. And if this were not a Capon in white broth, I am one i' the Coope.

Shak. All, all's transform'd, looke you what I have !

Bant. And I.

Whet. And I ! Yet I feare nothing thank my Aunt.

Greg. I had a Pie that is not open'd yet, Ile fee what's in that—live Birds as true as I live, look where they flye !   *Exit Spirit.*

Dough. Witches, live Witches, the houfe is full of witches, if we love our lives let's out on't.

Enter *Joane and Win.*

Ioan. O husband, O guefts, O fonne, O Gentle-men, fuch a chance in a Kitchin was never heard of, all the meat is flowne out o' the chimney top I thinke, and nothing inftead of it, but Snakes, Batts, Frogs, Beetles, Hornets, and Humble-bees ; all the Sallets are turn'd to Iewes-eares, Mufhromes, and Puckfifts ; and all the Cuftards into Cowfheards !

Dought. What fhall we doe, dare we ftay any longer ?

Arth. Dare we ! why not, I defie all Witches, and all their workes ; their power on our meat, cannot reach our perfons.

Whet. I fay fo too, and fo my Aunt ever told me, fo long I will feare nothing ; be not afrayd Mr. *Doughty.*

Dough. Zookes, I feare nothing living that I can fee more then you, and that's nothing at all, but to thinke of thefe invifible mifchiefes, troubles me I confeffe.

Arth. Sir I will not goe about to over-rule your reafon, but for my part I will not out of a houfe on a Bridall day, till I fee the laft man borne.

Dough. Zookes thou art fo brave a fellow that I I will ftick to thee, and if we come off handfomely,

I am an old Batchelour thou know'ft, and muft have an heyre, I like thy fpirit, where's the Bride ? where's the Bridegroome ? where's the Muficke ? where be the Laffes ? ha' you any wine i' the houfe, though we make no dinner, lets try if we can make an afternoone.

Ioan.   Nay fir if you pleafe to ftay, now that the many are frighted away, I have fome good cold meates, and halfe a dozen bottles of Wine.

Seel.   And I will bid you welcome.

Dough.   Say you me fo, but will not your fonne be angry, and your daughter chide you.

Greg.   Feare not you that fir, for look you I obey my Father.

Win.   And I my Mother.

Ioan.   And we are all at this inftant as well and as fenfible of our former errors, as you can wifh us to be.

Dough.   Na, if the Witches have but rob'd of your meat, and reftor'd your reafon, here has beene no hurt done to day, but this is ftrange, and as great a wonder as the reft to me.

Arth.   It feemes though thefe Hags had power to make the Wedding cheere a *Deceptio vifus*, the former ftore has fcap'd 'em.

Dough.   I am glad on't, but the divell good 'hem with my Surloyne, I thought to have fet that by mine owne Trencher——But you have cold meat you fay ?

Joan.   Yes Sir.

Dought.   And Wine you fay ?

Ioan.   Yes fir.

Dought.   I hope the Country wenches and the Fidlers are not gone.

Win.   They are all here, and one the merrieft Wench ; that makes all the reft fo laugh and tickle.

Seel.   Gentlemen will you in ?

All.   Agreed on all parts.

Dough.   If not a Wedding we will make a Wake

on't, and away with the Witch; I feare nothing now
you have your wits againe : but look you, hold 'em
while you have 'em.　　　　　　　　　　*Exeunt.*

Enter Generous, and Robin, with a Paper.

Gener. I confeſſe thou haſt done a Wonder in
fetching me ſo good Wine, but my good Servant
Robert, goe not about to put a Myracle upon me, I
will rather beleeve that *Lancaſter* affords this Wine,
which I thought impoſſible till I taſted it, then that
thou coo'dſt in one night fetch it from *London.*

Rob. I have known when you have held mee for
an honeſt fellow, and would have beleev'd me.

Gener. Th' art a Knave to wiſh me to beleeve
this, forgi' me, I would have ſworne if thou had'ſt
ſtayd but time anſwerable for the journey (to his that
flew to *Paris* and back to *London* in a day) it had
been the ſame Wine, but it can never fall within the
compaſſe of a Chriſtians beleefe, that thou cou'dſt
ride above three hundred miles in 8. houres : You
were no longer out, and upon one Horſe too, and in
the Night too !

Rob. And carry a Wench behind me too, and did
ſomething elſe too, but I muſt not ſpeak of her leſt I
be divell-torne.

Gen. And fill thy bottles too, and come home
halfe drunke too, for ſo thou art, thou wouldſt never a
had ſuch a fancy elſe !

Rob. I am ſorry I have ſayd ſo much, and not let
Lancaſter have the credit o' the Wine.

Gen. O are you ſo ! and why have you abus'd me
and your ſelfe then all this while, to glorifie the *Myter*
in *Fleet-ſtreet* ?

Rob. I could ſay ſir, that you might have the
better opinion of the Wine, for there are a great many
pallats in the Kingdome that can reliſh no Wine,
unleſſe it be of ſuch a Taverne, and drawne by ſuch
a Drawer——

Gen. I ſayd, and I ſay againe, if I were within ten mile of *London*, I durſt ſwear that this was *Myter* Wine, and drawn by honeſt *Iacke Paine.*

Rob. Nay then ſir I ſwore, and I ſweare againe, honeſt *Iack Paine* drew it.

Gener. Ha, ha, ha, if I coo'd beleeve there were ſuch a thing as Witchcraft, I ſhould thinke this ſlave were bewitch'd now with an opinion.

Rob. Much good doe you ſir, your Wine and your mirth, and my place for your next Groome, I deſire not to ſtay to be laught out of my opinion.

Gen. Nay be not angry *Robin*, we muſt not part ſo, and how does my honeſt Drawer? ha, ha, ha ; and what newes at *London*, *Robin* ? ha, ha, ha; but your ſtay was ſo ſhort I think you coo'd heare none, and ſuch your haſte home that you coo'd make none : is't not ſo *Robin*? ha, ha, ha, what a ſtrange fancy has good Wine begot in his head ?

Rob. Now will I puſh him over and over with a peece of paper : Yes ſir, I have brought you ſome-thing from *London.*

Gen. Come on, now let me heare.

Rob. Your honeſt Drawer ſir, conſider'd that you conſider'd him well for his good wine——

Gen. What ſhall we heare now ?

Rob. Was very carefull to keepe or convay this paper to you, which it ſeemes you dropt in the roome there.

Gener. Bleſſe me ! this paper belongs to me in-deed, 'tis an acquittance, and all I have to ſhow for the payment of one hundred pound, I tooke great care for't, and coo'd not imagine where or how I might looſe it, but why may not this bee a tricke? this Knave may finde it when I loſt it, and conceale it till now to come over me withall. I will not trouble my thoughts with it further at this time, well *Robin* looke to your buſineſſe, and have a care of my Guelding.   *Exit Generous.*

Robin. Yes Sir. I think I have netled him now,

but not as I was netled laſt night, three hundred
Miles a Night upon a Rawbon'd Divell, as in my
heart it was a Divell, and then a Wench that ſhar'd
more o' my backe then the ſayd Divell did o' my
Bum, this is ranke riding my Maſters : but why had I
ſuch an itch to tell my Maſter of it, and that he
ſhould beleeve it ; I doe now wiſh that I had not told,
and that hee will not beleeve it, for I dare not tell him
the meanes : 'Sfoot my Wench and her friends the
Fiends, will teare me to pieces if I diſcover her ; a
notable rogue, ſhe's at the Wedding now, for as good
a Mayd as the beſt o' em——O my Miſtreſſe.

Enter Mrs. Generous, with a Bridle.

Mrs. *Robin.*
Rob. I Miſtreſſe.
Mrs. Quickly good *Robin*, the gray Guelding.
Rob. What other horſe you pleaſe Miſtreſſe.
Mrs. And why not that ?
Rob. Truly Miſtreſſe pray pardon me, I muſt be
plaine with you, I dare not deliver him you ; my
maſter has tane notice of the ill caſe you have brought
him home in divers times.
Mrs. O is it ſo, and muſt he be made acquainted
with my actions by you, and muſt I then be con-
troll'd by him, and now by you ; you are a ſawcy
Groome.
Rob. You may ſay your pleaſure.
                                        He turnes from her.
Mrs. No ſir, Ile doe my pleaſure.
                                        She Bridles him.
Rob. Aw.
Mrs. Horſe, horſe, ſee thou be,
And where I point thee carry me. *Exeunt Neighing.*

Enter Arthur, Shakſton, and Bantam.

Arth. Was there ever ſuch a medley of mirth,
madneſſe, and drunkenneſſe, ſhuffled together.

Shak. Thy Vnckle and Aunt, old Mr. *Seely* and his wife, doe nothing but kiffe and play together like Monkeyes.

Arth. Yes, they doe over-love one another now.

Bant. And young *Gregory* and his fifter doe as much over-doe their obedience now to their Parents.

Arth. And their Parents as much over-doat upon them, they are all as farre beyond their wits now in loving one another, as they were wide of them before in croffing.

Shak. Yet this is the better madneffe.

Bant. But the married couple that are both fo daintily whitled, that now they are both mad to be a bed before Supper-time, and by and by he will, and fhe wo' not : ftreight fhe will and he wo' not, the next minute they both forget they are married, and defie one another.

Arth. My fides eene ake with laughter.

Shak. But the beft fport of all is, the old Batchelour Mafter *Doughty*, that was fo cautious, & fear'd every thing to be witchcraft, is now wound up to fuch a confidence that there is no fuch thing, that hee dares the Divell doe his worft, and will not out o' the houfe by all perfuafion, and all for the love of the husbandmans daughter withbin, *Mal Spencer*.

Arth. There I am in fome danger, he put me into halfe a beliefe I fhall be his heire, pray love fhee be not a witch to charme his love from mee. Of what condition is that wench do'ft thou know her ?

Sha. A little, but *Whetftone* knowes her better.

Arth. Hang him rogue, he'le belye her, and fpeak better than fhe deferves, for he's in love with her too. I faw old *Doughty* give him a box o' the eare for kiffing her, and he turnd about as he did by thee yefterday, and fwore his Aunt fhould know it.

Bant. Who would ha' thought that impudent rogue would have come among us after fuch a baffle.

Sha. He told me, hee had complain'd to his Aunt
on us, and that ſhe would ſpeak with us.

Arth. Wee will all to her, to patch vp the buſineſſe,
for the refpeɛt I beare her husband, noble *Generous.*

Bant. Here he comes.

Enter *Whetſtone.*

Arth. Hearke you Mr. *Byblow,* do you know the
laſſe within ? What do you call her, *Mal Spencer* ?

Whet. Sir, what. I know i'le keepe to my ſelfe, a
good civile merry harmleſſe rogue ſhe is, and comes
to my Aunt often, and thats all I know by her.

Arth. You doe well to keepe it to your ſelfe ſir.

Whet. And you may do well to queſtion her if
you dare. For the teſty old coxcombe that will not
let her goe out of his hand.

Sha. Take heed, he's at your heels.

Enter *Doughty, Mal, and two countrey Laſſes.*

Dongh. Come away Wenches, where are you
Gentlemen ? Play Fidlers : lets have a dance, ha my
little rogue.   *Kiſſes Mal.*
Zookes what ayles thy noſe.

Mal. My noſe ! Nothing ſir.——*turnes about*——
Yet mee thought a flie toucht it. Did you ſee any
thing ?

Dou. No, no, yet I would almoſt ha' ſworn, I
would not have ſprite or goblin blaſt thy face, for all
their kingdome. But hangt there is no ſuch thing :
Fidlers will you play ?

Selengers Round.

Gentlemen will you dance ?

All. With all our hearts.

Arth. But ſtay wheres this houſhold ?
This Family of love ? Let's have them into the
    revels.

Dou. Hold a little then.

Sha. Here they come all
In a True-love knot.

Enter Seely, Ioane, Greg, Win.

Greg. O Father twentie times a day is too little to
aske you bleſſing.

See. Goe too you are a raſcall : and you houſwife
teach your daughter better manners : i'le ſhip you all
for New England els.

Bant. The knot's untied, and this is another
change.

Ioane. Yes I will teach her manners, or put her
out to ſpin two penny tow : ſo you deare husband will
but take mee into favor : i'le talke with you dame
when the ſtrangers are gone.

Greg. Deare Father.

Win. Deare Mother.

Greg. Win. Deare Father and Mother pardon us
but this time.

See. Ioa. Never, and therefore hold your peace.

Dough. Nay thats unreaſonable.

Greg. Win. Oh !——— *Weepe.*

See. But for your ſake i'le forbeare them, and
beare with any thing this day.

Arth. Doe you note this ? Now they are all
worſe than ever they were, in a contrary vaine : What
thinke you of Witchcraft now ?

Dou. They are all naturall fooles man, I finde it
now.
Art thou mad to dreame of Witchcraft ?

Arth. He's as much chang'd and bewitcht as they
I feare.

Dough. Hey day ! Here comes the payre of boyld
Lovers in Sorrell ſops.

Enter Lawrence and Parnell.

Lawr. Nay deare hunny, nay hunny, but eance,
eance.

Par.   Na, na, I han' fwarne, I han' fwarne, not a bit afore bed, and look yeou it's but now dauncing time.

Dough.   Come away Bridegroome, wee'll ftay your ftomack with a daunce.   Now mafters play a good : come my Laffe wee'l fhew them how 'tis.

Muficke.   Selengers round.

As they beginne to daunce, they play another tune, then fall into many.

Ar. Ban. Sha.   Whether now, hoe ?

Dou.   Hey day ! why you rogues.

Whet.   What do's the Divell ride o' your Fiddle-ftickes.

Dou.   You drunken rogues, hold, hold, I fay, and begin againe foberly the beginning of the World.

Muficke.   Every one a feverall tune.

Arth. Bant. Shak.   Ha, ha, ha, How's this ?

Bant.   Every one a feverall tune.

Dou.   This is fomething towards it.   I bad them play the beginning o' the World, and they play, I know not what.

Arth.   No 'tis running o' the country feverall waies.

But what do you thinke on't.   *Muficke ceafe.*

Dough.   Thinke ! I thinke they are drunke.   Pri-thee doe not thou thinke of Witchcraft ; for my part, I fhall as foone thinke this maid one, as that theres any in *Lancafhire*.

Mal.   Ha, ha, ha.

Dough.   Why do'ft thou laugh ?

Mal.   To thinke this Bridegroome fhould once ha' bin mine, but he fhall rue it, ile hold him this point on't, and thats all I care for him.

Dough.   A witty Rogue.

Whet.   I tell you fir, they fay fhee made a payle follow her t'other day up two payre of ftayres.

Dough. You lying Rascall.

Arth. O sir forget your anger.

Mal. Looke you Mr. Bridegroome, what my care provides for you.

Lawrence. What, a point?

Mal. Yes put it in your pocket, it may stand you instead anon, when all your points be tane away, to trusse up your trinkits, I meane your slopes withall.

Lawr. *Mal* for awd acquaintance I will ma' thy point a point of preferment. It shan bee the Foreman of a haell Iewrie o' points, and right here will I weare it.

Par. Wy'a, wy'a, awd leove wo no be forgetten, but ay's never be jealous the mare for that.

Arth. Play fidlers any thing.

Dou. I, and lets see your faces, that you play fairely with us.

Musitians shew themselves above.

Fid. We do sir, as loud as we can possibly.

Sha. Play out that we may heare you.

Fid. So we do sir, as loud as we can possibly.

Dough. Doe you heare any thing?

All. Nothing not we sir.

Dough. 'Tis so, the rogues are brib'd to crosse me, and their Fiddles shall suffer, I will breake em as small as the Bride cake was to day.

Arth. Looke you sir, they'l save you a labour, they are doing it themselves.

Whet. Oh brave Fidlers, there was never better scuffling for the Tudberry Bull.

Mal. This is mother *Iohnson* and Gooddy *Dickisons* roguerie, I finde it, but I cannot helpe it, yet I will have musicke : sir theres a Piper without, would be glad to earne money.

Whet. She has spoke to purpose, & whether this were witchcraft or not : I have heard my Aunt say twentie times, that no Witchcraft can take hold of a *Lancashire* Bag-pipe, for it selfe is able to charme the Divell, ile fetch him.

Dough. Well said, a good boy now; come bride and bridegroome, leave your kissing and fooling, and prepare to come into the daunce. Wee'le have a Horne-pipe, and then a posset and to bed when you please. Welcome Piper, blow till thy bagge cracke agen, a lusty Horne-pipe, and all into the daunce, nay young and old.

Daunce. Lawrence and Parnell reele in the daunce. At the end, Mal vanishes, and the piper.

All. Bravely performd.

Dou. Stay, wheres my lasse?

Arth. Ban. Shak. Vanisht, she and the Piper both vanisht, no bodie knowes how.

Dou. Now do I plainly perceive again, here has bin nothing but witcherie all this day; therfore into your posset, & agree among your selves as you can, ile out o' the house. And Gentlemen, if you love me or your selves, follow me.

Ar. Bant. Sha. Whet. I, I, Away, away.
Exeunt.

See. Now good son, wife and daughter, let me in-treat you be not angry.

Win. O you are a trim mother are you not?

Ioa. Indeed childe, ile do so no more.

Greg. Now sir, i'le talke with you, your champions are al gon.

Lawr. Weell sir, and what wun yeou deow than?

Par. Whay, whay, whats here to doe? Come awaw, and whickly, and see us into our Brayd Chember, & delicatly ludgd togeder, or wee'l whap you out o' dores ith morne to sijourne in the common, come away.

All. Wee follow yee.   *Exeunt.*

ACTVS, IIII.   SCÆNA, I.

Enter Miftreffe Generous and Robin.

Now you this gingling bridle, if you fee'
agen ?   I wanted but a paire of gingling
fpurs to make you mend your pace, and
put you into a fweat.

Robin.   Yes, I have reafon to know it after my
hard journey, they fay there be light women, but for
your owne part, though you be merry.   Yet I may be
forry for your heavineffe.

Mrs. Gener.   I fee thou art not quite tyr'd by
fhaking of thy felfe, 'tis a figne that as thou haft
brought mee hither, fo thou art able to beare mee
backe, and fo you are like good *Robert.*   You will
not let me have your mafters gelding, you will not.
Wel fir, as you like this journey, fo deny him to me
hereafter.

Rob.   You fay well miftreffe, you have jaded me
(a pox take you for a jade.)   Now I bethinke my
felfe how damnably' did I ride laft night, and how
divellifhly have I bin rid now.

Mrs.   Doe you grumble you groome ?   Now the
bridl's of, I turne thee to grazing, gramercy my good
horfe, I have no better provender for thee at this
time, thou hadft beft like *Æfops* Affe to feed upon
Thiftles, of which this place will affoord thee plenty.
I am bid to a better banquet, which done, ile take
thee up from graffe, fpur cutt, and make a fhort cutt
home.   Farewell.

Robin.   A pox upon your tayle.

Enter all the Witches and Mal, at feverall dores.

All.   The Lady of the feaft is come, welcome, welcome.

Mrs. Is all the cheare that was prepared to grace
the wedding feaſt, yet come ?

Gooddy Dick. Part of it's here.
The other we muſt pull for. But whats hee ?

Mrs. My horſe, my horſe, ha, ha, ha.

All. Ha, ha, ha.   *Exeunt.*

Rob. My horſe, my horſe, I would I were now
ſome country Major, and in authority, to ſee if I
would not venter to rowze your Satanicall ſiſterhood :
Horſe, horſe, ſee thou be, & where I point thee, cary
me : is that the trick on't ? the divel himſelfe ſhall be
her carrier next if I can ſhun her : & yet my Mr. will
not beleeve theres any witches : theres no running
away, for I neither know how nor whether, beſides to
my thinking, theres a deepe ditch, & a hye quick-ſet
about mee, how ſhall I paſſe the time ? What place
is this ? it looks like an old barne : ile peep in at ſome
cranny or other, and try if I can ſee what they are
doing. Such a bevy of beldames did I never behold ;
and cramming like ſo many Cormorants : Marry choke
you with a miſchiefe.

Gooddy Dickiſon. Whoope, whurre, heres a ſturre,
never a cat, never a curre, but that we muſt have this
demurre.

Mal. A ſecond courſe.

Mrs. Gen. Pull, and pull hard
For all that hath lately bin prepar'd
For the great wedding feaſt.

Mal. As chiefe.
Of *Doughtyes* Surloine of roſt Beefe.

All. Ha, ha, ha.

Meg. 'Tis come, 'tis come.

Mawd. Where hath it all this while beene ?

Meg. Some
Delay hath kept it, now 'tis here,
For bottles next of wine and beere,
The Merchants cellers they ſhall pay for't.

Mrs. Gener. Well,
What fod or roſt meat more, pray tell.

Good. Dick.   Pul for the Poultry, Foule, & Fifh,
For emptie fhall not be a difh.

Robin.   A pox take them, muft only they feed upon
hot meat, and I upon nothing but cold fallads.

Mrs. Gener.   This meat is tedious, now fome
Farie,
Fetch what belongs unto the Dairie.

Mal.   Thats Butter, Milk, Whey, Curds and
Cheefe,
Wee nothing by the bargaine leefe.

All.   Ha, ha, ha.

Goody Dickifon.   Boy, theres meat for you.

Boy.   Thanke you.

Gooddy Dickif.   And drinke too.

Meg.   What Beaft was by thee hither rid?

Mawd.   A Badger nab.

Meg.   And I beftrid
A Porcupine that never prickt.

Mal.   The dull fides of a Beare I kickt.
I know how you rid Lady Nan.

Mrs. Gen.   Ha, ha, ha, upon the knave my man.

Rob.   A murrein take you, I am fure my hoofes
payd for't.

Boy.   Meat lie there, for thou haft no tafte, and
drinke there, for thou haft no relifh, for in neither of
them is there either falt or favour.

All.   Pull for the poffet, pull.

Robin.   The brides poffet on my life, nay if they
come to their fpoone meat once, I hope theil breake
up their feaft prefently.

Mrs. Gen.   So thofe that are our waiters nere,
Take hence this Wedding cheere.
We will be lively all, and make this barn our hall.

Gooddy Dick.   You our Familiers, come,
In fpeech let all be dumbe,
And to clofe up our Feaft,
To welcome every geft
A merry round let's daunce.

Meg.   Some Muficke then ith aire

Whileſt thus by paire and paire,
We nimbly foote it ; ſtrike.   *Muſick.*
  Mal.   We are obeyd.
  Sprite.   And we hels miniſters ſhall lend our aid.

*Dance and Song together.   In the time of which the Boy
    ſpeakes.*

  Boy.   Now whileſt they are in their jollitie, and do
not mind me, ile ſteale away, and ſhift for my felfe,
though I loſe my life for't.   *Exit.*
  Meg.   Enough, enough, now part,
To ſee the brides vext heart,
The bridegroomes too and all,
That vomit up their gall
For lacke o'th wedding chere.
  Gooddy Dickiſon.   But ſtay, wheres the *Boy*, looke
out, if he eſcape us, we are all betrayed.
  Meg.   No following further, yonder horſemen
    come,
In vaine is our purſuit, let's breake up court.
  Gooddy Dickiſon.   Where ſhall we next met?
  Mawd.   At Mill.
  Meg.   But when ?
  Mrs.   At Night.
  Meg.   To horſe, to horſe.
  2.   Where's my *Mamilian.*
  1.   And my *Incubus.   Robin ſtands amaz'd at this.*
  3.   My Tyger to beſtri'd.
  Mal.   My Puggie.
  Mrs. Gen.   My horſe.
  All.   Away, away,
The night we have Feaſted, now comes on the
    day.
  Mrs.   Come ſirrah, ſtoope your head like a tame
    jade,
Whil'ſt I put on your Bridle.
  Rob.   I pray Miſtreſſe ride me as you would be
rid.
  Mrs.   That's at full ſpeed.

Rob. Nay then Ile try Conclusions.
               A great noyfe within at their parting.
Mare Mare, fee thou be,
And where I point thee carry me.   *Exeunt.*

     Enter Mr. Generous, making him ready.

  Gen. I fee what Man is loath to entertaine,
Offers it felfe to him moft frequently,
And that which we moft covet to embrace,
Doth feldome court us, and proves moft averfe ;
For I, that never coo'd conceive a thought
Of this my woman worthy a rebuke,
(As one that in her youth bore her fo fairely
That fhe was taken for a feeming Saint)
To render me fuch juft occafion,
That I fhould now diftruft her in her age ;
Diftruft ! I cannot, that would bring me in
The poore afperfion of fond jealoufie ;
Which even from our firft meeting I abhorr'd.
The Gentile fafhion fometimes we obferve
To funder beds ; but moft in thefe hot monthes
Iune, Iuly, Auguft, fo we did laft night.
Now I (as ever tender of her health)
And therefore rifing early as I ufe,
Entring her Chamber to beftow on her
A cuftom'd Vifite ; finde the Pillow fwell'd,
Vnbruis'd with any weight, the fheets unruffled,
The Curtaines neither drawne, nor bed layd down ;
Which fhowes, fhe flept not in my houfe to night.
Should there be any contract betwixt her
And this my Groome, to abufe my honeft truft ;
I fhould not take it well, but for all this
Yet cannot I be jealous.   *Robin——*

          Enter Robin.

  Gen. Is my horfe fafe, lufty, and in good plight ?
What, feeds he well ?

Rob.   Yes ſir, he's broad buttock'd and full flanck'd, he doth not bate an ace of his fleſh.

Gen.   When was he rid laſt ?

Rob.   Not ſir ſince you backt him.

Gen.   Sirrah, take heed I finde you not a Knave, Have you not lent him to your Miſtreſſe late ? So late as this laſt Night ?

Rob.   Who I ſir, may I dye ſir, if you finde me in a lye ſir.

Gen.   Then I ſhall finde him where I left him laſt.

Robin.   No doubt Sir.

Gener.   Give me the Key o'th Stable.

Robin.   There Sir.

Gen.   Sirrah, your Miſtreſſe was abroad all night, Nor is ſhe yet come home, if there I finde him not, I ſhall finde thee, what to this preſent houre I never did ſuſpect ; and I muſt tell thee Will not be to thy profit.   *Exit.*

Rob.   Well ſir, finde what you can, him you ſhall finde, and what you finde elſe ; it may be for that, inſtead of Gramercy horſe, you may ſay Gramercy *Robin* ; you will beleeve there are no Witches ! had I not been late brideled, I coo'd have ſayd more, but I hope ſhe is ty'd to the racke that will confeſſe ſome-thing, and though not ſo much as I know, yet no more then I dare juſtifie——

Enter Generous.

Have you found your Gelding ſir ?

Gen.   Yes, I have.

Rob.   I hope not ſpurr'd, nor put into a ſweat, you may ſee by his plump belly and ſleeke legs he hath not bin ſore travail'd.

Gener.   Y'are a ſawcy Groome to receive horſes Into my Stable, and not aske me leave. Is't for my profit to buy Hay and Oates For every ſtrangers jades ?

Rob.   I hope ſir you finde none feeding there but

your owne, if there be any you ſuſpect, they have
nothing to champe on, but the Bridle.

Gener. Sirrah, whoſe jade is that ty'd to the
Racke?

Rob. The Mare you meane ſir?

Gener. Yes, that old Mare.

Rob. Old doe you call her? You ſhall finde the
marke ſtill in her mouth, when the Bridle is out of it?
I can aſſure you 'tis your owne Beaſt.

Gen. A beaſt thou art to tell me ſo, hath the
    wine
Not yet left working? not the *Myter* wine?
That made thee to beleeve Witchcraft?
Prithee perſwade me,
To be a drunken Sot like to thy ſelfe;
And not to know mine owne.

Rob. Ile not perſwade you to any thing, you will
beleeve nothing but what you ſee, I ſay the Beaſt is
your owne, and you have the moſt right to keepe her,
ſhee hath coſt you more the currying, then all the
Combs in your Stable are worth. You have paid for
her Provender this twentie yeares and upwards, and
furniſht her with all the Capariſons that ſhe hath
worne, of my Knowledge, and becauſe ſhe hath
been ridden hard the laſt Night, doe you renounce
her now?

Gener. Sirrah, I feare ſome ſtolne jade of your
    owne
That you would have me keepe.

Rob. I am ſure I found her no jade the laſt time
I rid her, ſhe carried me the beſt part of a hundred
Miles in leſſe then a quarter of an houre.

Gener. The divell ſhe did!

Robin. Yes ſo I ſay, either the divell or ſhe did;
an't pleaſe you walke in and take off her Bridle,
and then tell me who hath more right to her, you
or I.

Gen. Well *Robert*, for this once Ile play the
    Groome,

And doe your office for you.   *Exit.*

Rob. I pray doe Sir, but take heed left when the
Bridle is out of her mouth, fhe put it not into yours ;
if fhe doe, you are a gone man : if fhe but fay once—
Horfe, horfe, fee thou be.
Be you rid (if you pleafe) for me.

*Enter Mr. Generous, and Mrs. Generous, he with
a Bridle.*

Gener. My blood is turn'd to Ice, and my all
    vitals
Have ceas'd their working ! dull ftupidity
Surprifeth me at once, and hath arrefted
That vigorous agitation ; Which till now
Expreft a life within me : I me thinks
Am a meere Marble ftatue, and no man ;
Vnweave my age O time, to my firft thread ;
Let me loofe fiftie yeares in ignorance fpent :
That being made an infant once againe,
I may begin to know, what ? or where am I
To be thus loft in wonder.

    Mrs. Gen. Sir.

    Gen. Amazement ftill purfues me, how am I
        chang'd
Or brought ere I can underftand my felfe,
Into this new World.

    Rob. You will beleeue no Witches ?

    Gen. This makes me beleeve all, I any thing ;
And that my felfe am nothing : prithee *Robin*
Lay me to my felfe open, what art thou,
Or this new transform'd Creature ?

    Rob. I am *Robin*, and this your wife, my Mrs.

    Gen. Tell me the Earth
Shall leave it's feat, and mount to kiffe the
    Moone ;
Or that the Moone enamour'd of the Earth,
Shall leave her fpheare, to ftoope to us thus low.
What ? what's this in my hand, that at an inftant

Can from a foure leg'd Creature, make a thing
So like a wife ?

Rob.   A Bridle, a jugling Bridle Sir.

Gage.   A Bridle, hence inchantment,
A Viper were more ſafe within my hand
Then this charm'd Engine.

                Caſts it away.   Robin takes it up.

Rob.   Take heed Sir what you do, if you caſt it
hence, and ſhe catch it up, we that are here now, may
be rid as far as the *Indies* within theſe few houres,
Miſtreſſe down of your Mares bones, or your Mary-
bones whether you pleaſe, and confeſſe your ſelfe to
be what you are ; and that's in plaine *Engliſh* a Witch,
a grand notorious Witch.

Gen.   A Witch ! my wife a Witch !

Rob.   So it appeares by the ſtorie.

Gener.   The more I ſtrive to unwinde
My ſelfe from this *Meander*, I the more
Therein am intricated ; prithee woman
Art thou a Witch ?

Mrs.   It cannot be deny'd,
I am ſuch a curſt Creature.

Gen.   Keep aloofe,
And doe not come too neareme, O my truſt ;
Have I ſince firſt I underſtood my ſelfe,
Bin of my foule ſo charie, ſtill to ſtudie
What beſt was for it's health, to renounce˜all
The workes of that black Fiend with my beſt force
And hath that Serpent twin'd me ſo about,
That I muſt lye ſo often and ſo long
With a Divell in my boſome !

Mrs.   Pardon ſir.

Gen.   Pardon !   Can ſuch a thing as that be
    hop'd ?
Lift up thine eyes (loſt woman) to yon Hils ;
It muſt be thence expeſted : look not down
Vnto that horrid dwelling, which thou haſt ſought
At ſuch deare rate to purchaſe, prithee tell me,
(For now I can beleeve) art thou a Witch ?

Mrs. I am.

Gen. With that word I am thunderſtrooke,
And know not what to anſwer, yet reſolve me
Haſt thou made any contract with that Fiend
The Enemy of Mankind ?

Mrs. O I have.

Gen. What ? and how farre ?

Mrs. I have promis'd him my foule.

Gen. Ten thouſand times better thy Body had
Bin promis'd to the Stake, I and mine too,
Then ſuch a compact ever had bin made.   Oh——

Rob. What cheere ſir, ſhow your ſelfe a man,
though ſhe appear'd ſo late a Beaſt ; Miſtreſſe confeſſe all, better here than in a worſe place, out
with it.

Gen. Reſolve me, how farre doth that contract
     ſtretch ?

Mrs. What intereſt in this Soule, my ſelfe coo'd
     claime
I freely gave him, but his part that made it
I ſtill reſerve, not being mine to give.

Gen. O cunning Divell, fooliſh woman know
Where he can clayme but the leaſt little part,
He will uſurpe the whole ; th'art a loſt woman.

Mrs. I hope not ſo.

Gen. Why haſt thou any hope ?

Mrs. Yes Sir I have.

Gen. Make it appeare to me.

Mrs. I hope I never bargain'd for that fire,
Further then penitent teares have power to quench.

Gen. I would ſee ſome of them.

Mrs. You behold them now.
(If you looke on me with charitable eyes)
Tinctur'd in blood, blood iſſuing from the heart,
Sir I am ſorry ; when I looke towards Heaven
I beg a gracious Pardon ; when on you
Me thinkes your Native goodneſſe ſhould not be
Leſſe pittifull than they : 'gainſt both I have err'd,
From both I beg attonement.

Gener.   May I preſum't ?

Mrs.   I kneele to both your Mercies.

Gener.   Know'ſt thou what a Witch is ?

Mrs.   Alas, None better,
Or after mature recollection can be
More ſad to thinke on't.

Gen.   Tell me, are thoſe teares
As full of true hearted penitence,
As mine of ſorrow, to behold what ſtate
What deſperate ſtate th'art falne in.

Mrs.   Sir they are.

Gen.   Riſe, and as I doe, ſo heaven pardon me ;
We all offend, but from ſuch falling off,
Defend us.   Well, I doe remember wife,
When I firſt tooke thee, 'twas for good and bad ;
O change thy bad to good, that I may keep thee,
As then we paſt our faiths, till Death us ſever.
I will not aggravate thy griefe too much,
By Needles iteration : *Robin* hereafter
Forget thou haſt a tongue, if the leaſt Syllable
Of what hath paſt be rumour'd, you looſe me ;
But if I finde you faithfull, you gaine me ever.

Rob.   A match ſir, you ſhall finde me as mute as if
I had the Bridle ſtill in my mouth.

Gen.   O woman thou had'ſt need to weepe thy
   ſelfe
Into a fountaine, ſuch a penitent ſpring
As may have power to quench inviſible flames
In which my eyes ſhall ayde ; too little all,
If not too little, all's forgiven, forgot ;
Only thus much remember, thou had'ſt extermin'd
Thy ſelfe out of the bleſt ſociety
Of Saints and Angels, but on thy repentance
I take thee to my Boſome, once againe,
My wife, ſiſter, and daughter : ſaddle my Gelding,
Some buſineſſe that may hold me for two dayes
Calls me aſide.   *Exeunt.*

Rob.   I ſhall Sir, well now my Miſtreſſe hath promis'd to give over her Witchery, I hope though I ſtill

continue her man, yet ſhe will make me no more her journey-man ; to prevent which the firſt thing I doe ſhall be to burne the Bridle, and then away with the Witch.   *Exit.*

Enter Arthur and Doughty.

Arth. Sir you have done a right noble courteſie, which deſerves a memory, as long as the name of friendſhip can beare mention.

Dough. What I have done, I ha' done, if it be well, 'tis well, I doe not like the bouncing of good Offices, if the little care I have taken ſhall doe theſe poore people good, I have my end in't, and ſo my reward.

Enter Bantam.

Bant. Now Gentlemen, you ſeeme very ſerious.

Arth. 'Tis true we are ſo, but you are welcome to the knowledge of our affayres.

Bant. How does thine Vncle and Aunt, *Gregory* and his ſiſter, the Families of *Seelyes* agree yet, can you tell ?

Arth. That is the buſineſſe, the *Seely* houſhold is divided now.

Bant. How ſo I pray ?

Arth. You know, and cannot but with pitty know
Their miſerable condition, how
The good old couple were abus'd, and how
The young abus'd themſelves ; if we may ſay
That any of them are their ſelves at all
Which ſure we cannot, nor approve them fit
To be their owne diſpoſers, that would give
The governance of ſuch a houſe and living
Into their Vaſſailes hands, to thruſt them out on't
Without or Law or order, this conſider'd
This Gentleman and my ſelfe have taken home

By faire entreaty, the old folkes to his houſe,
The young to mine, untill ſome wholeſome order
By the judicious of the Common-wealth,
Shall for their perſons and eſtate be taken.

Bant. But what becomes of *Lawrence* and his *Parnell*? The luſty couple, what doe they now?

Dough. Alas poore folks, they are as farre to ſeeke of how they doe, or what they doe, or what they ſhould doe, as any of the reſt, they are all growne *Ideots*, and till ſome of theſe damnable jades, with their divelliſh deviſes bee found out, to diſcharme them, no remedy can be found, I mean to lay the Country for their Hagſhips, and if I can anticipate the purpoſe, of their grand Mr. Divell to confound 'em before their leaſe be out, be ſure ile do't.

A ſhout within.

Cry. A Skimington, a Skimmington, a Skiming-ton.

Dough. Whats the matter now, is Hell broke looſe?

Enter Mr. Shakſtone.

Arth. Tom *Shakſtone*, how now, canſt tell the newes?

Sha. The news, ye heare it up i'th aire, do you not?

Within. A Skimington, a Skimington, a Skiming-ton.

Sha. Hearke ye, do you not heare it? theres a Skimington, towards gentlemen.

Dou. Ware Wedlocke hoe.

Bant. At whoſe ſuit I prithee is Don Skimington come to towne.

Sha. Ile tell you gentlemen, ſince you have taken home old *Seely* and his wife to your houſe, and you their ſon and daughter to yours, the houſe-keepers

Lawrence, and his late bride *Parnell* are fallen out by
themſelves.

Arth. How prithee?

Sha. The quarell began they ſay upon the wedding night, and in the bride bed.

Bant. For want of bedſtaves?

Sha. No but a better implement it ſeemes the
bridegroome was unprovided of, a homely tale to
tell.

Dou. Now out upon her ſhee has a greedy worme
in her, I have heard the fellow complain'd on, for an
over mickle man among the maids.

Arth. Is his haſte to goe to bed at afternoone
come to this now?

Dough. Witchery, witchery, more witcherie ſtill
dat and plaine witchery. Now do I thinke upon the
codpeece point the young jade gave him at the wedding: ſhee is a witch, and that was a charme, if there
be any in the World.

Arth. A ligatory point.

Bant. Alas poore *Lawrence*.

Sha. He's comming to make his mone to you
about it, and ſhe too, ſince you have taken their
maſters & miſtreſſes to your care, you muſt do them
right too.

Dough. Marry but ile not undertake her at theſe
yeares, if luſty *Lawrence* cannot do't.

Bant. But has ſhe beaten him?

Sha. Grievouſly broke his head in I know not
how many places: of which the hoydens have taken
notice, and will have a Skimmington on horſe-backe
preſently. Looke ye, here comes both plaintiffe and
defendant.

Enter Lawrence and Parnell.

Dough. How now *Lawrence*, what has thy wed-
lock brought thee already to thy night-cap?

Lawr. Yie gadwat ír, I ware wadded but aw to
ſeun.

Par. Han yeou reeſon to complayne or ay trow yeou gaffer Downought? Wa warth the day that ever I wadded a Downought.

Ar. Ban. Sha. Nay hold *Parnel* hold.

Dough. We have heard enough of your valour already, wee know you have beaten him, let that ſuffice.

Parn. Ware ever poore mayden betrayed as ay ware unto a ſwagbellied Carle that cannot aw waw that cannot.

Dou. What ſaies ſhe?

Dou. I know not, ſhe catterwawles I think. *Parnel* be patient good *Parnell*, and a little modeſt too, 'tis not amiſſe, wee know not the reliſh of every eare that heares vs, lets talke within our ſelves. Whats the defect? Whats the impediment? *Lawrence* has had a luſty name among the Batchellors.

Par. What he ware when he ware a Batchelor, I know better than the beſt maid ith tawne. I wad I had not.

Ar. Ba. Sha. Peace *Parnell*.

Par. 'Tware that, that coſſen'd me, he has not now as he had than?

Ar. Ba. Sha. Peace good *Parnell*.

Parn. For then he could, but now he connot, he connot.

Ar. B. Sha. Fie *Parnel* fie.

Par. I ſay agean and agean, hee connot, he connot.

Ar. Ba. Sha. Alas poore *Parnel*.

Par. I am not a bit the better for him ſin wye ware wad.   *Cries.*

Dou. Heres good ſtuffe for a jurie of women to paſſe upon.

Arth. But *Parnel*, why have you beaten him ſo grievouſly? What would you have him doe in this caſe?

Dou. He's out of a doing caſe it ſeemes.

Par. Marry ſir, and beat him will I into his grave,

or backe to the Priest, and be unwadded agone, for I wonot bee baund to lig with him and live with him, the laife of an honest woman for aw the layves good i' *Loncoshire.*

Dou. An honest woman : thats a good mind *Parnel.* What say you to this *Lawrence ?*

Law. Keepe her of o'me, and I shan teln yeou, and she be by I am no body : But keep her off and search me, let me be searcht as never witch was fearcht, and finde ony thing mor or lasse upo me than a sufficient mon shold have, and let me me be honckt by't.

Art. Do you heare this *Parnell ?*

Par. Ah leear, leear, deell tacke the leear, troist yee and hong yee.

Dou. Alasse it is too plaine, the poore fellow is
    bewitcht.
Heres a plaine *Maleficium versus hanc* now.

Ar. And so is she bewitcht too into this im-modesty.

Ban. She would never talke so else.

Law. I prayn yeow gi' me the lere o' that Latine sir.

Dough. The meaning is, you must get halfe a dozen bastards Within this twelvemoneth, and that will mend your next mariage.

Law. And I thought it would ma' *Parnel,* love me i'd be sure on't, and gang about it now right.

Sha. Y'are soone provided it seems for such a journey.

Dou. Best tarry till thy head be whole *Lawrence.*

Pa. Nay, nay, ay's white casten away ent I be un-wadded agen : And then ine undertack to find 3 bet-ter husbands in a bean cod.

Sha. Hearke gentlemen, the shew is comming.

Ar. What shall we stay & see't.

Ban. O by all means Gent.

Dou. 'Tis best to have these away first.

Par. Nay mary shan yeou not sir, I heare yeou

well enogh, & I con the meaning o' the ſhow well
enogh, & I ſtay not the ſhow & ſee not the ſhow, &
ma' one i' the ſhow, let me be honckt up for a ſhow ile
ware them to mel or ma with a woman that mels or
mae's with a teſtril a longie, a dowlittle loſell that
connot, & if I skim not their skimingtons cockskeam
for't, ma that warplin boggle me a week lonker, &
thats a curſe eno' for any wife I tro.

Dough. Agreed, perhaps 'twill mend the ſport.

*Enter drum (beating before) a Skimington, and his wife
on a horſe; Divers country ruſticks (as they paſſe)
Par. (puls Skimington of the horſe: and Law.
Skimingtons wife: they beat em. Drum beats alar.
horſe comes away: The hoydens at firſt oppoſe the
Gentlemen: who draw: the clownes vaile bonnet,
(make a ring Par. and Skim. fight.*

Dou. Beat drum alarum.
Enough, enough, here my maſters: now patch up
your ſhew if you can, and catch your horſe again, and
when you have done drinke that.

Rabble. Thanke your worſhip. *Exeunt ſhout.*

Par. Lat'hem as they laik this gang a proceſſion
with their aydoll Skimington agean.

Arth. Parnel, thou didſt bravely.

Parn. I am ſure I han drawne blood o' theyr
aydoll.

Law. And I thinke I tickled his waife.

Par. Yie to be ſure, yeou bene eane of the owd
ticklers.
But with what con yeou tell?

Law. Yieu with her owne ladel.

Par. Yie marry a ladell is ſomething.

Dou. Come you have both done well, goe in to my
houſe, ſee your old maſter and miſtreſſe, while I tra-
vell a courſe to make yee all well againe, I will now a
witch hunting.

Par. Na courſe for hus but to be unwadded agone.

Arth. Sha. Bant.   Wee are for *Whet.* and his
Aunt you know.
   Dou.   Farewell, farewell.   *Exeunt.*

Enter Mrs. Generous, and Mal. Spencer.

Welcome, welcome, my girle, what hath thy puggy
Yet fuckt upon thy pretty duggy?
   Mal.   All's well at home, and abroad too.
What ere I bid my Pug, hee'l doo.   You fent for
   mee?
   Mrs.   I did.
   Mal.   And why?
   Mrs.   Wench ile tell thee, thou and I
Will walk a little, how doth *Meg*?
And her Mamillion.
   Mal   Of one leg
Shee's growne lame.
   Mrs.   Becaufe the beaft
Did miffe us laft *Goodfriday* Feaft,
I geft as much.
   Mal.   But *All-Saints* night
She met though fhe did halt downe right.
   Mrs.   *Dickifon* and *Hargrave* prithee tel,
How do they?
   Mal.   All about us well.
But Puggy whifperd in mine eare
That you of late were put in feare.
   Mrs.   The flave my man.
   Mal.   Who *Robin*?
   Mrs.   Hee.
   Mal.   My Sweet-heart?
   Mrs.   Such a tricke ferv'd me.
   Mal.   About the bridle, now alacke.
   Mrs.   The villain brought me to the rack.
Tyed was I both to rack and manger.
   Mal.   But thence how fcap't you?
   Mrs.   Without danger,
I thank my fpirit.
   Mal.   I but than

How pacified was your good man ?

   Mrs. Some paſſionate words mixt with forc t tears

Did ſo inchant his eyes and eares

I made my peace, with promiſe never

To doe the like ; but once and ever

A Witch thou know'ſt.   Now underſtand

New buſineſſe wee tooke in hand.

My Husband packt out of the towne

Know that the houſe, and all's our owne.

Enter Whetſtone.

   Whet. Naunt, is this your promiſe Naunt ? (What *Mal*! How doeſt thou *Mal*?) You told mee you would put a tricke upon theſe Gentlemen, whom you made mee invite to ſupper, who abuſed and called me baſtard. (And when ſhall I get one upon thee my ſweet Rogue ?) And that you would doe I know not what ; for you would not tell mee what you would doe. (And ſhall you and I never have any doing together) ſupper is done, and the table ready to withdraw : And I am riſen the earlieſt from the boord, and yet for ought I can ſee I am never a whit the neerer. What not one kiſſe at parting *Mal* ?

   Mrs. Well Cozen this is all you have to do :

Retire the Gallants to ſome privat roome,

Where call for wine, and junckets what you pleaſe,

Then thou ſhalt need to do no other thing

Than what this note directs thee, obſerve that

And trouble me no farther.

   Whet. Very good, I like this beginning well : for where they ſleighted me before, they ſhall finde me a man of note.   *Exit.*

   Mal. Of this the meaning.

   Mrs. Marry Laſſe

To bring a new conceit to paſſe.

Thy Spirit I muſt borrow more,

To fill the number three or foure ;
Whom we will ufe to no great harm,
Only affift me with thy charme.
This night wee'l celebrate to fport :
'Tis all for mirth, we mean no hurt.

Mal. My Spirit and my felfe command ;
Mamillion, & the reft at hand,
Shall all affift.

Mrs. Withdraw then, quicke,
Now gallants, ther's for you a trick.   *Exeunt.*

Enter Whetstone, Arthur, Shakstone, Bantam.

Whet. Heer's a more privat roome gentlemen, free
from the noife of the Hall.   Here we may talke, and
throw the chamber out of the cafements.   Some wine
and a fhort banquet.

Enter with a Banquet, Wine, and two Tapers.

Whet. So now leave us.

Arth. Wee are much bound to you mafter *Whetftone* for this great entertainment : I fee you command
the houfe in the abfence of your vnkle.

Whet. Yes, I thanke my Aunt ; for though I
be but a daily gueft yet I can be welcome to her at
midnight.

Shak. How fhall we paffe the time ?

Bant. In fome difcourfe.

Whet. But no fuch difcourfe as we had laft, I befeech you.

Bant. Now mafter *Whetftone* you reflect on me.
'Tis true, at our laft meeting fome few words
Then paft my lips, which I could wifh forgot :
I thinke I call'd you Baftard.

Whet. I thinke fo too ; but whats that amongft
friends, for I would faine know which amongft you all
knowes his owne father.

Bant. You are merrie with your friends, good

maſter *By-Blow*, and wee are gueſts here in your
Vnckles houſe, and therefore priviledged.

Enter Miſtreſſe Generous, Mal and Spirits.

Whet.   I preſume you had no more priviledge in
your getting than I.   But tell me gentlemen, is there
any man here amongſt you, that hath a minde to ſee
his father ?

Bant.   Why, who ſhall ſhew him ?

Whet.   Thats all one ; if any man here deſire it, let
him but ſpeake the word, and 'tis ſufficient.

Bant.   Why, I would ſee my father.

Miſtreſſe Gener.   Strike.   *Muſique.*

Enter a Pedant dauncing to the muſique ; the ſtrain
  don, he points at Bantam, & looks full in his
  face.

Whet.   Doe you know him that lookes ſo full in
your face ?

Bant.   Yes well, a pedant in my fathers houſe.
Who beeing young, taught me my A, B, C.

Whet.   In his houſe, that goes for your father you
would ſay : For know one morning, when your mothers
husband rid early to have a *Niſi prius* tryed at *Lancaſter* Syzes, hee crept into his warme place, lay cloſe
by her ſide, and then were you got.   Then come,
your heeles and tayle together, and kneele unto your
own deare father.

All.   Ha, ha, ha.

Bant.   I am abuſed.

Whet.   Why laugh you Gentlemen ?   It may be
more mens caſes than his or mine.

Bant.   To be thus geer'd.

Arth.   Come, take it as a jeſt.
For I preſume 'twas meant no otherwiſe.

Whet.   Would either of you two now ſee his father
in earneſt.

Shak.   Yes, canft thou fhew me mine ?
Mrs. Gen.   Strike.

*Enter a nimble Taylor dauncing, ufing the fame pofture
to Shakftone.*

Whet.   Hee lookes on you, fpeake, doe yon know
him ?
Shak.   Yes, he was my mothers Taylor, I remember
him ever fince I was a childe.
Whet.   Who when hee came to take meafure of her
upper parts had more minde to the lower, whileft the
good man was in the fields hunting, he was at home
whoring.
Then, fince no better comfort can be had,
Come downe, come downe, aske bleffiing of your
      dad.
All.   Ha, ha, ha.
Bont.   This cannot be indur'd.
Arth.   It is plaine Witchcraft.
Nay fince we are all bid unto one feaft,
Lets fare alike, come fhew me mine too.
Mrs. Gener.   Strike.

*Enter Robin with a fwitch and a Currycombe,
he points at Arthur.*

Whet.   He points at you.
Arth.   What then ?
Whet.   You know him.
Arth.   Yes, *Robin* the groome belonging to this
houfe.
Whet.   And never ferved your father ?
Arth.   In's youth I thinke he did.
Whet.   Who when your fuppofed father had bufi-
neffe at the Lord Prefidents Court in Yorke, ftood for
his Atturney at home, & fo it feems you were got by
deputy : what all a mort ? if you will have but a little
patience, ftay & you fhall fee mine too :

And knew I ſhow you him the rather,
To finde who hath the beſt man to his Father.
    Mrs. Strike——

    Muſicke. Enter a Gallant, as before to him.

    Whet. Now Gentlemen make me your Preſident,
learne your duties, and doe as I doe——A bleſſing
Dad.
    Bant. Come, come, let's home, we'l finde ſome
        other time,
When to diſpute of theſe things——
    Whet. Nay Gent. no parting in ſpleene, ſince we
have begun in mirth, let's not end in melancholy; you
ſee there are more By-blowes than beare the name; It
is growne a great kindred in the Kingdome. Come,
come, all friends; Let's into the Cellar and conclude
our Revels in a luſty health.
    Shak. I faine would ſtrike, but cannot.
    Bank. Some ſtrange fate holds me.
    Arth. Here then all anger end,
Let none be mad at what they cannot mend.
                                  Exeunt.

    Mal. Now ſay what's next?
    Mrs. I'th' Mill there lyes
A Souldier yet with unſcratcht eyes,
Summon the Siſter-hood together
For we with all our Spirits will thither;
And ſuch a Catterwalling keepe,
That he in vaine ſhall thinke to ſleepe.
Call *Meg*, and *Doll*, *Tib*, *Nab*, and *Iug*,
Let none appeare without her Pug.
We'l try our utmoſt Art and skill.
To fright the ſtout Knave in the Mill.   *Exeunt.*

ACTVS, V. SCENA I.

Enter Doughty, Miller, Boy in a Cap.

Doughty.

Hou art a brave Boy, the honour of thy Country; thy Statue fhall be fet up in braffe upon the Market Croffe in *Lancafter*, I bleffe the time that I anfwered at the Font for thee : 'Zookes did I ever thinke that a Godfon of mine fhould have fought hand to fift with the Divell !

Mil. He was ever an unhappy Boy Sir, and like enough to grow acquainted with him ; and friends may fall out fometimes.

Dought. Thou art a dogged Sire, and doeft not know the vertue of my Godfonne, my fonne now ; he fhall be thy fonne no longer : he and I will worry all the Witches in *Lancafhire.*

Mil. You were beft take heed though.

Dough. I care not, though we leave not above three untainted women in the Parifh, we'll doe it.

Mil. Doe what you pleafe Sir, there's the Boy ftout enough to juftifie anything he has fayd. Now 'tis out, he fhould be my Sonne ftill by that : Though he was at Death's dore before he would reveale any thing, the damnable jades had fo threatned him, and as foone as ever he had told he mended.

Dought. 'Tis well he did fo, we will fo fwing them in twopenny halters Boy.

Mil. For my part I have no reafon to hinder any

thing that may root them all out; I have tafted enough
of their mifchiefe, witneffe my ufage i' the Mill, which
could be nothing but their Roguerie. One night in
my fleepe they fet me a ftride ftark naked a top of my
Mill, a bitter cold night too; 'twas daylight before I
waked, and I durft never fpeake of it to this houre,
becaufe I thought it impoffible to be beleeved.

Dought. Villanous Hags!

Mil. And all laft Summer, my Wife could not make
a bit of butter.

Dough. It would not come, would it?

Mill. No Sir, we could not make it come, though
fhe and I both together, churn'd almoft our harts out,
and nothing would come, but all ran into thin water-
ifh geere : the Pigges would not drinke it.

Dought. Is 't poffible?

Mil. None but one, and he ran out of his wits upon't,
till we bound his head, and layd him a fleepe, but he
has had a wry mouth ever fince.

Dought. That the Divell fhould put in their hearts
to delight in fuch Villanies! I have fought about
thefe two dayes, and heard of a hundred fuch mif-
chievous tricks, though none mortall, but could not
finde whom to miftruft for a Witch till now this boy,
this happy boy informes me.

Mil. And they fhould neere have been fought for
me if their affrightments and divellifh devices, had not
brought my Boy into fuch a ficknesse; Whereupon indeed I thought good to acquaint your worfhip, and
bring the Boy unto you being his Godfather, and as
you now ftick not to fay his Father.

Dought. After you I thanke you Goffip. But my
Boy thou haft fatisfied me in their names, and thy
knowledge of the women, their turning into fhapes,
their dog-trickes, and their horfe trickes, and their great
Feaft in the Barne (a pox take them with my Surloyne, I fay ftill.) But a little more of thy combat
with the Divell, I prithee; he came to thee like a Boy
thou fayeft, about thine owne bigneffe?

Boy. Yes Sir, and he asked me where I dwelt, and what my name was.

Dough. Ah Rogue !

Boy. But it was in a quarrelſome way; Whereupon I was as ſtout, and ask'd him who made him an examiner ?

Dough. Ah good Boy.

Mil. In that he was my Sonne.

Boy. He told me he would know or beat it out
 of me,
And I told him he ſhould not, and bid him doe his
 worſt ;
And to't we went.

Dough. In that he was my ſonne againe, ha boy ; I ſee him at it now.

Boy. We fought a quarter of an houre, till his ſharpe nailes made my eares bleed.

Dough. O the grand Divell pare 'em.

Boy. I wondred to finde him ſo ſtrong in my hands, ſeeming but of mine owne age and bigneſſe, till I looking downe, perceived he had clubb'd cloven feet like Oxe feet : but his face was as young as mine.

Dovgh. A pox, but by his feet, he may be the Club-footed Horſe-courſers father, for all his young lookes.

Boy. But I was afraid of his feet, and ran from him towards a light that I ſaw, and when I came to it, it was one of the Witches in white upon a Bridge, that ſcar'd me backe againe, and then met me the Boy againe, and he ſtrucke me and layd mee for dead.

Mil. Till I wondring at his ſtay, went out and found him in the Trance ; ſince which time, he has beene haunted and frighted with Goblins, 40. times ; and never durſt tell any thing (as I ſayd) becauſe the Hags had ſo threatned him till in his ſickneſ he revealed it to his mother.

Dough. And ſhe told no body but folkes on't.

VVell Goffip *Gretty*, as thou art a Miller, and a clofe thiefe, now let us keepe it as clofe as we may till we take 'hem, and fee them handfomly hanged o' the way : Ha my little Cuffe-divell, thou art a made man. Come, away with me.   *Exeunt.*

Enter Souldier.

   Soul. Thefe two nights I have flept well and heard
      no noife
Of Cats, or Rats ; moft fure the fellow dream't,
And fcratcht himfelfe in 's fleep. I have traveld'
      Defarts,
Beheld Wolves, Beares, and Lyons : Indeed what
      not ?
Of horrid fhape ; And fhall I be afrayd
Of Cats in mine owne Country ? I can never
Grow fo Moufe-hearted.   It is now a Calme
And no winde ftirring, I can beare no fayle ;
Then beft lye downe to fleepe.   Nay reft by me
Good *Morglay*, my Comrague and Bedfellow
That never fayl'd me yet ; I know thou did'ft not.
If I be wak'd, fee thou be ftirring too ;
Then come a *Gib* as big as *Afcapart*
We'l make him play at Leap-frog.   A brave Soul-
      diers lodging,
The floore my Bed, a Milftone for my Pillow,
The Sayles for Curtaines. So good night.
                        Lyes downe.

Enter Mrs. Generous, Mall, *all the Witches and their
      Spirits(at feverall dores.*)

   Mrs. Is *Nab* come ?
   Mal. Yes.
   Mrs. Where's *Jug* ?
   Mal. On horfeback yet,
Now lighting from her Broome-ftaffe.
   Mrs. But where's *Peg* ?

Mal. Entred the Mill already.

Mrs. Is he faſt ?

Mal. As fenceleſſe as a Dormouſe.

Mrs. Then to work, to work my pretty Lap-
lands

Pinch, here, fcratch,

Doe that within, without we'l keep the watch.

*The Witches retire : the Spirits come about him with a
dreadfull noiſe ; he ſtarts.*

Sold. Am I in Hell, then have among'ſt you
divels ;

This fide, and that fide, what behinde, before ?

Ile keep my face unfcratch'd difpight you all :

What, doe you pinch in private, clawes I feele

But can fee nothing, nothing pinch me thus ?

Have at you then, I and have at you ſtill ;

And ſtil have at you.

Beates them off, followes them in, and Enters againe.

One of them I have pay'd,

In leaping out oth' hole a foot or eare

Or fomething I have light on.   What all gone ?

All quiet ? not a Cat that's heard to mew ?

Nay then Ile try to take another nap,

Though I ſleepe with mine eyes open.   *Exit.*

Enter Mr. *Generous, and Robin.*

Gen. *Robin*, the laſt night that I lodg'd at home

My Wife (if thou remembreſt) lay abroad,

But no words of that.

Rob. You have taught me filence.

Gen. I rofe thus early much before my houre,

To take her in her bed ; 'Tis yet not five :

The Sunne fcarce up.   Thofe horfes take and lead
'em

Into the Stable, fee them rubb'd and dreſt,
We have rid hard. Now in the interim I
Will ſtep and fee how my new Miller fares,
Or whether he ſlept better in his charge,
Than thoſe which did precede him.

    Rob. Sir I ſhall.

    Gen. But one thing more——   *Whiſpers.*

Enter Arthur.

    Arth. Now from the laſt nights witchcraft we are freed,
And I that had not power to cleare my ſelfe
From baſe aſperſion, am at liberty
For vow'd revenge : I cannot be at peace
(The night-ſpell being took of) till I have met
With noble Mr. *Generous* : in whoſe ſearch
The beſt part of this morning I have ſpent,
His wife now I ſufpeĉt.

    Rob. By your leave Sir.

    Arth. O y'are well met, pray tell me how long is't
Since you were firſt my Father ?

    Rob. Be patient I befeech you, what doe you meane Sir ?

    Arth. But that I honour
Thy Maſter, to whoſe goodneſſe I am bound,
And ſtill muſt remaine thankfull, I ſhould prove
Worfe then a Murderer, a meere Paricide
By killing thee my Father.

    Rob. I your Father ? he was a man I alwayes lov'd
And honour'd. He bred me.

    Arth. And you begot me ? oh you us'd me finely laſt night ?

    Gen. Pray what's the matter Sir ?

    Arth. My worthy friend, but that I honour you
As one to whom I am ſo much oblig'd,
This Villaine could not ſtirre a foot from hence

Till periſht by my ſword.

    Gener. How hath he wrong'd you ?
Be of a milder temper I intreat,
Relate what and when done ?

    Arth. You may command me,
If aske me what wrongs, know this Groome pre-
    tends
He hath ſtrumpeted my mother, if when, blaz'd
Laſt night at midnight. If you aske me further
Where, in your owne houſe ; when he pointed
    to me
As had I been his Baſtard.

    Rob. I doe this ? I am a horſe agen if I got you,
Maſter, why Maſter.

    Gen. I know you Mr. *Arthnr*, for a Gentle-
    man
Of faire endowments, a moſt ſolid braine,
And ſetled underſtanding. Why this fellow
Theſe two dayes was ſcarce ſundred from my ſide,
And for the laſt night I am moſt aſſur'd
He ſlept within my Chamber, 12. miles off,
We have nere parted ſince.

    Arth. You tell me wonders.
Since all your words to me are Oracles,
And ſuch as I moſt conſtantly beleeve.
But Sir, ſhall I be bold and plaine withall,
I am ſuſpitious all's not well at home ;
I dare proceed no farther without leave,
Yet there is ſomething lodged within my breaſt
Which I am loath to utter.

    Gen. Keepe it there,
I pray doe a ſeaſon (O my feares)
No doubt ere long my tongue may be the Key
To open that your ſecret : Get you gone ſir
And doe as I commanded.

    Rob. I ſhall Sir. Father quoth he
I ſhould be proud indeed of ſuch a ſonne.   *Exit.*

    Gen. Pleaſe you now walk with me to my Mill, I
    faine would ſee

How my bold Soldier ſpeeds. It is a place
Hath beene much troubled.

Enter Soldier.

Arth. I ſhall waite on you.—See he appeares.
Gen. Good morrow Soldier.
Sold. A bad night I have had
A murrin take your Mill-ſprights.
Gen. Prithee tell me, haſt thou bin frighted then?
Sold. How frighted Sir,
A Doungcart full of Divels coo'd not do't.
But I have bin ſo nipt, and pull'd, and pinch'd,
By a company of Hell-cats.
Arth. Fairies ſure.
Sold. Rather foule fiends, Fairies have no ſuch
clawes;
Yet I have kept my face whole thanks my Semiter,
My truſty Bilbo, but for which I vow,
I had been torne to pieces. But I thinke
I met with ſome of them. One I am ſure
I have ſent limping hence.
Gen. Didſt thou faſten upon any?
Sold. Faſt or looſe, moſt ſure I made them flye,
And skip out of the Port-holes. But the laſt
I made her ſqueake, ſhe had forgot to mew,
I ſpoyl'd her Catter-wawling.
Arth. Let's ſee thy ſword.
Sold. To look on, not to part with from my
hand,
'Tis not the Soldiers cuſtome.
Arth. Sir, I obſerve 'tis bloody towards the
point.
Sold. If all the reſt ſcape ſcot-free, yet I am
ſure
There's one hath payd the reckoning.
Gen. Looke well about,
Perhaps there may be ſeene ſome tract of bloud.
Lookes about and findes the hand.

Sold. What's here? is't poffible Cats fhould have hands
And rings upon their fingers.
  Arth. Moft prodigious.
  Gen. Reach me that hand.
  Sold. There's that of the three I can beft fpare.
  Gen. Amazement upon wonder, can thls be ;
I needs muft know't by moft infallible markes.
Is this the hand once plighted holy vowes,
And this the ring that bound them? doth this laft age
Afford what former never durft beleeve?
O how have I offended thofe high powers?
That my great incredulity fhould merit
A punifhment fo grievous, and to happen
Vnder mine owne roofe, mine own bed, my bofome.
  Arth. Know you the hand Sir?
  Gen. Yes and too well can reade it.
Good Mafter *Arthur* beare me company
Vnto my houfe, in the fociety
Of good men there's great folace.
  Arth. Sir Ile waite on you.
  Gen. And Soldier do not leave me, lock thy Mill,
I have imployment for thee.
  Sold. I fhall fir, I think I have tickled fome of your Tenants at will, that thought to revell here rent-free; the beft is if one of the parties fhall deny the deed, we have their hand to fhew.   *Exeunt.*

A Bed thruft out, Mrs. Gener. in't ; Whetftone,
        Mall Spencer by her.

  Whet. Why Aunt, deere Aunt, honey Aunt, how doe you, how fare you, cheere you, how is't with you! you have bin a lufty woman in your time, but now you look as if you could not doe with all.
  Mrs. Good *Mal* let him not trouble me.
  Mal. Fie Mr. *Whetftone* you keep fuch a noife in

the chamber that your Aunt is deſirous to take a little
reſt and cannot.

 Whet. In my Vncles abſence who but I ſhould
  comfort my Aunt,
Am not I of the Bloud, am not I next of Kin ?
Why Aunt ?

 Mrs. Gen. Good Nephew leave me.

 Whet. The Divell ſhall leave you ere ile forſake
you, Aunt, you know, *Sic* is *So,* and being ſo ſicke doe
you thinke ile leave you, what know I but this Bed
may prove your death-bed, and then I hope you
will remember me, that is, remember me in your
Will.—(*Knocke within.*) Who's that knocks with
ſuch authority. Ten to one my Vncles come to
towne.

 Mrs. Gen. It it be ſo, excuſe my weaknes to him,
ſay I can ſpeake with none.

 Mal. I will, and ſcape him if I can ; by this accident all muſt come out, and here's no ſtay for me—
(*Knock again*) Againe, ſtay you here with your Aunt,
and ile goe let in your Vncle.

 Whet. Doe good *Mal,* and how, and how ſweet
Aunt ?

 Enter Mr. Gener., Mal, Arthur, Soldier, and Robin.

 Gen. Y'are well met here, I am told you oft
  frequent
This houſe as my Wives choyſe companion,
Yet have I ſeldome ſeene you.

 Mal. Pray, by your leave Sir,
Your wife is taken with a ſuddaine qualme
She hath ſent me for a Doctor.

 Gen. But that labour ile ſave you, Soldier take her
  to your charge.
And now where's this ſicke woman.

 Whet. O Vncle you come in good time, my Aunt
is ſo ſuddainly taken as if ſhe were ready to give up
the ſpirit.

Gen. 'Tis almoſt time ſhe did, ſpeake how is't
　　wife
My Nephew tels me you were tooke laſt night
With a ſhrewd ſickneſſe, which this Mayde con-
　ſirmes.

Mrs. Yes ſir, but now deſire no company.
Noyſe troubles me, and I would gladly ſleepe.

Gener. In company there's comfort, prithee wife
Lend me thy hand, and let me feele thy pulſe,
Perhaps ſome Feaver, by their beating I
May gueſſe at thy diſeaſe.

Mrs. Gen. My hand, 'tis there.

Gen. A dangerous ſicknes, and I feare t death,
'Tis oddes you will not ſcape it. Take that backe
And let me prove the t' other, if perhaps
I there can finde more comfort.

Mrs. Gen. I pray excuſe me.

Gener. I muſt not be deny'd,
Sick folkes are peeviſh, and muſt be ore-rul'd, and ſo
　　ſhall you.

Mrs. Gen. Alas I have not ſtrength to lift it up.

Gener. If not thy hand Wife, ſhew me but thy
　　wriſt,
And ſee how this will match it, here's a Teſtate
That cannot be out-fac'd.

Mrs. Gener. I am undone.

Whet. Hath my Aunt bin playing at handee dan-
dee, nay then if the game goe this way I feare ſhe'l
have the worſt hand on't.

Arth. 'Tis now apparant
How all the laſt nights buſineſſe came about,
In this my late ſuſpicion, is conſirm'd.

Gen. My heart hath bled more for thy curſt re-
　　lapſe
Than drops hath iſſu'd from thy wounded arme.
But wherefore ſhould I preach to one paſt hope?
Or where the divell himſelfe claimes right in all,
Seeke the leaſt part or intereſt? Leave your Bed,

Vp, make you ready ; I muſt deliver you
Into the hand of Iuſtice.   O deare friend
It is in vaine to gueſſe at this my griefe
'Tis ſo inundant.   Soldier take away that young
But old in miſchiefe.
And being of theſe *Apoſtat*'s rid ſo well,
Ile ſee my houſe no more be made a Hell.
Away with them.   *Exeunt.*

Enter Bantam, and Shakſton.

Ban. Ile out o' the Country, and as ſoone live in
Lapland as *Lancaſhire* hereafter.
Shak. What for a falſe illuſive apparition ? I hope
the divell is not able to perſwade thee thou art a
Baſtard.
Bant. No, but I am afflicted to thinke that the
divell ſhould have power to put ſuch a trick upon us,
to countenance a Raſcal, that is one.
Shak. I hope *Arthur* has taken a courſe with his
Vncle about him by this time, who would have
thought ſuch a foole as hee could have beene a
Witch ?
Bant. Why doe you thinke there's any wiſe folks
of the quality ; Can any but fooles be drawne into a
Covenant with the greateſt enemy of mankind ? yet I
cannot thinke that *Whetſtone* is the Witch ? The young
Queane that was at the Wedding was i' th houſe yee
know.

Enter Lawrence and Parnell, in their firſt Habits.

Shak. See *Lawrence* and *Parnell* civilly accorded
againe it ſeems, and accoutred as they were wont to be
when they had their wits.
Law. Bleſt be the houre I ſay may hunny, may
ſweet *Pall*, that Ay's becom'd thaine agone, and thou's

becom'd maine agone, and may this ea kiffe ma us tway become both eane for ever and a day.

Parn. Yie marry *Lall*, and thus fhadden it be, there is nought getten by fawing out, we mun faw in or we get nought.

Bant. The world's well mended here; we cannot but rejoyce to fee this, *Lawrence.*

Lawr. And you been welcome to it Gentle-men.

Parn. And we been glad we han it for you.

Shak. And I proteft I am glad to fee it.

Parn. And thus fhan yeou fee't till our deeing houre.
Ween eon leove now for a laife time, the Dewle fhonot ha the poore to put us to peeces agone.

Bant. Why now all's right and ftraight and as it fhould be.

Lawr. Yie marry that is it, the good houre be bleffed for it, that put the wit into may head, to have a miftruft of that peftilent Codpeece-point, that the witched worch *Mal Spencer* go me, ah woe worth her, that were it that made aw fo nought.

Bant. & Shak. Is 't poffible?

Parn. Yie marry it were an Inchauntment, and about an houre fince it come intill our hearts to doe, what yeou thinke, and we did it.

Bant. What *Parnell*?

Parn. Marry we take the point, and we caften the point into the fire, and the point fpitter'd and fpatter'd in the fire, like an it were (love bleffe us) a laive thing in the faire; and it hopet and skippet, and riggled, and frisket in the faire, and crept about laike a worme in the faire, that it were warke enough for us both with all the Chimney tooles to keepe it into the faire, and it ftinket in the faire, worfen than ony brim-ftone in the faire.

Bant. This is wonderfull as all the reft.

Lawr. It wolld ha fcar'd ony that hadden their wits till a feen't, and we werne mad eont it were deone.

Parn. And this were not above an houre fine, and you cannot devaife how we han lov'd t' on t' other by now, yeou woud een bliffe your feln to fee't.

Lawr. Yie an han pit on our working geere, to fwinke and ferve our Mafter and Maiftreffe like intill painfull fervants agone, as we fhudden.

Bant. 'Tis wondrous well.

Shak. And are they well agen?

Parn. Yie and weel's laike heane bliffe them, they are awas weel becom'd as none ill had ever beene aneaft 'hem; Lo ye, lo ye, as they come.

Enter Seely, Ioane, Gregory, and Win.

Greg. Sir, if a contrite heart ftrucke through with fence
Of it's fharpe errors, bleeding with remorfe
The blacke polluted ftaine it had conceived
Of foule unnaturall difobedience
May yet by your faire mercy finde Remiffion;
You fhall upraife a Sonne out o' the gulph
Of horrour and defpaire, unto a bliffe
That fhall for ever crowne your goodneffe, and
Inftructive in my after life to ferve you,
In all the duties that befit a fonne.

Seel. Enough, enough, good boy, 'tis moft appa-
rant
We all have had our errors, and as plainly
It now appeare, our judgments, yea our reafon
Was poyfon'd by fome violent infection,
Quite contrary to Nature.

Bant. This founds well.

Seely. I feare it was by Witchcraft: for I now
(Bleft be the power that wrought the happy means
Of my delivery) remember that
Some 3. months fince I croft a wayward woman
(One that I now fufpect) for bearing with
A moft unfeemly difobedience,
In an untoward ill-bred fonne of hers,

When with an ill looke and an hollow voyce
She mutter'd out thefe words.　Perhaps ere long
Thy felfe fhalt be obedient to thy fonne.
She has play'd her pranke it feemes.

Greg.　Sir I have heard, that Witches apprehended
under hands of lawfull authority, doe loofe their
power ;
And all their fpells are inftantly diffolv'd.

Seel.　If it be fo, then at this happy houre,
The Witch is tane that over us had power.

Joane.　Enough Childe, thou art mine and all
is well.

Win.　Long may you live the well-fpring of my
　　bliffe,
And may my duty and my fruitfull Prayers,
Draw a perpetuall ftreame of bleffings from you.

Seely.　Gentlemen welcome to my beft friends
　　houfe,
You know the unhappy caufe that drew me hether.

Bant.　And cannot but rejoyce to fee the remedy
fo neere at hand.

Enter Doughty, Miller, and boy.

Dought.　Come Goffip, come Boy——Gentlemen
you are come to the braveft difcovery——Mr. *Seely*
and the reft, how is't with you ? you look reafonable
well me thinkes.

Seely.　Sir, we doe find that we have reafon enough
to thank you for your Neighbourly and pious care of
us.

Doughty.　Is all fo well with you already ? goe to,
will you know a reafon for't Gentlemen : I have catcht
a whole Kennel of Witches.　It feemes their Witch is
one of 'hem, and fo they are difcharm'd, they are all
in Officers hands, and they will touch here with two
or three of them for a little private parley, before they
goe to the Iuftices.　Mafter *Generous* is comming

hither too, with a ſupply that you dreame not of, and your Nephew *Arthur.*

Bant.   You are beholden Sir to Maſter *Generous* in behalfe of your Nephew for ſaving his land from forfeiture in time of your diſtraction.

Seely.   I will acknowledge it moſt thankfully.

Shak.   See he comes.

Enter Mr. Generous, Mrs. Generous, Arthur, Whet-
ſtone, Mal, Soldier, and Robin.

Seel.   O Mr. *Generous,* the noble favour you have ſhew'd

My Nephew for ever bindes me to you.

Gener.   I pittyed then your miſery, and now
Have nothing left but to bewayle mine owne
In this unhappy woman.

Seel.   Good Miſtreſſe *Generous――*

Arth.   Make a full ſtop there Sir, ſides, ſides, make
ſides,

You know her not as I doe, ſtand aloofe there Miſ-treſſe with your darling Witch, your Nephew too if you pleaſe, becauſe though he be no witch, he is a wel-willer to the infernal ſcience.

Gener.   I utterly diſcard him in her blood
And all the good that I intended him
I will conferre upon this vertuous Gentleman.

Whet.   Well Sir, though you be no Vnckle, yet mine Aunt's mine Aunt, and ſhall be to her dying day.

Doug.   And that will be about a day after next Sizes I take it.

Enter Witches, Conſtable, and Officers.

O here comes more o' your Naunts, Naunt *Dickenſon* & Naunt *Hargrave,* ods fiſh and your Granny *John-ſon* too ; we want but a good fire to entertaine 'em.

Arth.   See how they lay their heads together?

Witches charme together.

Gill. No fuccour.

Maud. No reliéfe.

Peg. No comfort!

All. *Mawfy*, my *Mawfy*, gentle *Mawfy* come.

Maud. Come my fweet *Puckling.*

Peg. My *Mamilion.*

Arth. What doe they fay?

Bant. They call their Spirits I thinke.

Dough. Now a fhame take you for a fardell of fooles, have you knowne fo many of the Divels tricks, and can be ignorant of that common feate of the old Iugler; that is, to leave you all to the Law, when you are once feized on by the tallons of Authority? Ile undertake this little *Demigorgon* Conftable with thefe Common-wealth Characters upon his ftaffe here, is able in fpite of all your bugs-words, to ftave off the grand Divell for doing any of you good till you come to his Kingdome to him, and there take what you can finde.

Arth. But Gentlemen, fhall we try if we can by examination get from them fomething that may abbreviate the caufe unto the wifer in Commiffion for the peace before wee carry them before 'em.

Gen. & Seel. Let it be fo.

Dought. Well fay, ftand out Boy, ftand out Miller, ftand out *Robin*, ftand out Soldier, and lay your accufation upon 'em.

Bant. Speake Boy doe you know thefe Creatures, women I dare not call 'em?

Boy. Yes Sir, and faw them all in the Barne together, and many more at their Feaft and Witchery.

Rob. And fo did I, by a Divellifh token, I was rid thither, though I rid home againe as faft without fwitch or fpur.

Mill. I was ill handled by them in the Mill.

Sold. And I fliced off a Cats foot there, that is fince a hand, who ever wants it.

Seel. How I and all my family have fuffered you all know.

Lawr. And how I were betwitcht my *Pall.* here knowes.

Parn. Yie *Lall,* and the Witch I knaw, an I prayen yeou goe me but leave to ſcrat her well-favorely.

Bant. Hold *Parnell.*

Parn. Yeou can blame no honeſt woman, I trow, to ſcrat for the thing ſhe leoves.

*Mal.*Ha, ha, ha.

Dough. Doe you laugh Gentlewoman ? what ſay you to all theſe matters ?

Mrs. Gen. I will ſay nothing, but what you know
                  you know,
And as the law ſhall finde me let it take me.

Gil. And ſo ſay I.

Mawd. And I.

Mal. And I, other confeſſion you get none from us.

Arth. What ſay you Granny ?

Peg. *Mamilion,* ho *Mamilion, Mamilion.*

Arth. Who's that you call ?

Peg. My friend, my Sweet-heart, my *Mamilion.*

Witches. You are not mad ?

Dought. Ah ha, that's her Divell, her *Incubus* I warrant ; take her off from the reſt they'l hurt her. Come hether poore old woman. Ile dandle a Witch a little, thou wilt ſpeake, and tell the truth, and ſhalt have favour doubt not. Say art not thou a Witch ?

They ſtorme.

Peg. 'Tis folly to diſſemble yie ſir, I am one.

Dought. And that *Mamilion* which thou call'ſt upon
Is thy familiar Divell is't not ? Nay prithee ſpeake.

Peg. Yes Sir.

Dough. That's a good woman, how long haſt had's acquaintance, ha ?

Peg. A matter of ſixe yeares Sir.

Dough. A pretty matter. What was he like a man ?

Peg.   Yes when I pleas'd.

Dought.   And then he lay with thee, did he not fometimes ?

Peg.   Tis folly to diffemble; twice a Weeke he never fail'd me.

Dough.   Humh—and how ? and how a little ? was he a good Bedfellow ?

Peg.   Tis folly to fpeake worfe of him than he is.

Dough.   I truft me is't.   Give the Divell his due.

Peg.   He pleas'd me well Sir, like a proper man.

Dought.   There was fweet coupling.

Peg.   Onely his flefh felt cold.

Arth.   He wanted his great fires about him that he has at home.

Dough.   Peace, and did he weare good clothes ?

Peg.   Gentleman like, but blacke blacke points and all.

Dought.   I, very like his points were blacke enough.   But come we'l trifle w' yee no longer.   Now fhall you all to the Iuftices, and let them take order with you till the Sizes, and then let Law take his courfe, and *Vivat Rex.*   Mr. *Generous* I am forry for your caufe of forrow, we fhall not have your company ?

Gener.   No fir, my Prayers for her foules recovery
Shall not be wanting to her, but mine eyes
Muft never fee her more.

Rob.   *Mal,* adiew fweet *Mal,* ride your next journey with the company you have there.

Mal.   Well Rogue I may live to ride in a Coach before I come to the Gallowes yet.

Rob.   And Mrs. the horfe that ftayes for you rides better with a Halter than your gingling bridle.

> *Exeunt Gen. &> Robin.*

Dought.   Mr. *Seely* I rejoyce for your families attonement.

Seel.   And I praife heaven for you that were the means to it.

Dough. On afore Drovers with your untoward Cattell. *Exeunt feverally.*

Bant. Why doe not you follow Mr. *By-blow.* I thanke your Aunt for the tricke fhe would have father'd us withall.

Whot. Well Sir, mine Aunt's mine Aunt, and for that trick I will not leave her till I fee her doe a worfe.

Baut. Y'are a kinde Kinfman. *Exeunt.*

Flourifh.

FINIS.

Song. II. Act.

Come Mawſy, *come* Puckling,
And come my ſweet Suckling,
  My pretty Mamillion, *my Ioy,*
Fall each to his Duggv,
While kindly we huggie,
  As tender as Nurſe over Boy.
    Then suck our blouds freely, and with it be jolly,
    While merrily we ſing, hey Trolly Lolly.

We'l dandle and clip yee,
We'l ſtroke yee, and leape yee,
  And all that we have is your due;
The feates you doe for us,
And thoſe which you ſlore us
  Withall, tyes us onely to you.
    Then suck our blouds freely, and with it be jolly,
    While merrily we ſing, hey Trolly Loſly.

THE EPILOGVE.

Ow while the Witches muſt expeƈt their due
By lawfull Iuſtice, we appeale to you
For favourable cenſure; what their crime
May bring upon 'em, ripenes yet of time
Has not reveal'd.   Perhaps great Mercy may
After juſt condemnation give them day
Of longer life.   We repreſent as much
As they have done, before Lawes hand did touch
Vpon their guilt; But dare not hold it fit,
That we for Iuſtices and Iudges fit,
And perſonate their grave wiſedomes on the Stage
Whom we are bound to honour; No, the Age
Allowes it not.   Therefore unto the Lawes
We can but bring the Witches and their cauſe,
And there we leave 'em, as their Divels did,
Should we goe further with 'em ?   Wit forbid;
What of their ſtorie, further ſhall enſue,
We muſt referre to time, our ſelves to you.

Londons Ius Honorarium.

Expreſt in ſundry Triumphs, pagiants, and ſhews :
At the Initiation or Entrance of the Right Honourable
George Whitmore, into the Maioralty of the famous and
farre renouned City of London..

All the charge and expence of the laborious pro-
iects, and obiects both by Water and Land, being the
ſole vndertaking of the Right Worſhipfull, the
ſociety of the Habburdaſhers.

Redeunt ſpeEtacula.

Printed at *London* by N ICHOLAS OKES. 1631.

To the Right Honourable, *George*
Whitmore, Lord Maior of this renowned
Metrapolis, London.

Right Honorable,

I T was the fpeech of a Learned and
grave Philofopher the Tutor and
Counfeler to the Emperour *Gra-*
tianus, Pulcrius multo parari,
quam creari nobilem. More faire and
famous it is to be made, then to be borne
Noble, For that Honour is to be moft
Honored, which is purchaft by merrit, not
crept into by defcent: For you; whofe
goodneffe, hath made you thus great, I
make my affectionate prefentment of this annuall Celebration, concerning which : (without flattery be it fpoken) there is nothing
fo much as mentioned (much lefs enforced)
in this your *Ius honorarium,* which rather
commeth not fhort, then any way exceedeth
the hope and expectation which is now
vpon you, and therefore worthily was your

fo free Election, (without either emulation,
or competitorfhip conferd vpon you, fince
of you it may be vndeniably fpoken : that
none euer in your place was more fufficient
or able, any caufe whatfoeuer fhall be
brought before you, more truly to difcerne ;
being apprehended more aduifedly to difpofe, being digefted, more maturely to
defpatch.   After this fhort tender of my
feruice vnto you, I humbly take my leaue,
with this fentence borrowed from *Seneca :*
Decet timeri Magiftratum, at plus diligi.

Your Lordfhips in all
obferuance,

Thomas Heywood.

To the Right Worſhipfull *Samuell*
Cranmer, and *Henry Pratt,* the two
Sheriffs of the Honourable Citty of
London, Lately Elected.

Right Worſhipfull,

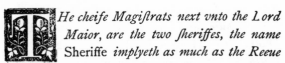

He cheife Magiſtrats next vnto the Lord
Maior, are the two ſheriffes, the name
Sheriffe *implyeth as much as the Reeue*
and Gouernour of a Sheire, for Reeue : *is Graue*
Count *or* Earle *(for ſo ſaith Maſter* Verſtigan :)
and theſe, were of like authority with the Cenſors,
who were reputed in the prime and beſt ranke
amongſt the Magiſtrates of Rome ? *They were*
ſo cal'd a Ceſſendo, *of ceaſing, for they ſet a rate*
vpon euery mans eſtate : regiſtring their names,
and placing them in a fit century : A ſecond part
of their Office conſiſted in the reforming of maners,
as hauing power to inquire into euery mans life
and carriage. The Embleame of which Autho-
rity was their Tirgula cenſoria *borne before them :*
they are (by others) reſembled to the Tribunes *of*

the people, and thefe are cal'd Sacro Sancti, *whofe perfons might not be iniured, nor their names any way fcandaliz'd, for whofoeuer was proued to be a delinquent in either, was held to be* Homo facer; *an excommunicated perfon, and hee that flew him was not liable vnto any Iudgement: their Houfes ftand open continually, not onely for Hofpitality, but for a Sanctuary to all fuch as were diftreft: neither was it lawfull for them to be abfent from the Colledge one whole day together, during their Yeare. Thus you fee how neere the Dignities of this Citty, come neere to thefe in* Rome, *when it was moft flourifhing. The firft* Sheriffes *that bore the name and office in this* Citty, *were* Peter Duke, *and* Thomas Neale, *Anno* 1209. *The nouiffimi, now in prefent* Samuell Cranmer *and* Henry Pratt. *Anno* 1631. *To whom I direct this fhort Remembrance.*

Your Worfhips euer

Attendant,

Thomas Heywood.

LONDONS

Ius Honorarium.

Hen *Rome* was erected: at the firſt eſta-
bliſhing of a common weale, *Romulus* the
founder of it, inſtituted a prime officer to
gouerne the Citty, who was cald *præfectus
vrbis, i.e.* the præfect of the City, whoſe vncontroul-
able authority, had power, not onely to examine, but
to determine, all cauſes & controuerſies, & to ſit vpon,
and cenſure all delinquents, whether their offences
were capitall or criminall : *Intra centiſſimum lapidem,*
within an hundred miles of the City, in proceſſe of
time the *Tarquins* being expeld, & the prime ſoueraignty
remaining in the conſuls. They (by reaſon of their forraigne imployments) hauing no leaſure to adminiſter
Iuſtice at home, created two cheife officers, the one
they cald *prætor vrbanus,* or *Maior,* the other *peregri-
nus* : The firſt had his iuriſdiction, in and ouer the
Citty, the other excerciſed his authority meerely vpon
ſtrangers.

The name *Prætor* is deriued from *Præfsendo* or
Præeundo, from priority of place, which as a learned
Roman Author writs, had abſolute power ouer all

publique aud priuat affaires, to make new Lawes, and abolifh old, without controwle, or contradiction : His authority growing to that height, that whatfoeuer he decreed or cenfured in publique, was cald *Ius Honorarium*, the firft on whome this dignity was conferd in *Rome*, was *fpur* : *furius Camillus*, the fonne of *Marcus* : And the firft *Prætor* or Lord Maior appointed to the Gouernment of the Honorable Citty of *London*, was *Henry Fitz Allwin*, aduaunced to that Dignity, by King *Iohn*, *Anno.* 1210. fo much for the Honor and Antiquity of the name and place, I proceede to the fhowes.

Vpon the water.

Are two craggy Rockes, plac'd directly oppofit, of that diftance that the Barges may paffe betwixt them : thefe are full of monfters, as Serpents, Snakes, Dragons, &c. fome fpitting Fier, others vomiting water, in the bafes thereof, nothing to be feene, but the fad relicks of fhipwracke in broken Barkes and fplit Veffels, &c. The one is cald *Silla*, the other *Charibdis*, which is fcituate directly againft *Meffana* ; *Scilla* againft *Rhegium* : and what foever fhippe that paffeth thefe Seas, it it keepe not the middle Channell, it is either wrackt upon the one, or deuoured by the other ; *Medio tutifsimus ibit.* Vpon thefe Rocks are placed the *Syrens*, excellent both in voyce and Inftrument : They are three in number, *Telfipio, Iligi, Aglaofi* ; or as others will have them called, *Parthenope*, skilfull in muficke ; *Leucofia*, upon the winde Inftrument ; *Ligni*, upon the Harpe. The morrall intended by the Poets, that whofoever fhall lend an attentive eare to their muficke, is in great danger to perifh ; but he that can warily avoyd it by ftopping his eares againft their inchantment, fhall not onely fecure themfelves, but bee their ruine : this was made good in *Vliffes* the fpeaker, who by his wifedome and pollicy not onely preſerved himſelfe and his people, but was the cauſe that they from the rocks caſt themſelves headlong into the Sea. In him is perſonated a wiſe and diſcreete Magiſtrate.

Vliſſes *his speech.*

BEhold great Magiſtrate, on either hand
    Sands, ſhelves, and Syrtes, and upon them ſtand
Two dangerous rocks, your ſafety to ingage,
Boaſting of nought ſave ſhipwrake ſpoyle and ſtrage.
This Sylla, *that* Charibdis, *(dangerous both)*
Plac't in the way you rowe to take your oath.

   Yet though a thouſand monſters yawne and gape
To ingurdge and ſwallow you, ther's way to ſcape ;
Vliſſes *by his wiſedome found it, ſteare*
You by his Compaſſe, and the way lyes cleare,
Will you know how ? *looke upward then ; and ſayle*
By the ſigne Libra, *that Celeſtiall ſcale,*
In which (ſome write) the Sunne at his creation
Firſt ſhone ; and is to theſe times a relation
Of Divine Juſtice : It in juſtice ſhind,
Doe you ſo (Lora) and be like it divind.

   Keepe the even Channell, and be neither ſwayde,
To the right hand nor left, and ſo evade
Malicious envie (never out of aĉtion,)
Smooth viſadgd flattery, and blacke mouthd detraĉtion,
Sedition, whiſprings, murmuring, private hate,
All ambuſhing, the godlike Magiſtrate.

   About theſe rockes and quickſands Syrens *haunt,*
One ſinges connivence, th' other would inchaunt
With partiall ſentence ; and a third aſcribes,
In pleaſing tunes, a right to gifts and bribes ;
Sweetning the eare, and every other ſence,
That place, and office, may with theſe diſpence.
But though their tones be ſweete, and ſhrill their
   notes,

They come from foule brefts, and impoftum'd throats,
Sea monfters they be ftiled, but much (nay more,
'Tis to be doubted,) they frequent the fhoare.
　　Yet like Vliffes, *doe but ftop your eare*
To their inchantments, with an heart fincere;
They fayling to indanger your eftate,
Will from the rocks themfelves precipitate.
　　Proceede then in your bleft Inauguration,
And celebrate this Annual Ovation;
Whilft you nor this way, nor to that way leane,
But fhunne th' extreames, to keepe the golden meane.
This glorious City, Europs *chiefeft minion,*
Moft happy in fo great a Kings dominion:
Into whofe charge this day doth you inveft,
Shall her in you, and you in her make bleft.

The firft fhow by land.

THe firft fhow by Land, (prefented in *Pauls*
Church yard, is a greene and pleafant Hill,
adorned with all the Flowers of the fpring, upon
which is erected a faire and flourifhing tree, furnifhed
with variety of faire and pleafant fruite, under which
tree, and in the moft eminent place of the Hill, fitteth
a woman of beautiful afpect, apparrelled like Summer:
Her motto, *Civitas bene Gubernata. i.* a Citty well
governed. Her Attendants (or rather Affociats) are
three Damfels habited according to their qualitie, and
reprefenting the three Theologicall vertues, *Faith*,
Hope, and *Charity*: Amongft the leaves and fruits of
this Tree, are inferted diverfe labels with feverall
fentences expreffing the caufes which make Cities to
flourifh and profper: As, *The feare of God, Religious*
zeale, a Wife Magiftrate, Obedience to rulers, Vnity,
Plaine and faithfull dealing, with others of the like
nature. At the foot of the Hill fitteth old Time, and

by him his daughter Truth, with this infcription ; *Veritas
eſt Temporis Filia, i.* Truth is the Daughter of Time ;
which Time fpeaketh as followeth.

Tymes ſpeech.

Non nova funt fem-
per, & quod fuit Ante
relictum eft fit que
quod haud fuerat, &c.

IF Time (*ſome ſay*) *have bin here
oft in view*
Yet not the ſame, old Time *is each day
new,*
*Who doth the future lockt up houres in-
large,*
To welcome you to this great Cities charge.
Time, *who hath brought you hither* (*grave and great*)
To inaugure you, in your Prætorium feate :
Thus much with griefe doth of him felfe profeſſe
Nothing's more precious, and eſteemed leſſe.
Yet you have made great uſe of me, to aſpire
This eminence, by defert, when in full quire
Avees and Acclamations, with loud voyce,
Meete you on all ſides, and with Time *re'oyce.*
   This Hill, that Nimph apparreld like the Spring,
Theſe Graces that attend her, (*every thing*)
As fruitful trees, greene plants, flowers of choiſe ſmell,
All Emblems of a City governd well ;
Which muſt be now your charge. The Labels here
*Mixt with the leaves will ſhew what fruit they
      beare :*
The feare *of* God, *a* Magiftrate difcreete,
Iuſtice *and* Equity : *when with theſe meete,*
Obedience unto Rulers, Vnity,
Plaine *and* juft dealing, Zeale, *and* Induftry :
In ſuch bleſt ſymptoms where theſe ſhall agree,
Cities, ſhall like perpetuall Summers bee.
   You are now Generall, doe but bravely lead,
And (*doubtleſſe*) *all will march, as you ſhall tread :*
You are the Captaine, doe but bravely ſtand
To oppoſe vice, ſee, all this goodly band
Now in their City Liveries will apply
Themſelves to follow, where your Colours fly.
You are the chiefe, defend my daughter Truth,

And then both Health and Poverty, Age and Youth,
Will follow this your Standard, to oppofe
Errour, Sedition, Hate, (the common foes.)
 But pardon Time *(grave Lord) who fpeaks to thee,*
 As well what thou now art, as ought to be.

Then Time maketh a paufe, and taking up a leave-
leffe & withered branch, thus proceedeth.

 See you this withered branch, by Time *o're growne*
 A Cities Symbole, ruind, and trod downe.
 A Tree that bare bad fruit ; Diffimulation,
Pride, Malice, Envy, Atheifme, Supplantation,
Ill Government, Prophannes, Fraud, Oppreffion,
Neglect of vertue, Freedome to tranfgreffion,
Obedience, *here with power did difagree,*
All which faire London *be ftill farre from thee.*

The fecond fhow by Land, is prefented in the upper part of Cheapfide,
which is a Chariot; The two beafts that are placed
before it, are a Lyon paffant, and a white Vnicorne in
the fame pofture, on whofe backs are feated two
Ladies, the one reprefenting *Iuftice* upon the Lyon,
the other *Mercy* upon the Vnicorne. The motto
which *Iuftice* beareth, is *Rebelles protero* ; the infcription which *Mercy* carrieth, is *Imbelles protego* : Herein
is intimated, that by thefe types and fymboles of
Honour (reprefented in thefe noble beafts belonging
to his Majeftie) all other inferiour magiftracies and
governments either in Common weales, or private
Societies, receive both being and fupportance.

The prime Lady feated in the firft and moft eminent place of the Chariot, reprefenteth *London*, behinde whom, and on either fide, diverfe others of the
chiefe Cities of the Kingdome take place : As *Weft-*
minfter, Yorke, Briftoll, Oxford, Lincolne, Exeter, &c.
All thefe are to be diftnguifhed by their feverall
Efcutchons ; to them *London* being Speaker, directeth
he firft part of her fpeech as followeth.

London the fpeaker. *You noble Cities of this generous Ifle,*
May thefe my two each Ladies ever
fmile.

(Iuftice, and mercy) on you. You we know
Are come to grace this our triumphant fhow.
And of your curtefy, the hand to kiſte
Of London, this faire lands Metropolis.

Why fifter Cittyes fit you thus amazd?
Iſt to behold above you, windows glaf'd
With Diamonds 'fted of glaffe? Starres hither fent,
This day to deck our lower Firmament?

Is it to fee my numerous Children round
Incompaffe me? So that no place is found.
In all my large ftreets empty? My yffue fpred
In number more then ftones whereon they tread.
To fee my Temples, Houfes, even all places,
With people covered, as if Tyl'd with faces?

Will you know whence proceedes this faire increafe,
This ioy? the fruits of a continued peace,
The way to thrive; to profper in each calling,
The weake, and fhrinking ftates, to keepe from falling,

Serve and obey: the Motto of the Worfhp. Company of the Hab-berd.
Behold; my motto fhall all this dif-
play,
Reade and obferve it well: Serve
and obay.

Obedience *though it humbly doth begin,*
It foone augments unto a Magazin
Of plenty, in all Cities 'tis the grownd,
And doth like harmony in muficke found:
Nations and Common weales, by it alone
Flourifh: It incorporates, many into one,
And makes vnanimous peace content and joy,
Which pride, doth ftill Infidiate to deftroy.

And you grave Lord, on whom right honour calls.
Both borne and bred i' th circuit of my wals,
By vertue and example, have made plaine,
How others may like eminence attaine.

Perfift in this bleft concord, may we long,
That Citties to this City may ftill throng,

To view my annuall tryumphs, and fo grace,
Thofe honored Pretors *that fupply this place.*

Next after the Chariot, are borne the two rocks,
Sylla and *Caribdis*, which before were prefented upon
the water : upon the top of the one ftands a Sea Lyon
vpon the other a Meare-maide or *Sea-Nimphe*, the
Sirens and *Monfters*, beeing in continuall agitation
and motion, fome breathing fire, others fpowting
water, I fhall not neede to fpend much time in the
Defcription of them, the worke being fufficiently able
to Commend it felfe.

The third fhew by Land Prefented neere vnto the
great Crofle in Cheape-fide, beareth the title of the
Palace of *Honour* : A faire and curious ftructure archt
and Tarreft aboue, on the Top of which ftandeth
Honour, a Glorious prefens, and richtly habited, fhee
in her fpeech directed to the right Honorable : the
Lord Maior, difcouers all the true and direct wayes
.o attaine vnto her as, firft :

A King : Eyther by fucceffion or Election.

A Souldier, by valour and martiall Difcipline.

A Churchman by Learning and degrees in fcooles.

A Statesman by Trauell and Language, &c.

A Lord Maior by Commerce and Trafficke both by Sea
    and Land, by the Inriching of the Kingdome,
    and Honour of our Nation.

The Palace of Honour is thus governed
            Induftry *Controwler*, his Word
                        Negotior
            Charity *Steward*, the Word
                        Miferior.
            Liberality *Trefurer*, the Word
                        Largior.

Innocence and ⎱ *Henchmen*, the words,
Deuotion ⎰

            Patior : *Precor.*

And fo of the reft, and according to this Pallace of
Honour is facioned not onely the management of the

whole *Citty* in generall : but the Houfe and Family of the *Lord Maior* in particular.

Before in the Front of this pallace is feated Saint *Katherin*, the Lady and Patroneffe of this Worfhipfull Society of whom I will giue you this fhort Chara&ter, the name it felfe imports in the Originall, *Omnis ruina*, which (as fome interpret it) is as much as to fay, the fall and ruin of all the workes of the Diuell : Others deriue the word from *Catena*, a Chaine wherein all cheife Vertues and Graces are concatinated and link't together, fo much for her name.

For her birth, fhee was lineally defcended from the Roman Emperours, the daughter of *Coflus* the fonne of *Conflantine* which *Coflus* was Crowned King of *Armenia*, for *Conflantine* hauing conquered that King dome, grew Inamored of the Kings Daughter by whom he had Iffue, this *Coflus* who after fucceeded his Grand Father.

Conflantine after the death of his firft Wife made an expedition from *Roome*, and hauing Conquered this Kingdome of Great Britaine : he tooke to his Second Wife *Helena*, which *Helena* was fhe that found the Croffe vpon which the Sauiour of the World was Cru-cified, &c.

Coflus Dying whilft *Katherine* was yet young, and fhee being all that Time liuing in *Famogofta*, (a cheife *City*) becaufe fhee was there Proclaimed and Crowned was called *Queene* of *Famogofta*, fhe liued and dyed a Virgin and a *Martyr* vnder the Tiranny of *Maxentius*, whofe Empreffe, with many other great and eminent perfons fhe had before conuerted to the Faith. So much for her chara&ter. Her fpeech to the Lord Maior as followeth.

I Katherine, *long fince Sainted for true piety,*
  The Lady patroneffe of this Society,
A queene, a Virgin, and a Martir : All
My Attributes : Inuite you to this Hall

Cald Honours pallace : nor is this my Wheele,
Blind Fortunes Embleame, ſhe that makes to reele ;
Kingdomes and Common weales, all turning round,
Some to aduance, and others to Confound :
  Mine is the Wheele of Faith, (*all wayes in motion*)
Stedfaſt in Hope, *and Conſtant in Deuotion.*
It imitates the Spheres ſwift agitation,
Orbicularly, ſtill mouing to Saluation :
That's to the Primus motor *: from whom Flowes,*
All Goodneſſe, Vertue : There, true Honour growes.
  Which : If you will attaine t' muſt be your care,
(*Graue Magiſtrate*) *Inſtated as you are,*
To keepe this Curoular action, in your charge,
To Curbe the' opreſſor, the oppreſt to inlarge ;
To be the Widdowes Husband, th' Orphants Father,
The blindmans eye, the lame mans foot : ſo gather
A treaſure beyond valew, by your place ;
(*More then Earths Honour,*) *trew Cœleſtiall grace,*
Ayme firſt at that : what other Honors be,
Honour Her ſelfe can beſt Inſtruct thats ſhee.

At that word ſhee poynteth vpward to a Glorious
prefens which perſonates *Honor* in the top of the pallace, who thus fecondeth *Saint Katherens Speech.*

Honours Speech.

The way to me though not debard,
Yet it is dificult and hard.
If Kings arrive to my profection
Tis by Succeſſion, or Election
When Fortitude *doth Action grace,*
The Souldier then with me takes place
When Stooddy, Knowledge and degree
Makes Scollers *Eminent heere with mee ;*
They 'are liſted with the Honored : and
The Trauilar, *when many a land*

He hath 'peirſt for language, and much knowes
A great reſpeﬅed ﬅateſman growes.
  So you, and ſuch as you (Graue Lord)
Who weare this Scarlet, vſe that Sword
Collar, and Cap of Maintenance.
Theſe are no things, that come by chance
Or got by ﬂeeping but auerſe
From theſe I am gain'd : by care, Commerce,
The hazarding of Goods, and men
To Pyrats Rocks, ﬁhelues, Tempeﬅ, when ?
You through a Wilderneſſe of Seas,
Dangers of wrack, Surpriſe, Deſeaſe
Make new deſcoueryes, for a laﬅing ﬅory
Of this our Kingdomes fame and Nations glory
Thus is that Collar, and your Scarlet worne,
And for ſuch cauſe, the Sworde before you Borne.
They are the emblems of your Power, and heere
Though curb'd within the Limmet of one yeare,
Yet manadge as they ought by your Indeuour,
Shall make your name (as now) Honored for euer.
Vnto which Pallace of peace, reﬅ and bliſſe,
Supply of all things, where nought wanting is
Would theſe that ﬁhall ſucceede you know the way ?
Tis plaine, God, the King Serue *and* Obay.

I cannot heare forget that in the preſentment of my
papers to the Maﬆer, Wardens, & Committies of this
Right Worſhipfull Company of the Haberdaſhers (at
whoſe ſole expence and charges all the publick Triumphes of this dayes Solemnity both by water and land,
were Celebrated) nothing here deuiſed or expreſſed was
any way forraigne vnto them, but of all theſe my con-
ceptions, they were as able to Iudge, as ready to Heare,
and to direct as well as to Cenſure ; nether was there
any dificulty which needed a comment, but as ſoone
known as ſhowne, and apprehended as read : which
makes me now confident of the beﬆ ranke of the
Cittiſens : That as to the Honour and ﬆrength both of
the Citty and Kingdome in generall, they excerciſe

Armes in publicke, fo to the benefit of their Iudge-
ments, and inriching of their knowledge, they neglect
not the ftuddy of arts, and practife of literature in
priuate, fo that of them it may be truly faid they are,
Tam Mercurio quam Marte periti : I proceede now to
the laft Speech at night in which *Vliffes* at the taking
leaue of his Lordfhip at his Gate, vfeth this fhort
Commemoration, of all that hath been included in the
former pageants, poynting to them in order, the manner thereof thus.

Night growes, Inuiting you to reft, prepare
To rife to morrow to a whole Yeares care,
Enuy ftill waites on Honour, *then prouide*
Vliffes *Wifdome may be ftill your guide*
To ftere you through all dangers : Husband Time
That this day brings you to a place fublime,
By the Supporture of his daughter Truth
This Ancient Citty *in her priftine Youth,*
Your fword may reeftablifh : and fo bring
Her ftill to florifh; like that lafting Spring
That London *in whofe Circuit you were bred*
And borne therein, to be the Cheife and Head
Drawne by thefe two beafts in an Equall line
May in your Mercy *and your* Iuftice *fhine.*
So Honour *who this day did you Inuite*
Vnto Her palace bids you thus Good Night,
No following day but adde to your Renowne
And   this   your   Charge,   with   numerous Bleffings
    crowne.

I have forborne to fpend much paper in needeleffe
and Inpertinent deciphering the worke, or explaining
the habits of the perfons, as being freely expofed to
the publicke view of all the Spectators. The maine
fhow, being performed by the moft excellent in that
kind, Maifter *Gerard Chriftmas* hath expreft his
Modals to be exquifite (as hauing fpared nei-ther Coft

nor care, either in the Figures or ornaments. I fhall not neede to point vnto them to fay, this is a Lyon, and that an Vnicorne, &c. For of this Artift, I may bouldly and freely thus much fpeake, though many about the towne may enuie their worke, yet with all their indeuor they fhall not be able to compare with their worth. I Conclude with *Plautus in fticho* : *Nam curiofus eft nemo qui non fit malevolus.*

F I N I S.

Londini Sinus Salutis,

OR,

LONDONS *Harbour of Health,*
and Happineſſe.

Expreſſed in ſundry Triumphs, Pageants
and Showes ; at the Initiation of the
Right Honorable,

CHRISTOPHER CLETHROWE,

Into the Maioralty of the farre Renowned
City LONDON.

All the Charges and Expences of this preſent
Ovation ; being the ſole undertaking of the Right
Worſhipfull Company of the
Ironmongers.

The 29. *of Oĉtober, Anno Salutis.* 1635.

Written by THOMAS HEYWOOD.

———Redeunt Speĉtacula,———

Printed at *London* by *Robert Raworth.* 1635

TO THE RIGHT

Honorable, *Chriſtopher Clethrowe*,

Lord Maior of this Renowned

Metropolis, L O N D O N,

RIGHT HONOURABLE,

T is one of Eraſmus *his undeniable Apothegms, that there is no Citie can bee ſo ſtrongly immur'd or Defenc'd, but may bee either by Engins defaced, by Enemies inuaded, or by Treaſon ſurprized*; *but the Counſells and Decrees of a wiſe Magiſtrate, are in-expugnable. Time, and your Merit, have call'd you to this Office and Honor* : *As all eyes are upon you, ſo all hearts are towards you*; *never was any more freely voyc't in his Election, and therfore none more hopefull in expectation*: *your Abilitie, what you can doe, is known*; *your purpoſe, what you intend, you have amply delivered*; *your purpoſe, what you intend, you have amply delivered*; *onely the Performance remaines* : *In which, there is no queſtion, but that you will accommodate all yeur future Proceedings to theſe three heads* : Pro Rege, pro Lege, pro Grege ; *for as you are a Magiſtrate, ſo you are a Iudge*: *A calling, both of* Truſt, *and* Trouble : *Of* Truſt ; *becauſe all ſuch as ſit in Iudicature, are Perſons ordained by* GOD, *to examine Cauſes diſcreetely* ; *Heare both Parties Conſiderately,*

and Cenſure all matters unpartially : *For* Iuſtice *is the Badge of* Vertue, *the ſtaffe of* Peace, *and the maintainance of* Honor. *Of* Trouble ; *becauſe in no part of your Time* ; *during your regency, neither in publicke, or private, forraine, or domeſtick things, whether you meditate alone, or conuerſe with others, you ſhall find the leaſt vacancie, which remembers me of that which* Dion *witneſſeth of one* Similis, *who living long in great Place and Authoritie under the Emperour* Adrian, *after much intreaty, got leave to retire himſelfe into the Countrey, where after ſeaven contented yeeres expiring, hee cauſed this Epitaph to be Inſculpt upon his tombe* : Similis hic jacet, cujus ætas multorum fuit annorum. Septem tamen Duntaxat, Annos vixit. Lanctantius *further teacheth us, that it is moſt requiſite, in all ſuch as have charge in the Common Weale, under their Prince and Governour, ſo to know the bownds of their Calling, and underſtand the full effects of their dutie, that by executing* Iuſtice, *they may be feared, and by ſhewing* Mercy, *bee loved* : *I conclude all in this ſhort ſentence,* Non, quid Ipſe velis, ſed quod lex & Religio Cogat, Cogita, *Ever ſubmitting my ſelfe to your better Iudgement, and remaining, to your Lordſhip moſt obſequious.*

Tho. Heywood.

LONDONS

SINVS SALVTIS.

 fhall not neede to borrow my Induction
from the Antiquitie of this Famous *Metropolis*, nor to enter into a large difcourfe, of
the noble Magiftracy and government
thereof ; being Arguments already granted, and therefore unneceffary to be difputed : and yet I hold it not
altogether Impertinent to remember fome few things
of remarke, which have happened in the Prætorfhips
of the Right Honourable, the Lord Maiors of this Renowned Citie, who have beene Free of the Right
Worfhipfull Company of the *Iron-mongers.*

In the year 1409, RICHARD MARLOE, of the fame
Fraternitie, bearing the Sword, there was a Show prefented by the Parifh *Clerkes* of *London*, at a place
called *Skinners Well*, and now *Clerken Well*, which
was of matter from the Creation of the World ; and
lafted for the fpace of Eight Intyre dayes : EDWARD
the *Fourth* (then King) being prefent with his Queene,
and the greateft part of his Nobilitie, which RICHARD
MARLOE, was after Inaugurated Into the fame
Honor, *Anno* 1417. In the yeere 1566. Sir CHRIS-
TOPHER DRAPER, being Lord Maior, King IAMES, of
late and moft Sacred memory, was borne the Sixth
day of *June, Anno* 1569. In Sir ALEXANDER AVE-

NONS Maioralty, was the fuppreffion of the Rebells in the *North*, *Anno* 1581. Sir FRANCIS HARVEY being Mayor, was the *French Mounfiers* comming over into *England*, and his Royall entertainement by Queene ELIZABETH, *Anno* 1607. Sir THOMAS CAMBEL being Invefted into the fame Honor : All the like Showes and Triumphs belonging unto the folemnitie of this day, which for fome yeeres, had beene omitted and neglected, were by a fpeciall commandement from his Majeftie, King IAMES, againe retained, and have beene till this prefent day continued ; whom fince hath fucceeded in the fame Honor, Sir IAMES CAMBEL, his Sonne, a worthy Senator of this Citie, yet living. (The laft of this worthy and Worfhipfull Company, who hath fate in that feate of Iuftice) now this day fucceeded by the Right Honourable, CHRISTOPHER CLETHROWE : but I leave all circumftances, and come to the Showes, now in prefent Agitation.

The firft Showe by Water :

IS an Artificiall Moddell, partly fafhioned like a Rock, and beautified with fundry varieties, and rarities, in all which Art (in Imitating) ftriveth to exceed Nature : The Decorements that adorne the Structure, I omit, and defcend to the Perfons that furnifh it, which are the Three Cæleftiall Goddeffes, *Iuno*, *Pallas*, *Venus* : In *Iuno*, is figured Power and State ; In *Pallas* or *Minerua*, Arms and Arts ; In *Venus*, Beautie and Love : The firft beft knowne by her *Peacocks* ; the fecond by her *Owles* ; the third by her *Swans* & *Turtles*, who is alfo attended by her Sonne *Cupid*, in whom is Emblem'd *Love;* by whom fome have thought, the Vniverfe to have beene Created, becaufe of the Beautie, Glory, and Flourifhing forme thereof, as alfo, that *Love* (though pictured young) yet in Age exceeds all things : But *Venus*, becaufe borne of the Seas, I hold moft proper to fpeake upon the Waters : Thefe Three Goddeffes are

fent from *Jupiter*, with feverall Prefents, to honour
this dayes Triumphs, and him to whom they are de-
voted ; *Iuno* brings Power, *Pallas* Wifedome, *Venus*
Love ; whofe Speech is as followeth :

Venus the Speaker.

THe Three *Cœleftiall goddeffes this day*
       Defcend (Grave Prætor) *to prepare your way*
To your new Oath, and Honor : Iove, *whofe ftation*
Is ftill above, hath fent to this Ovation
And glorious Triumph, Vs : Iuno *the great*
And Potent Queene ; who to your Iurall feat,
Brings State and Power : Pallas, *who from* Ioves
       brain
Derives her felfe, and from the higheft ftraine
Of all the other gods, claimes her defcent,
Her Divine Wifedome, doth this day prefent.
    But I, Emergent Venus, *Loves faire Queene,*
Borne of the Seas ; and therefore beft befeene
To fpeake upon the Waters, bring a gift,
Priz'd equally with theirs ; that which fhall lift
You up on voyces, and from the low frame
Of fordid Earth, give you (above) a name :
From iuft affeftions. and pure thoughts, Love *fprings,*
And thefe are Impt with no Icarian *wings,*
But Plumes Immortall, fuch as Angels beare,
To fixe your Name in an eternall fpheare.
    Which to attaine ; Take Iuno *for your guide,*
Maintaine her Peacocks riches, not her pride ;
Who to prove all Earths glory is but vaine,
Lookes but upon her feete, and flaggs her traine.
    Obferue next Pallas *Owles, and from them take*
This notion ; you muft watch even as they wake :
For all fuch as the management of ftate
Shall undergoe, rife earlie, and bed lcte,
So Wifedome is begot ; from Wifedome Love,
(Sweete Child of fuch a Parent) may't then prove :
That as this day you doe attraft the eyes,

And expectation of the great, and wise,
So in the happy progresse of your yeere,
You may their hearts and soules to you Indeere :
From Love, *your Waters passage vnderstand,*
But Power *and* Wisedome *wellcoms you on land.*

THe next Modell by Land, which was onely showne upon the Water, is one of the twelue Cælestiall signes: *Sagitarius* called *Croton*; hee, before he was translated into the Heavens, was said to bee the Sonne of *Pan*, and the Nimph *Euphemes*, and in his Infancy, was *Conlacteus Musarum. i.* Hee suckt of the same brest with the *Muses*, his mother being their Nurse and dwelt in *Helicon*; hee was Famous for his skill in Archerie, wonderous swift of foote, and when the Nine *Sisters* sung to their severall instruments of Musick, his custome was to dance before them in sundry active figures and postures. For which, and other indowments, knowne to be eminent in, hee was at their request to *Iupiter* translated amongst the starres, in the plat-forme, on which hee is borne: at the foure corners, are seated foure other dignified with the like Constellations: *Virgo*, best knowne by the name of *Astrea* and *Iusta*, the daughter of *Iupiter*, and *Themis*; and for her Iustice and Integritie, thither transferr'd, and numbred amongst the Twelue: Next *Ariadne*, best knowne amongst the *Astrologians*, by the name of *Corona*, the Crowne, which was said to bee forged by *Vulcan* in *Lemnos*, the materialls thereof were Gold, and *Indian* Gemmes, of extraordinary splendor, which shee lending to *Theseus* at that time when her Father *Minos* had expos'd him to the *Minotaure*, by the luster thereof, hee passed freely through the darknesse of the Laborinth : Some say, it was first given her by *Liberpater*, or *Bacchus*, the Sonne of *Iupiter* and *Semele*, and was the price of her Virginitie : but howsoever, shee being most ingratefully forsaken by *Theseus*, in the Ile of *Naxos*; was there found by *Bacchus*, who having

Sagitarius.

Virgo.

Ariadne.

efpoufed her with great folemnitie, caufed her after
her death, with this Crowne to bee Inuefted
in the Firmament. The Third, *Caffiopeia*,   Caffiopeia.
the wife of *Cepheus*, who preferring her owne
beautie before the *Nereides*, who were the daughters of
Neptune, was for that infolence, doom'd to be bownd
in a chayre, hand and foote, and fo placed amongft
the fpheares, where fhee remaines Confpicuous, in
Thirteene Starres. The Fourth, is *Andro-*
meda, the Daughter of *Cepheus* and *Caffio-* Andromeda.
peia, who by the wrath of *Neptune*, being
chain'd unto a Rocke, and ready to bee devoured by
a Sea Monfter, was delivered thence by *Perfeus*, the
Sonne of *Iupiter*, and *Danaæ*, to whom being after
married, was call'd *Perfa*, and Stellified by *Minerua* :
The Speaker is an *Aftrologian.*

¶ The Speech followeth :

L Ate *rifen in the Heaven is* Sagitary,
   (*With you, great Lora*) *who doth about him carry*
Fifteene bright Starres, moft Influent, and thefe all
Appearing in the Circle hiemall :
His Bow devided in that beaten roade,
Call'd Galaxia, *where the gods have troade*
So oft ; that looke upon it in the night,
When all the reft's dull, that alone fhines bright :
(*As you now at this inftant* :) *Hee fifteene*
Starres, did I fay ? How you then ; who betweene
Your landing and repofe, by power divine,
Have full Three-fcore, about your ftate to fhine :
For every Company's *a Starre this day,*
Vifible to all, and over thefe you fway :
But twelue in chiefe ; and thofe wee muft confeffe,
Of greater luftere made, to guide the leffe :
All enioy one like Freedome, all are Free,
And all (*Great* Prætor) *to bee rul'd by thee* :
Commanding all the reft, who in thy fpheare,
Now rifing, art to fhine a compleate yeere.

You may obferue his Bow ftill ready bent,
In which there is a perfect Emblem ment
Of Divine Iuftice : *Th' Arrow, with a Starre*
Headed, Implies, that her power reacheth farre ;
And no oppofure, fraude, violence, or rape,
Can (when fhee aimes to ftrike) her vengeance fcape ;
Yet though the ftring be drawne up to his eare,
(As alwayes preft) hee rather feemes with feare
To threat, then punifh, and though hee can ftill
Let loofe his fhafts, hee feldome fhoots to kill.
    Obferue it well, the Morrall doth imply,
All Iuftice *fhould be mixt with lenitie,*
So, Imitate the gods, fince them wee know,
Apt ftill to Mercie, but to vengeance flow :
And the Cœleftiall bodies, though they trade
Above, yet were for our example made.
As oft as man finnes, fhould Ioue *punnifh vice,*
His Quiver would be emptied in a trice,
And man-kind, at once perifh : O mixe them
Mercy *with* Iuftice, *Interweave againe*
Iuftice *with* Mercy ; *fo fhall you in your ftate,*
Not Starres alone, but the gods Imitate :
So fhall your Terrene body, in the end,
All the Cœleftiall bodies farre tranfcend,
And deckt with better lights then thofe you fee
Above the fpheares, fhine to eternitie.

THe Third Plat-forme, is contrived onely for
    Paftime, to pleafe the vulgar, and therefore
deferves no further Charractar, then a plaine nomi-
nation, as devifed onely to pleafe the eye, but no way
to feaft the eare : and fo I leave it to proceede to
the next.

THe Fourth Moddell, is a Caftle munified with
    fundry Peeces of Ordnance ; and Accomodated
with all fuch Perfons as are needfull for the defence
of fuch a Citadell : the Gunner being ready to give
fire upon all occafions ; as for the curious Art in the

contriving thereof, I make no queftion but the worke
it felfe is fufficiently able to commend the Worke-
man, being knowne to be an excellent Artift, of which,
the fpectatours may beft cenfure; I will onely deliver
unto you a word or two concerning the prefenter,
which is *Mars*.

Mars. Hee is ftyled the third amongft the gods,
becaufe hee ftands in that degree amongft the Planets:
and is faid to be the fonne of *Iupiter*; fome write
that *Bellona* was his Nurffe, others that fhe was his
Mother, and fome his fifter. Yet none of thefe
improper, for *Ennio* which is *Bellona*, implies no
more then an incouragement of the minde to hardi-
neffe and valour in all Skyrmifhes and Battailes. He
His fundry is alfo cal'd *Ares* which fignifieth Dammage
Denomina-
tions. or detriment, and *Mavors* quafi *Mares vorans*,
of devouring of men; and by the *Gentiles*, had the
Denomination of the god of Battailes. He was an-
tiently figured an angry man fitting in a Chariot,
armed with a fheild and other weapons, both offenfiue,
and defenfiue. Vpon his head a plumed Helmet, his
fword mounted vpon his thigh, hee held in one hand
a whip, in the other, the Raines, being drawne in his
Chariot by wylde and vntam'd Horfes. Before him
was portraied a Wolfe devouring a Lambe, the Wolfe
being the beaft particularly offered vpon his fhrine,
and becaufe the two *Romane* Twinnes the firft
founders of *Rome*, ROMVLVS and REMVS, were fained
to be the fonnes of *Mars* (of which the one flewe the
other) therefore ROMVLVS is figured vpon his Chariot
as the vnnatural furvivor. The *Athenians* were the
firft that ever facrificed to this god of Warre, which
Celebration was call'd *Ekaton pephomena* for whofoever
had flaine an Hundred of the publike Enemies, was
bownd to facrifice a man upon his Altar, fituate in the
Ile *Lemnos*, but after the bloodineffe, and inhumanitie
thereof, difpleafing the *Athenians*, they changed that
cuftome, and in ftead of a man, offered a gelded
Hogge, which they call'd *Nefrendes*: *Varro* writes,

that amongſt the *Romans*, SICINNIVS DENTATVS,
having fought one hundered and Ten ſeverall Duells,
and being Victor in them all, receiving Forty five
wounds, whoſe skarres were viſible upon his body, all
before, and none backward : Hee was for his Valour,
honoured with Twenty five ſeverall Crownes, and
received moreover, an Hundred and Forty golden
Bracelets ; and was the firſt amongſt the *Romanes*, that
ever made oblation to this Deity : *Mars* ſitting in the
front of the Tower, ſpeakes as followeth.

The *Speech* of Mars.

BEllipotent Mars *is from his ſpheare come downe,*
    To heighten theſe brave Triumphs of Renowne,
Seated in this mur'd Citadel, defenc'd   A Peece goes off.
With Bullets wrapt in Fire, and Cloudes condenſt.
    The Tormentary Art, *not long ſince found,*
Which ſhatters Towers, & by which Ships are drown'd,
I bring along ; to let you underſtand
Theſe guard your ſafety, both by Sea, and Land.
    O, when I late ſaw from mine orbe Divine,
So many Sonnes of Mars, *amongſt you, ſhine*
In compleat Arms, *Plum'd Casks, and Enſigns ſpred*
By ſuch brave Captaines, *and* Commanders *led* :
No Souldier, but his Poſture to the life,
Acting to'th Muſick of the Drum and Fyffe,
Some practiſing ſmall Bombards, ſome the great,
Whoſe very thunder, rowſ'd mee from my ſeate :
This Peacefull Citie, *I much prayſ'd, whoſe power*
Could to a Campe, *it ſelfe change in an houre* :
Proceed in your brave Practiſe ; whilſt I tell
Wherein your Iron *and* Steele *doth moſt excell.*
    Without theſe Metalls, *Nature could produce*
Nothing that is conducefull to mans uſe :
The Plow, *without the* Coulter *and the* Share,
Could make no Furrows, and thoſe Graines that are
Vpon them throwne, were loſt to them that ſowe them,
Without the Sickle, *or the* Sythe *to mowe them* :

The Gardeners Art, *would ceaſe to be a trade,*
If take from him the Matocke, *and the* Spade.
In Denns and Caves wee ſhould be forc'd to dwell,
Were there no Axes *made, that* Timber *fell* :
Nor on the Seas could wee have Shipps *to ſayle,*
Without the Sawe, *the* Hammer, *and the* Nayle :
Aske thoſe that take in Angling *moſt delight,*
Without the baited Hooke, *no fiſh will bite.*
The Iron Crowe *turnes up the* Indian *mould,*
Trenching the Earth untill they dig out Gold.
If with the Iron *the* Adamant *ſhould contend,*
There ſhould be no more Compaſſe, *but an end*
Of all Diſcovery : *Even the Horſe wee ride*
Vnſhod, *would founder, who takes greateſt pride,*
When the moſt curb'd, *and playing with the* bit,
Hee ſnowes the ground, and doth the Spurre *forgit.*
There is no Art, Craft, Faculty, or Trade,
Without it, can ſubſiſt : *Your* Sword *is made*
Of theſe mixt Metalls (*Sir*) Iuſtice *would ceaſe,*
If (*as in Warre*) *it were not us'd in Peace* :
Power makes it yours, your wiſedome now direct you ;
Whilſt Peace ſwayes heere, Mars *ſhall abroad protect*
    you.

THe ſpeech being ended, the Ordnance goeth off
    from the Caſtle ; and now I come to the fift
and laſt.

Heere I might enter into large diſcourſe, concerning the commodiouſneſſe of *Iron* and *Steele,* and to
ſpeake of *Tuball Cain,* who made the firſt *Forge,* and
found out the vſe of theſe Metalls : as alſo *Vulcan* the
deified Smith and of his *Cyclopean Hammers* with
which hee was ſaid to have beaten out *Ioves* Thunder-
boults, with other fixions to the like purpoſe, theſe
having before been expoſed to the publick view vpon
occaſion of the like ſolemnity, & knowing withall that
Cibus his coctus, reliſheth not the queſie ſtomackes of
theſe times. I therefore purpoſly omit them proceed-
ing to the laſt Pageants, ſtyled *Sinus ſalutis,* firſt the

Boofome, or harbour of Health and Happineffe. The fculpture being adorned with eight feveral perfons, reprefenting fuch vertues as are neceffary to bee imbraced by all fuch Majeftrates, who after their ftormy and tempeftuous progreffe through all judicature caufes incident to their places, feeke to anchor in that fafe and fecure Port fo ftyled.

Every Magiftrate is a minifter vnder God, appointed by his divine ordinance to that calling to be a protector of the Church, a preferuer of difcipline and Peace, confonant with his lawes, the lawes of nature, and the land, which hee ought faithfully to execute, with corporall punifhment, correcting the proud and difobedient, and againft all unjuft oppreffors, defending the conformable and humble. The firft vertue adorning the ftructure is ftiled *Fortitudo togata*, which gowned Fortitude is thus defined.

Fortitudo togata.

A conftancy of minde perfevering in honeft purpofe rightly undertaken and according to his place and calling, tollerating private injuries for lawdable caufe, difpifing pleafures, corrupt guifts, detraction, and the like : and thefe meerly for vertues fake and preferring the publike good before his owne private gaine, &c. Of which *Fabritius* was a noble prefident, who refufing the gold fent him by *Pyrhus* was no whit affrighted with the terror of his Elephants ; to fpeake or act any thing againft the dignity of the Republicke. Of whom *Eutropius* reports, *Pyrhus* to have faid : the Sunne is more eafie to bee altered in his courfe, then this *Fabritius* to be removed from his honefty.

Manfuetudo.

Manfuetudo, or gentleneffe is a vertue mediating wrath and fuppreffing all defire of revenge and remitting offences, for publicke concords fake, which notably appeared in *Pericles*, who when one had bitterly rayled on him, for fpace of one whole after noone, in the open market place : night comming, hee caufed his fervants to light him to his houfe with Torches.

Candor, or fincerity is when without fimulation we
our felues fpeake, and with no diffidence fuf-
Candor. pect the good meaning of others : wifhing all
juft men well, rejoycing at theire profperity, and com-
miſſerating their difafter : It is reported of *Trajanus*
the Emperour, that when *Sura Licinius* one of the
Tribunes, was accufed unto him, to have Infidiated his
life, not queftioning the faith of fo knowre a friend ;
the fame night, un-invited, fupt with him privately in
his houfe, and the Table being with-drawne, trufted
himfelfe to be trim'd by *Sura's* Barbar.

Patientia Philofophica, Is a Vertue obe-
Patientia
Phylofo- dient unto reafon, in bearing wrongs, and fuf-
phica. fering adverfities ; it moderates griefe, and
bridles nature, fo that it never rebells againft Iuftice,
Modefty, Conftancy, or any other vertue ; *Xenophon*
ports *Cyrus* and *Agefolanus* to be of fuch Philofophi-
cal patience, that in their height of determination in
all their actions, and fpeech, they appeared to all
men affable, and offenceleſſe.

Placabilitie is a vertue, having corefpon-
Placabilitas. dence with that which I before ftil'd *Manfuetudo*, or Gentleneffe ; *Philofuchia*, or ftudy of
Peace, and Concord, is when a Magiftrate thinks
Humbly of himfelfe, moderating his owne anger, and
bearing with the Infirmities of others, pardoning Injuries, and maintaining unitie, being provident that
all unneceffary controverfie bee aton'd, leaft the publike Peace and Vnitie of the Church, or Common-
weale be difturbed, or hindred ; of which Vertue,
Abraham was a moft Imitable Prefident, who, though
in Authoritie, Wifedome, and age, hee had Prioritie
before *Lot*, yet not-with-ftanding, gave place to him ;
only for Concords fake.

Humanitie, which the *Greekes* call *Ethos*, Is Iuftice, coupled with Gentleneffe, Equitie, Vp-
Humanitas. right-life, Affabilitie, and the like, for which
are remark't, *Alexander*, *Cyrus*, *Octavius Cæfar*, &c. It
hath alfo beene obferued amongft Schollars (In which

number I may Catalogue your Lordſhip), that the more
learned they have beene, they have ſhewed themſelues
the more humane, and humble.

Nemeſis five Zealus. . The laſt is *Nemeſis*, or Zeale, which
is an ardent love of Gods glory, of
Iuſtice, Pietie, Sanctitie, &c. With an earneſt Indig-
nation againſt whatſoever is evill, ſupporting the Religious, and ſeverely puniſhing the wicked, and refractory. *Phinees zelo Inflammatus Confodit ſcortatorem,
&c.* So much to Illuſtrate the Perſons, I come now
to the Speech.

H EE that is call'd to bee a Majeſtrate,
    A Guide, a Ruler, or a Candidate,
Muſt of ſo great a burden know the weight;
But firſt the ſtepps that mount him to that height:
Shall I direct you then, what ſayle to beare?
(*Like a good Pilot*) *and what courſe to ſteare*:
(*Your pardon, Great Sir*) *daring to deſcry
A paſſage, which you better know then I.*
   There is a double Fortitude, *both Crown'd
With merited Palme*; *one Gunn'd, the other Gown'd*:
*The Souldier claymes the firſt, as his by due,
The next, the Civill Sword, now borne by you*:
*By which, as great a glory you ſhall win
In* Peace, *as hee in* Warre, *by curbing ſinne,
And cheriſhing vertue*; *In the ſecond place,
Stands* Gentleneſſe, *and* Mercy, *O what grace
Hath* Peace, *with* Pitty *mixt*? Metalls *beſt feele,
When* Iron *is well Incorporate with* Steele:
*A body ſo calcin'd to publike uſe,
As to ſupport Right, and ſuppreſſe abuſe*:
Sinceritie *may chalenge the third claſſe,
Next* Patience, *which by ſuffering, doth ſurpaſſe
All other Vertues*: Placability,
Study of Concord, *and* Fidelity;
Laſt, holy Zeale, *and that doth crowne the reſt*:
*All theſe being harbour'd in your honour'd breſt,
Shall* (*maugre ſhelues and rocks*) *your paſſage cleare,*

And bring you to the Port, *to which you ſteare* :
You are the Citties Chiefe, *the Prime, the Sole,*
In expeƈlation : *like the ſledfaſt Pole* :
Proove conſtant in your Courſe, be ſlill the ſame,
So let your Sword (tutch'd with Truth's Adamant)
 aime
In your yeeres compaſſe, that to all mens view
(Skilfull in ſlearage) it may ſtill goe true :
 So, thoſe that were before you, and rul'd well,
 Equall you ſhall, although not Antecell.

THere remaines the Speech at Night, which is
 onely a Sumnary, or reiteration of the former
Showes, Applied to the taking leave of his Lordſhip,
and to commend him to his reſt : *Mars* being the
Speaker.

¶ The Speech at Night.

PHœbus *his Steedes hath ſtabled in the* Weſt,
 And Night (ſucceeding Day) inuites to reſt :
The three Cœleſtiall Queenes, ſent from above,
Leaving with you their Power, *their* Wiſdom, Love
Now take their leaves : *The* Centaure *doth beſtow*
On you his Iuſtice, *with his ſhaft, and boue,*
Who to your beſt repoſe, bequeath's you heere,
To mount himſelfe againe uhto his ſpheare :
The Night being come, he cannot well be miſt :
For without him, his Orbe cannot ſubſiſt :
Neither can mine : *Now muſl my Starre diſplay*
It's Luminous Rays, being borrowed thence this day,
To waite upon your Triumphs, and ſhall ſtill
Proteƈt you, and your weighty charge, untill
Hee, which ſhall all your upright Aƈtions bleſſe,
Conduƈt you to your Port of Happineſſe.

THeſe Frames, Modells, and Struƈtures, were
 Faſhioned, Wrought, and Perfeƈted, by the Two
Artiſts, IOHN, and MATHIAS CHRISMAS ; Succeſſors to

their Father, Mr. GERALD CHRISMAS, late difceafed, as well in the Exquifite performance of his qualititie, as in his true finceritie, and honefty ; of whom I may confidently fpeake, as no man could out-vie him in thefe Workes, which hee underwent, fo none could out-match him in his word, For any thing hee undertooke ; concerning whom I make no fcruple, thus Ingenioufly to conclude : *Ars patris, in fili:s etiam, poſt fata viget.*

F I N I S.

Londini Speculum: or,

Londons Mirror, Expreft in fundry *Triumphs,*
Pageants, and *Showes,* at the Initiation of
the right Honorable *Richard Fenn,* into
the Mairolty of the Famous and
farre renowned City *LONDON.*

All the Charge and Expence of thefe laborious projects
both by Water and Land, being the fole undertaking of the Right Worfhipful Company
of the *Habberdafhers.*

Written by Tho. Heywood.

Imprinted at *London* by *I. Okes* dwelling in little *St.*
Barthtolmews. 1637.

To the Right Honour-

able *Richard Fenn*, Lord
Maior of this Renowned
Metropolis LONDON.

Right Honourable:

Xcufe (I intreate) this my boldneffe, which proceedeth rather from *Cuftome* in others, then *Curiofity* in my *Selfe*, in prefuming to prompt your *Memory* in fome things tending to the *greatnes* of your high *place* and *Calling* ; You are now entred into one of the moft famous *Mairolties* of the *Chriftian World.* You are alfo cald *Fathers, Patrons* of the *Afflicted*, and *Procurators of the Publicke good.* And whatfoever hath reference to the true confideration of *Juftice* and *Mercy*, may be *Analogically* conferd upon pyous and iuft *Magiftrates.*

And for the *Antiquity* of your yearely *Government*, I read that the *Athenians* elected theirs *Annually* : and for no longer continuance : And fo of the *Carthagians*, the *Thebans*, &c. And the *Roman* Senate held, that continued *Magiftracy* was in fome

reſpeᴄts unprofitable to the *Weale-publicke*, againſt
which there was an *Aᴄt* in the Lawes of the twelve
Tables. And it is thus concluded by the Learned,
that the Dominion of the *greateſt Magiſtrates* which
are *Kings* and *Princes*, ought to be perpetuall ; but
of the leſſe which be *Prætors*, *Cenſors*, and the like,
only *Ambulatory* and *Annuall*. I conclude with that
ſaying of a wiſe man, Prime Officers ought to Rule by
Good Lawes, and commendable Example, Iudge by
Providence, *Wiſdome* and *Iuſtice*, and Defend by
Prowes, *Care* and *Vigilancy* : Theſe things I can but
Diᴄtate, of which your *Lordſhip* knoweth beſt how to
Diſpoſe : ever (as now) remayning your Honors

Humble ſervant,

Thomas Heywood.

Londini Speculum,

OR,

Londons Mirrour.

LL Triumphes have their Titles, and fo this, according to the nature thereof, beareth a name : It is called *Londini* Κατόπτρον, that is, *Speculum*, more plainly, *Londons Mir-rour*, neither altogether unproperly fo termed, fince fhe in her felfe may not onely perfpicuoufly behold her owne vertues, but all forraigne Cities by her, how to correct their vices.

Her Antiquity fhe deriveth from *Brute*, lineally difcended from *Æneas*, the fonne of *Anchifes* and *Venus*, and by him erected, about the yeare of the world two thoufand eight hundred fifty five : before the Nativity of our bleffed Saviour, one thoufand one hundred and eight : firft cald by him *Trinovantum*, or *Troy-novant*, *New Troy*, to continue the remembancer of the old, and after, in the proceſſe of time *Caier Lud,* that is, *Luds Towne,* of King *Lud,* who not onely greatly repaired the City, but increaſed it with goodly and gorgeous buildings ; in the Weſt part whereof, he built a ſtrong gate, which hee called after his owne name *Lud-gate,* and ſo from *Luds Towne,* by contraction of the word and *dialect* uſed in thoſe times, it came ſince to be called *London.*

I will not inſiſt to ſpeake of the name of *Maior,* which implyeth as much as *the greater,* or more prime perſon ; ſuch were the *Prætors,* or *Præfecti* in *Rome,* neither were the *Dictators* any more, till *Julius Cæſar* aiming at the Imperiall Purple, was not content with that annuall *honour,* which was to paſſe ſucceſſively from one to another, but he cauſed himſelfe to be Elected *Perpetuus Dictator,* which was in effect no leſſe than Emperor.

And for the name of *Elder-man,* or *Alder-man,* it is ſo ancient, that learned Maſter *Cambden* in his *Britan,* remembreth unto us, that in the daies of Royal King *Edgar,* a noble Earle, and of the Royall blood, whoſe name was *Alwin,* was in ſuch favour with the King, that he was ſtiled *Healf Kunning,* or halfe King, and had the ſtile of Alderman of all *England* : This man was the firſt founder of a famous Monaſtery in the Iſle of *Ely,* where his body lies interred, upon whoſe Tombe was an inſcription in *Latin,* which I have, *verbatim,* thus turned into *Engliſh, Here reſteth* Alwin, *couzen to King* Edgar, *Alderman of all* England, *and of this Holy Abbey the miraculous founder.* And ſo much (being tide to a briefe diſcourſe) may ſerve for the Antiquity of London, and the Titles for *Maior* or *Alderman.*

I come now to the *Speculum,* or *Mirrour. Plutarch* tels us, *That a glaſſe in which a man or woman behold their faces, is of no eſtimation or value (though the frame thereof be never ſo richly deckt with gold & gemmes, unleſſe it repreſent unto us the true figure and object. Moreover, that ſuch are fooliſh and flattering glaſſes, which make a ſad face to looke pleaſant, or a merry countenance melancholy : but a perfect and a true Chriſtall, without any falſity or flattery, rendreth every obiect its true forme, and proper figure, diſtinguiſhing a ſmile from a wrincle; and ſuch are the meanes many times to bridle our refractory affections : for who being in a violent rage, would be pleaſed that his ſervant ſhould bring him a glaſſe wherein hee might be hold thetorvity and ſtrange alteration of his countenance ?* Minerva *playing upon a Pipe, was mockt by a Satyre in theſe words.*

Non te decet forma iſtæc, pone fiſtulas,
   Et Arma capeſſe componens recte genus.

That viſage miſ-becomes, thy Pipe
   Caſt from thee, Warlike dame,
Take unto thee thy wonted Armes,
   And keepe thy Cheekes in frame.

But though ſhe deſpiſed his Councell for the preſent, when after, playing upon the ſame Pipe, in which ſhe ſo much delighted, ſhee beheld in a river ſuch a change in her face, ſhee caſt it from her, and broke it aſunder, as knowing that the ſweetnes of her muſick could not countervaile or recompence that deformity which it put upon her countenance, and therefore I have purpoſed ſo true and exact a Mirrour, that in it may be diſcovered as well that which beautifies the governour, as deformes the government.

One thing more is neceſſitouſly to be added, and then I fall upon the ſhowes in preſent agitation : namely, that the fellowſhip of the Merchant Adventurers of *England* were firſt truſted with the ſole venting of the manufacture of Cloth out of this kingdome, & have for above this 4 hundred years traded in a priviledged, & wel governed courſe, in *Germany,* the *Low Countries, &c.,* and have beene the chiefe meanes to raiſe the manufacture of all wollen commodities to that height in which it

now exifteth, which is the moft famous ftaple
of the Land, and whereby the poore in all Countries are plentifully maintained : and of this Company
his Lordfhip is free ; as alfo of the *Levant,* or *Turkey,*
and of the *Eaft India* Company, whofe trading hath
beene, and is in thefe forraine adventures : alfo who
fpent many yeares and a great part of his youth in
other Countries.

Now the firft fhow by water is prefented by *St.
Katherine,* of whom I will give you this fhort Charac-
ter : *She was the daughter of King* Coftus, *and had the
generall title of Queene of* Famogofta, *becaufe crowned
in that City, being lineally difcended from the* Roman
*Emperors, who as fhe lived a Virgin fo fhe dyed a
Martyr, under the Tyrant* Maxentius, *whofe Empreffe
with divers other eminent perfons fhe had before con-
verted to the Faith : fhe rideth on a Scallop, which is
part of his Lordfhips Coate of Armes, drawne in a Sea-
Chariot, by two Sea-horfes with divers other adornments
to beautifie the peece : the Art of which, the eye may better difcover, than my pen defcribe, and why fhe being a
Princeffe, and Patroneffe of this Company of the Haberdafhers, who onely ruled on the Land, fhould at this time
appeare upon the water, and without any iuft taxation,
to make that cleare, fhee thus delivereth her felfe.*

St. Katherines *fpeech by Water.*

G Reat *Prætor,* and grave Senators, fhe craves
A free admittance on thefe curled waves,
Who doth from long antiquity profeffe
Her felfe to be your gratious Patroneffe :
Oft have I on a paffant Lyon fate,
And through your populous ftreets beene borne in
 ftate :
Oft have I grac't your Triumphes on the fhore,
But on the Waters was not feene before.
 Will you the reafon know why it doth fall,
That I thus change my Element ? you fhall :

When *Triton* with his pearly trumpets blew
A ſtreperous blaſt, to ſummon all the crew
Of Marine gods and goddeſſes to appeare,
(As the annuall cuſtome is) and meet you here :
As they were then in councell to debate,
What honour they might adde unto the ſtate
Of this Inauguration; there appear'd
God *Mercury*, who would from *Jove* be heard :
His *Caduæus* ſilence might command ;
Whilſt all attentive were to underſtand
The tenor of his meſſage : who thus ſpake.
 The Sire of gods, with what you undertake
Is highly pleas'd, and greatly doth commend
That faire deſigne and purpoſe you intend ;
But he beheld a Machine from an high,
Which at firſt ſight daz'd his immortall eye ;
A royall Arke, whoſe bright and glorious beams
Rivall the Sunnes, ready to proove your ſtreames :
A veſſell of ſuch beauty, burthen, ſtate,
That all the high Powers were amaz'd thereat ;
So beautified, ſo munified, ſo clad,
As might an eight to the ſeaven wonders adde :
Which muſt be now your charge ; 'twas *Ioves* owne
  motion,
That all of you attend her to the *Ocean.*
 This notwithſtanding, ſuch was their great care,.
(To ſhew that o're you they indulgent are)
That *Neptune* from his Chariot bad me chuſe
Two of his beſt Sea horſes, to excuſe
His inforc't abſence : *Thames* (whoſe breaſt doth
  ſwell
Still with that glorious burthen) bad me tell,
That *Ioves* command ſhall be no ſooner done,
But every Tide he'le on your errands runne
From hence to the Lands end, and thence againe
Backe, to conveigh your trafficke from the Maine :
My meſſage thus delivered ; now proceed
To take your oath ; there is no further need

Of my affiftance : who on Land will meete you,
And with the ftate of greater Triumphes greete you.

Thefe few following Lines may, (and not imperti-
nently) be added unto *Jupiters* meffage, delivered by
Mercury, which though too long for the Bardge, may
perhaps not fhew lame in the booke, as being leffe
troublefome to the Reader than the Rower.

Dance in thy raine-bow colours *Protœus*, change
Thy felfe to thoufand figures, 'tis not ftrange
With thee, thou old Sea-prophet, throng the feas
With *Phorcus* Daughters, the *Nereides*,
And all the blew-hair'd Nymphes, in number more,
Than Barkes that float, or Pibbles on the fhore :
Take *Æolus* along to fill her failes
With profperous windes, and keepe within his gailes
Tempeftuous gufts : which was no fooner faid,
But done : for all the Marine gods obey'd.

The fecond fhow, but the firft by Land, is prefented
by the great *Philofopher Pythagoras, Samius,* the fonne
of *Menarchus* ; which being outwardly *Sphericall* and
Orbicular, yet being opened it quadrates it felfe iuft
into fo many *Angles* as there be Scepters, over which
his Sacred Maiefty beareth title : namely, *England,
Scotland, France,* and *Ireland,* concerning which
number of *foure,* I thus Read : *Pythagoras* and his
Schollers, who taught in his fchooles, that *Ten* was the
nature and foule of all number; one Reafon which
he gave (to omit the reft) was, becaufe all nations, as
well civill as barbarous, can tell no farther than to the
Denary, which is *Ten,* and then returne in their
account unto the *Monady,* that is one : For example,
from *Tenne* wee proceed to *Eleven* and *Twelve,* which
is no more than *Ten* and *One, Ten* and *Two,* and fo of
the reft, till the number rife to an infinite.

Againe hee affirmeth, that the ftrength and vertue
of all number confifteth in the *quarternion* ; for begin-

ning with *one, two, three,* and *foure,* put them together
and they make *ten;* he faith further, that the nature of
number confifteth in *ten,* and the faculty of number
is comprized in *foure*: in which refpect the *Pythago-
reans* expreffe their holy oath in the *quaternion,*
which they cal'd τετρακτιν, as may appear in thefe
words.

Per tibi noſtræ animæ præbentem tetrada Iuro,
Naturæ fontemque & firmamenta perennis.

For they held the foule of man to fubfift in that number, proportionating it into thefe *foure* Faculties, *Mens,
Scientia, Opinio, Senſus,* the *Mind, Knowledge, Opinion,* and *Sence,* and therefore according to that number *Pythagoras* frames his *Speech,* alluding to thofe
four Kingdomes over which his Maiefty beareth
title.

The *Speech* of the fecond Show, delivered in *Paules*
Church-yard.

SAcred's the number foure, *Philoſophers ſay,*
   And beares an happy Omen; as this day
It may appeare : foure *Elements conſpire,*
Namely, the Water, Earth, the Aire, and Fire,
To make up man: *the colours in him bred*
Are alſo foure, White, Pallid, Blacke, and red :
Of foure *Complexions he exiſteth ſoly,*
Flegmaticke, Sanguine, Choler, Melancholy.
His meate foure *ſeverall digeſtions gaines,*
In Stomacke, Liver, Members, and the Veines.
Foure *qualities* cald primæ *within lie,*
Which are thus titled, Hot, Cold, Moiſt, and Drie.
He acts his whole life on this earthy ſtage,
In Child-hood, Youth, Man-hood, Decripit age.
The very day that doth afford him light,
Is Morning, the Meridian, Evening, Night.
Foure *ſeaſons ſtill ſucceſſively appeare,*

Which put together make a compleat yeare.
The earth, with all the Kingdomes therein guided,
Is into foure *diſtinguiſh'd parts devided.*
The foure *Windes from the Worlds* foure *quarters blow,*
Eurus, Favonius, Auſter, Aquilo.
All Morall vertues we in foure *include,*
As Prudence, Iuſtice, Temperance, Fortitude.
Court, City, Campe, and Countrey, the foure *C C C s;*
Which repreſent to us the foure *degrees,*
Requir'd in every faire and flouriſhing Land,
Subſtract but one a Kingdome cannot ſtand.
Foure Colonels *are in this City knowne,*
Of which you, honoured Sir, have long beene one :
And thoſe foure *Crownes, (for ſo the high Powers*
 pleaſe)
Embleme the Kings foure *Scepters, and* foure *Seas.*
The fift (1) *Imperiall Arch above, proclaimes*
That glorious Crowne, *at which his* Highneſſe *aimes.*
Thus is our round Globe ſquared, *figuring his power,*
And yours beneath Him, *in the* number foure.

The third Show.

THe third Pageant or Show meerly confiſteth of
 Anticke geſticulations, dances, and other Mimicke
poſtures, deviſed onely for the vulgar, who are better
delighted with that which pleaſeth the eye, than con-
tenteth the eare, in which we imitate *Cuſtome,* which alwaies carrieth with it excuſe : neither are they altogether
to be vilefied by the moſt ſupercilious, and cenſorious,
eſpecially in ſuch a confluence, where all Degrees,
Ages, and Sexes are aſſembled, every of them looking
to bee preſented with ſome fancy or other, according
to their expectations and humours : Since grave and
wiſe men have beene of opinion, that it is convenient,
nay neceſſitous, upon the like occaſions, to mixe *ſeria*

---

(1) Quinta perennis.

iocis; for what better can fet off matter, than when it is interlaced with mirth? From that I proceede to the fourth.

The fourth Show.

IT beareth the Title of an *Imperiall* Fort : nor is it compulfive, that here I fhould argue what a Fort is, a Skonce, or a Cittadall, nor what a Counterskarfe, or halfe Moone, &c. is ; nor what the oppofures or defences are : my purpofe is onely to exprefle my felfe thus farre, that this Fort which is ftil'd *Imperiall*, defenc'd with men and officers, fuiting their functions and places proper to fuch a muniment ; doth in the morall include his Majefties royall chamber, which is the City of *London*, for to that onely purpofe was the project intended.

The Speaker is *Bellona*, whom fome held to be the Daughter, fome the Sifter, others the Nurfe of *Mars* the god of Warre ; neither in any of thefe is any impropriety, or ought that is diftonant from authority, becaufe *Enyo*, which is *Bellona*, implyeth that which putteth fpirit and courage into an army, &c. Antiquity called her *Duellona*, that is, the goddeffe of warre, to whom their Priefts facrificed their owne blood, and before whofe Temple the *Fœcialis* fet a fpeare againft fome prime pillar thereof, when any publicke warre was to be denounced : Shee was moft honoured of the *Thracians*, the *Scithians*, and thofe wild and barbarous nations, upon whofe Altars they ufed to facrifice a Vulture, which is a ravenous hird, ufed to prey upon dead carcaffes, and affemble themfelves in great flocks after any fought battaile : but this Difcourfe may to fome appeare impertinent to the project in hand, and therefore I thus proceed to her fpeech.

Bellonaes *Speech upon the* Imperiall *Fort.*

THis Structure (*honour'd Sir*) *doth title beare
Of an* Imperiall Fort, *apt for that fpheare
In which you now moove, borrowing all her grace,*

As well from your owne perſon as your place ;
For you have paſt through all the degrees that tended
Vnto that height which you have now aſcended.

You have beene in this City *('tis knowne well)*
A Souldier, Captaine, *and a* Colonell.
And now in times faire progreſſe, to crowne all,
Of this Metropolis *chiefe Generall.*
You, of this Embleme, which this day we bring,
To repreſent the Chamber of the King,
Are the prime governour : a Royall Fort,
And ſtrongly ſcited, as not built for ſport,
But for example and defence : a Tower
Supported by no leſſe than Soveraigne power :
The Theologicke *vertues, the three* Graces,
And Charities *have here their ſeverall places.*
Here Piety, *true* Zeale, *ſtudy of* Peace,
(By which ſmall mites to Magozines *increaſe)*
Have reſidence : now oppoſite there are
To theſe, and with them at continuall warre,
Pride, Arrogance, Sloath, Vanity, Preſtigion,
Prophaneſſe, the contempt of true Religion,
With thouſands more, who aſſiduatly waite
This your Imperiall Fort *to inſidiate.*

Concordia
parvæ res
Creſcunt,
is the Motto
of the Com-
pany of the
right Wor-
ſhipfull
Habber-
daſhers.

You may obſerve i'th muſicke of your Bels
Like found in Triumphes, *and for funerall knels ;*
Marriage and death to them appeare all one,
Masking nor mourning cannot change their tone :
With our Fort *'tis not ſo, whoſe faire pretence, is*
To comply with the nature of offences,
Errors ; *ſhe knowes in low termes how to chide*
Great faults, with greater noiſe are terrifi'd :
But ſhe can load her Cannons, and ſpeake loud
To encounter with the arrogant and proud :
Whats further in your Prætorſhip *afsign'd,*
You, in your Londons Mirrour *there may find.*

The fifth fhow, cald Londons Mirrour.

THis beareth the title of the whole Triumphe ; of Glaffes pertinent to this our purpofe, there bee feverall forts, as *Opticke, Perfpective, Profpective, Multiplying, &c.* The prefenter is *Vifus,* or Sight ; for what the minde is to the foule, the fame is the eye to the body, being the moft precious part thereof. Sight is the moft foveraigne fence, the firft of five, which directeth man to the ftuddy & fearch of know-ledge & wifedome ; the eyes are placed in the head as in a Citadel, to be watch-towers and Centinels for the fafety, and guiders and conducters for the follace of the body.

We read that one *Marcus Varro* was fir-named *Strabo,* for the excellency and quickneffe of his fight, who from *Libæum,* a Province in *Scicilia,* could diftin-guifh and give an exact account of all fuch fhips as came out of the haven of *Carthage,* which two places fome hold to be more than an hundred *Italian* leagues diftant : indeed no man can better efti-mate the vertue and value of the fight, than he that is made blinde and wants it, neither could I devife a more apt Speaker to prefent this *Mirrour,* than the fence of the fight, without which, the pureft Chriftall is of no ufe at all.

The Pageant it felfe is decored with glaffes of all forts : the perfons upon or about it are beautifull Chil-dren, every one of them expreffing their natures and conditions in the imprefaes of their fhields, eight of the prime of which fuiting with the quality of the *Optick* fence, beare thefe feverall Infcriptions : *Afpice, Defpice, Confpice, Profpice, Perfpice, Infpice, Circumfpice, Refpice :*

Οψσις, or *Opfis* the Speaker.

BEhold me Sight, *of the five fences prime ;* (*Now beft complying with the place and time*) *Prefenting* Londons Mirrour, *and this Glaffe*

Shewes not alone what fhe is, or once was,
But that the fpacious Vniverfe might fee
In her, what their great Cities ought to be ;
That every forraigne Magiftrate from hence
Might learne how to difpofe his Opticke *fence.*
    Afpice *faith, Looke toward and upon*
Defartfull men whom this Age frowneth on.
And Defpice *caft downe thy powerfull eye*
On the poore wretch that doth beneath thee lye.
Then Confpice *take counfell firft and paufe*
With meditation, ere thou iudge a caufe.
Profpice *bids looke afarre off, and view*
(Before conclude) what dangers may infue.
Perfpice *wils, in fifting doubts, then fcan*
The nature of the matter with the man.
Let every caufe be fearcht, and duely fought,
Saith Infpice, *ere thou determinft ought.*
Circumfpice *faith, looke about to immure*
So great a charge, that all within be fure.
Confiderate *Refpice inioynes thee laft,*
To caft thine eyes backe upon all things paft.
    For Londons *felfe, if they fhall firft begin*
To examine her without, and then within,
What Architectures, Palaces, what Bowers,
What Citadels, what turrets, and what towers ?
Who in her age, grew pregnant, brought a bed
Of a New Towne, *and late delivered*
Of fuch a burthen, as in few yeares fpace,
Can almoft fpeake all tongues, (to her more grace.)
Then her Cathedrals, Temples *new reparing,*
An act of true devotion, no man fparing
His helping hand ; and many, 'tis well knowne,
To further Gods houfe have forgot their owne.
    Vnto her outward fhape I doe not prize her,
But let them come within to anatomize her.
Her Prætor, *fcarlet Senate, Liveries,*
The ordering of her brave focieties :
Divine Aftræa *here in equall fcale*
Doth ballance Iuftice, *Truth needes not looke pale,*

Nor poverty deiected, th' Orphants caufe,
And Widowes plea finde helpe ; no fubtile claufe
Can make demurre in fentence : a faire hearing,
And upright doome in every Court appearing :
 Still to preferve her fo, be 't your indeavour,
 And fhe in you ; you her fhall live for ever.

I come now to the Linvoy, or laft Speech, when his Lordfhip, after his dayes long and tedious trouble, retireth himfelfe to his reft at night, in which *Pythago-ras* the Speaker briefly runs over the paffages of the Pageant before expreffed, after this manner.

The Speech at Night.

WE to a Valediction *are confin'd,*
 (Right Honoured) *and intreat You beare in*
  minde
What was this Day prefented : Your *chiefe* Saint
A Martyr *once of the* Church militant,
But now of the tryumphant, *bids You fpare*
Your felfe this Night : *for to a World of Care*
You are ingag'd to morrow, which muft laft
Till the whole progreffe of Your Yeere *be paft.*
The Spheare-like Globe quadrated, lets You know,
What Pro-Rex *doth to the foure Scepters owe.*
Your Military honours, (*in your Dayes*
Of leffe command) *th'* Imperiall Fort *difplayes,*
And Londons Mirrour, *that all men may fee*
What Magiftrates *have beene, and ought to be.*
Set is the Sunne *long fince, and now the Light*
Quite fayling us, Thrice Honourd Sir, *good Night.*

For the Artifts, and directors of thefe Pageants and fhowes, *John Chriftmas* and *Mathias*, the two Sonnes of *Gerard*, their now deceafed Father, a knowne Mafter in all thofe Sciences he profeft : I can fay no more but thus, that proportioning their Workes according to the limits of the gates through which they were to paffe, being ty'de not to exceede one Inch either in height, or breadth : My Opinion is, that few Workemen about the Towne can paralell them, much leffe exceede them. But if any fhall either out of Curiofity or malice taxe their ability, in this kind of Art, I referre them to the Carving of his Majefties *Great Ship* lately built at *Woolwitch*, which Worke alone is able both to fatisfie *Emulation*, and qualifie *Envie*.

F I N I S.

NOTES AND ILLUSTRATIONS.

PAGE 1.

THE ENGLISH TRAVELLER.

Reprinted in the Sixth Volume of Dilke's *Old Plays* (1816).

Of the *Englifh Traveller* the ftory, as far as it relates to Young Lionel and Reignald, is (as Langbaine obferves) borrowed from the *Mortellaria* of Plautus. Indeed, fo confiderable a part of the play is clofely copied from that performance, that it is curious Heywood did not think it neceffary to acknowledge the obligation.

The *Englifh Traveller*, it may be added further, is not the only drama which has been very deeply indebted to the *Mortellaria*. The *Intriguing Chambermaid* of Fielding is evidently founded upon it : and the entertainment given by the rakifh fon, the old man's return from a voyage, the projeft of the knavifh fervant to prevent the father's furprifing the company that were caroufing in his houfe by making him believe it was haunted, and his pretending that the young gentleman had purchafed another in the room of it, are all introduced with little variation from the original. And thefe obfervations apply as clofely to *The Englifh Traveller*, as to the *Intriguing Chambermaid*.

PAGE 16.

Drinke Whig *and fowre Milke*.

" Whig" was formed from the whey of milk after the cheefe curd had been feparated from it by runnet, a fecond and inferior curd being feparated from the whey by an acid mixture ; the remainder, after a flight fermentation, was called *whig*, and drunk by the poorer claffes inftead of fmall beer.

Page 26.

Alfareſſe.

Alſarez, or *alſares*, ſeems to have been a ſubordinate officer (an enſign, ſays Reed). Don Juan, in Maſſinger's *Rule a Wife and have a Wife*, ſays, Leon had been recommended to him as his "Alferez."

Ib.

rebellings.

Qy. "*Ravelines?*"

Page 28.

In the height of their carouſing, all their braines
Warm'd with the heate of wine, &c.

"This piece of pleaſant exaggeration," ſays Charles Lamb, "(which, for its life and humour might have been told, or acted, by Petruchio himſelf) gave riſe to the title of Cowley's Latin play, *Naufragium Ioculare*, and furniſhed the idea of the beſt ſcene in it."

Hazlitt conſiders this account of ſhipwreck by drink "the moſt ſplendid paſſage in Heywood's comedies."

Page 48.

Pollute the Nuptiall bed with Michall *ſinne.*

The word "michall," or "mechal," has been already explained.

Mr. Dilke, not being able to underſtand it, ſubſtituted "mickle," though he confeſſed himſelf "not altogether ſatisfied with the alteration"!

Page 63.

What braue car'u'd poaſts ; Who knowes but heere,
In time, Sir, you may keepe your Shreualtie.

It appears from many of our old writers, that it was cuſtomary for the ſheriff to have poſts in front of his houſe, ornamented in ſome particular way, probably for the purpoſe of pointing out his reſidence, or, as Warburton conjectures, "that the King's proclamations, and other public acts, might be affixed thereon by way of publication."

PAGE 65.
Chauelah.

A corruption of *Qui va là ?*

PAGE 167.
THE LATE LANCASHIRE WITCHES.

In 1633 Pendle Foreſt again became the ſcene of pretended witchcrafts : and from various circumſtances the trial which took place then has acquired even greater notoriety than that which preceded it twenty years before.   The particulars are ſub-ſtantially compriſed in the *Examination of Edmund Robinſon* (1) ſon of Edm. Robinſon, of Pendle Foreſt, Maſon, taken at Padi-ham, before Richard Shuttleworth and John Starkie, Eſqs., two of his Majeſty's juſtices of the peace, within the county of Lan-caſter, 10th February, 1633.

Heywood and Brome, in their play, *The late Lancaſhire Witches*, follow the terms of this depoſition very cloſely.   It is very probable that they had ſeen and converſed with the boy, to whom, when taken up to London, there was a great reſort of company.   The Lancaſhire dialect, as given in this play, and by no means unfaithfully, was perhaps derived from converſations with ſome of the actors in this drama of real life—a drama quite as extraordinary as any that Heywood's imagination ever bodied forth from the world of fiction.

Alice Nutter (concerning whom ſee *The Wonderfull Diſ-coverie of Witches in the Countie of Lancaſter by Thomas Potts*, 1613) (2) was doubtleſs the original of the ſtory of which Hey-wood availed himſelf in the *The late Lancaſhire Witches*—a ſtory frequently noticed by the writers of the ſeventeenth century—that the wife of a Lancaſhire country gentleman had been detected in

---

(1) This examination (which is too long to be given here) is printed *in extenſo* in Whitaker's *Whalley*, p. 213 ; Webſter's *Diſplaying of Witchcraft*, p. 347 ; and Baines's *Lancaſhire*, vol. i. p. 604.

(2) Reprinted for the Chetham Society (*Remains Hiſtorical and Literary, Vol. VI.*) in 1845, with an Introduction and Notes by James Croſſley, Eſq.; to which we are mainly indebted for the in-formation given above.

practifing witchcraft and unlawful arts, and had been condemned and executed. "In that play there can be little hefitation in afcribing to Heywood the fcenes in which Mr. Generous and his wife are the interlocutors, and to Brome the fubordinate and farcica portions. It is a very unequal performance, but not deftitute of thofe fine touches, which Heywood is never without, in the characters of Englifh country gentlemen and the pathos of domeftic tragedy."—CROSSLEY (*ubi fuprà*) : Introduction, lxv—lxx. Notes, pp. 34—38.

There is a reprint of this play by Mr. Halliwell, thus entitled " The Poetry of Witchcraft illuftrated by Copies of the Plays on the Lancafhire Witches by Heywood and Shadwell. Brixton Hill : Printed for Private Circulation only, 1853."

Mr. Harrifon Ainfworth has written a romance on the fubject of *The Lancafhire Witches*.

PAGE 262.
Londons Ius Honorarium.

An exact reprint from the only copy known to be extant of this pageant, kindly placed at our difpofal by H. Huth, Efq., of whofe invaluable library it is one of the many pricelefs treafures.

Heywood alfo wrote the pageants for 1632 and 1633 : to thefe we have not fucceeded in obtaining accefs ; but we are enabled to give fome account of them extracted from an interefting book publifhed fome thirty years ago by the Percy Society. (2).

That of 1632 is entitled : " Londini Artium et Scientiarum Scaturigo, Londons Fountain of Arts and Sciences ; expreft in fundrie Triumphes, Pageants and Shews, at the Initiation of the Right Honorable Nich. Raynton, in the Majoralty of the famous and far-renowned City of London. All the charge and Expenfe of the Laborious Projects, both by Sea and Land, being the fole Undertaking and Charge of the Right Worfhipfull Company of Haberdafhers. Written by Thomas Heywood. Lond. 1632."

The Pageant of 1633 is entitled :—"Londini Emporia, or London's

---

(2) Lord Mayor's Pageants : being Collections towards a hif tory of thefe Annual Celebrations. By F. W. Fairholt. Lond. (Percy Society), Part I., 1843.

Mercatura : expreſt in ſundry triumphs, pageants, and ſhowes, at the inauguration of the Right Honorable Ralph Freeman into the Maioralty of the famous and farre-renowned citty London. All the charge and expenſe of the laborious proieċts, both by water and land being the ſole undertaking of the Right Worſhip-full Company of the Cloath-workers. Written by Thomas Hey-wood. *Redeunt Speċtacula.* Printed at London by Nicholas Okes. 1633."

The pamphlet opens with the praiſe of merchantmen, detail-ing " the eight offices of piety in a merchant required :—" 1. Rec-titude of conſcience ; 2. Abſence of equivocation ; 3. Honeſty in bargaining ; 4. Juſtice ; 5. Humility ; 6. Charity to the poor ; 7. Abſence of Avarice ; 8. A renunciation of " all care and trouble of mind, which may hinder divine contemplation." Of courſe—" all theſe things deſireable being knowne to be eminent in your lordſhip," Heywood tells us, " was the maine induce-ment to entitle this preſent ſhow by this apt denomination *Lon-doni Emporia.*"

The firſt pageant is exhibited on the water ; " which is a ſea-chariot, beautified and adorned with ſhel-fiſhes of ſundry faſhion and ſplendour." It is drawn by two griffins ; upon them are ſeated two figures bearing pendants, " upon which are portrayed the armes of the two ſheriffes now in place." Thames rides in the chariot, ſurrounded by water nymphs, and appears to arouſe from a ſleep, as the mayor's barge approaches. He addreſſes him in a ſpeech, which contains an alluſion to the " clenſing of the river at this time by ſundry water engines," in theſe ſtrange words :—

> " Can Thameſis himſelf ſo far forget ?
> But 'tis long ſince Tame and Iſis met,
> That 'tis not rare ; for we two are groune old,
> And being rivers, ſubieċt to take cold ;
> Forc't with extremity of paine to grone,
> As troubled with the gravell and the ſtone,
> (Whole ſhelves are in our raines) but (Fates ſo pleaſe)
> By artiſts' helpe wee late have got ſome eaſe.
> Thanks to our patriots !"

After explaining the pageant and its myſtic alluſions, he ends :—

> " But why ſhould I, though beſt of Neptunes' ſons,

(Whofe ftreame almoft by your permiffion runnes)
Inftruct him who can teach? fince the laft yeare,
Till this day, never ran my tides fo cleare
As now they doe, were never fo become
With barges, enfignes, trumpets, fyfe and drum,
Methinkes you make mee young againe to view,
Old cuftomes kept, and (in them) all things new."

The firft fhow by land is placed in St. Paul's Churchyard. It is the trade-pageant of the company.—The fhepherd and fheep, with his dog guarding them from the ever-watchful wolf. He fits "upon a dyall, to which his fheep-hooke is the gnomon," and he explains this, in his fpeech to the mayor.—

" As I, fo you muft on a dyall fit,
    Which hath no gnomon but my ftaffe to it,
    And fuch your fword is now, your wakefull eye
    Muft ftill be ope, to watch where you can fpy
    The ravenous woolfe, to preffe, and blocke the way,
    Leaft hee on any of your flocke fhould prey.
.   .   .   .

    And that your charge fo carefully be borne,
    That they be neuer *but in feafon* fhorne."

The fecond pageant " is a fhip, moft proper to the trade of merchant-adventurers," with Mercury as pilot, who addreffes the mayor in a fpeech alluding to his own large mercantile occupation, and its confequent beneficial effects to the country.

" The third fhow by land, is a modell devifed to humour the throng, who come rather to fee than to heare : and without fome fuch intruded anti-maske, many who carry their ears in their eyes, will not fticke to fay, *I will not give a pinne for the Show.* Since therefore it confifts only in motion, agitation, and action, and thefe (expreffed to the life) being apparently vifible to all, in vaine fhould I imploy a fpeaker, where I prefuppofe all his words would be drown'd in noyfe and laughter. I therefore paffe to the fourth and laft."

" Which is a curious and neately framed architect, beautified with many proper and becoming ornaments : bearing the title of the Bower of Bliffe ; an embleme of that future happineffe which not onely all juft and upright magiftrates, but every good man, of what condition or quality foever, in the courfe of his life efpecially aimeth at." Herein are feated Prudence, Temperance, Juftice and Fortitude, and "the three theologicall vertues, Faith, Hope and Charity, as handmaides attending to conduct all fuch pious and religious magiftrates the way to the cœleftiall bower of bliffe." Prudence defcribes and defcants upon all in a moral fpeech, in which fhe delares it

"Aptly may be titled *Freeman's* bower."

"The fpeech at night" alludes "to the twelve celeftiall fignes, which may aptly be applied unto the twelve moneths during the lord mayor's goverment." The entire fpeech runs thus :—

"Sleepe may you foundly fir, to morrow preft.
To a yeares trouble, for this one nights reft,
In which may ftarres and planets all confpire,
To warme you fo by their celeftiall fire ;
Aries whofe Gold Fleece Greece doth fo renowne,
May both inrich you, and this glorious toune,
That *Taurus* in your ftrength may fo appeare,
You this great weight may on your fhoulders beare ;
That the two *Twins*, the mother's bleft increafe,
May in this citty ftill continue peace.
That *Caneer* who incites to hate and fpleene,
May not in your faire government be feene,
That *Leo* waiting on your iudgement feate,
May moderate his rage and fcorching heate ;
That the celeftial *Maide* may you aduife,
Virgins and orphans ftill to patronize ;
And rather then your juftice heere fhould faile,
Libra no more be feene with golden fcale ;
And that the *Scorpions* fting may be fo charm'd,
The poore may not be wrong'd nor innocent harm'd.
That *Chiron's* bent bow fo may guide your will,
You may ftill aime, but neuer fhoote to kill ;
And *Capricorne* though all things faid to dare,
Though he haue power, yet may have will to fpare ;
That as *Aquarius* doth his water power,
You may your goodnefs on this city fhower :

Pifces, the laft of twelve, the feet they guide,
From head to foot, O may you fo provide.

It ends with praife of "Mr. Gerald Chrifmas," who conftructed the pageant. Heywood having previoufly returned thanks to the wardens and committee of the Clothworkers company, "for their affability and courtefie, unto myfelfe, being at that time to them all a meere ftranger, who when I fent my then unperfect papers, were as able to judge of them, as attentively to heare them ; and rather judicially confidering all things, then nicely carping at any thing."

END OF FOURTH VOLUME.